What leaders
are saying about
CityServe . . .

"At Focus on the Family we know that the first line of defense for families is the local church. That's why I'm so excited about *CityServe*. This book will be a tremendous resource for churches as they engage in the critical work of helping troubled marriages, equipping parents in the challenges they face, and embracing struggling families with the hope of Christ."

—Jim Daly, president, Focus on the Family

"I can't imagine a more relevant and important resource for churches who are seeking to press into the transformation God is doing through us in our cities, communities, country, and world. *CityServe* equips the body of Christ to do what it does best—witness to Jesus in word and deed."

—Edgar Sandoval Sr., president, World Vision U.S.

"More than ever, churches need to make a difference in their communities. Habitat for Humanity is delighted to be a part of CityServe's efforts to engage churches in ministries that can alleviate suffering—ministries that stir the hearts of passionate and compassionate people."

—Jonathan Reckford, CEO, Habitat for Humanity International

"I buy a book hoping for one good idea; *CityServe* has a hundred."

—Rick Bezet, founder and lead pastor, New Life Church, AR; co-founder, Association of Related Churches (ARC)

"Performing the Great Commission with compassion becomes automatic with a lifetime commitment to move everyone, every day, closer to Jesus. *CityServe* is one of the best tools to inspire and equip you to do it."

—Barry Meguiar, president, Meguiar Inc.

"*CityServe* comes at a perfect time, when businesses are encouraging workplace compassion through volunteerism and giving. A top resource for any company team!"

—Anne Beiler, co-founder, Auntie Anne's Pretzels

"*CityServe* masterfully captures God's heart and strategy for transforming communities of all races, social backgrounds, and needs. God has designed the local church to be His hand extended to accomplish this. We are blessed to carry out His plan."

—Dan de León, pastor, Templo Calvario

"*CityServe* is an effective road map to bring together businesses, churches, and government to offer proven solutions to the systemic problems in our communities."

—Charlie O'Reilly, former chairman of the board, president, and CEO, O'Reilly Auto Parts

FOREWORD BY
TOMMY BARNETT
PASTOR AND FOUNDER, *DREAM CENTER*

CITY**SERVE**
YOUR GUIDE TO CHURCH-BASED COMPASSION

GENERAL EDITORS
DAVE DONALDSON
& WENDELL VINSON

SALUBRIS®
RESOURCES

Published by Salubris Resources
1445 N. Boonville Ave.
Springfield, Missouri 65802

ISBN: 978-1-68067-189-6

02-7392

22 21 20 19 • 1 2 3 4

Printed in the United States of America

Dedication

We dedicate *CityServe* to Lynda Vinson,

extraordinary wife, mother, grandmother, and friend,

because she reflects the truth that compassion begins at

home, and from home genuine compassion is shown.

Contents

PART 3—CHURCH-BASED COMPASSION MODELS

PART 6—CHURCH AND GOVERNMENT

PART 7—THE GREAT COMMISSION: WORD AND DEED

Foreword

Pure and undefiled religion before God and the Father is this:
to visit orphans and widows in their trouble. (James 1:27, NKJV).

After sixty-four years of ministry, I now realize that every church is in one of three stages: risk-taking, caretaking, or undertaking. Risk-taking churches press into God's future and focus on His dream and vision. Caretaking churches concern themselves only with the present. Undertaking churches look back at how God moved in the past. If you're reading this book, I believe you're a future-oriented risk-taker anointed by God to help accomplish His will on earth as it is in heaven!

God's future always involves the most important thing in all creation: people.

In Acts, the Early Church experienced multiplied growth because it was filled with givers who valued people over self-preservation or reputation. Since then, the harvest has been ripe, and the world is waiting for business executives, pastors, community leaders, government representatives, and congregations to join in a spirit of unity to share ideas, a helping hand, and prayer. This book is a testament to that kind of unity. A unity that will allow the Holy Spirit to move in full power through our churches to transform our communities.

There's no set formula for multiplication or compassion ministry, but there's an atmosphere for it. A risk-taking atmosphere is created when people seek the Lord, extend their arms to be used by Him to love their neighbor, and enable entrepreneurism by giving people permission to try new things. In such an atmosphere, nothing is impossible! At the L.A. Dream Center, risk-taking allowed us to love gang members, drug addicts, single mothers, orphans, released prisoners, homeless people, AIDS victims, and so many more. This kind of atmosphere can happen at your church and nonprofit too.

I believe the vision, models, and expertise shared in *CityServe: Your Guide to Church-Based Compassion* will spark a fire inside you to see the miracle God can do in your own neighborhood. I've known the general editors, Dave Donaldson and Wendell Vinson, for many years and have witnessed God's special anointing upon their leadership. Dave has been greatly used as the co-founder of Convoy of Hope and in Washington, DC, as part of the White House Faith-Based and Community Initiative. Wendell started attending our Pastor's School from the outset and has remained a close friend over the years. I'm so proud of him and how he has remained faithful to his church and community for over thirty years. Now he's innovating new ways to reach his community by spearheading a church-based compassion movement alongside Dave called CityServe.

If your church is in a difficult and broken community, you're in the perfect place for a miracle—a miracle that'll be accomplished through the words, hands, and feet of your congregation. Seek God, take risks, love people, and watch the impossible become possible!

—Tommy Barnett
Co-pastor of Dream City Church
Founder of Los Angeles Dream Center

Introduction

Over the past three decades, we've served together in various types of church-based ministries. Prior to my [Dave] serving at Operation Blessing, We Care America in Washington, DC, and co-founding Convoy of Hope, I served alongside Wendell as his associate pastor at Canyon Hills Church in Bakersfield, California. During those years, Canyon Hills experienced meteoric growth while piloting innovative church-based compassion programs and *Rock Solid*, which today is a best-selling discipleship program. Over the years we've remained close friends and are both passionate about empowering pastors and their neighborhood churches.

In 2018, we and a small group of business executives formally launched CityServe International. The vision was formed after our team repeatedly observed that the local church isn't adequately equipped to meet the growing complexity of spiritual, mental, and social brokenness in our communities, which has resulted in outsourcing compassion to government and national nonprofit organizations.

Paradoxically, there's a wealth of church-based compassion solutions to these civic and societal problems that remains isolated, and sometimes lost, because a pipeline to discover and share these models doesn't exist. We're grateful for the vision of Assemblies of God leadership and its Publishing division, My Healthy Church, to address the need by helping to produce this book, *CityServe*.

This is more than just a collection of thoughts. A wide variety of highly qualified leaders from church, business, government, and nonprofit sectors have furnished most of the content. Topics range from innovative leadership, community-based programs, corporate philanthropy, government funding, and much more. We developed the book to coordinate with the CityServe.us web-based platform designed to provide additional downloadable resources and networking opportunities with other compassionate leaders.

Communities across the nation can be transformed as church leaders are equipped with proven leadership principles and best practices from industry-leading professionals. This will help believers compassionately live out the gospel of Jesus Christ in their communities.

Our hope is that as you read and apply *CityServe*, it will inspire you, your leadership team, and church family to fulfill its destiny and become a strong catalyst for healthier communities and the restoration of broken lives from your neighborhood to the nations.

General Editors,

—Dave Donaldson   —Wendell Vinson
Co-founder   Co-founder
CityServe International   CityServe International

Part 1

IT'S YOUR SEAT, TAKE IT!

God has ordained for you to occupy a seat at the
table of influence to bring spiritual and physical
renewal to your community.
You are His For-Prophet Leader with
His prophetic voice!

—Dave Donaldson

1

For-Prophet Leadership

Dave Donaldson

The pastor walked slowly toward the podium as I sat on the stage behind him, waiting to be introduced. Clearing his throat, the pastor nervously shared, "My wife and I are grateful for the opportunity to serve here, but we've decided to resign as your pastors." Gasps from shocked congregants ricocheted around the room, followed by a deafening silence. My initial thought was, *Couldn't he have given me a little warning?* I began to dig into my mental archives for an appropriate sermon, but the pastor immediately introduced me as the morning's guest speaker. Unwilling to call a last-minute audible, I stayed with my planned message: "Never Quit, Never Give Up!"

Later that afternoon the pastor apologized for not forewarning me and confided that he had made the decision to resign prior to the service when a board member issued him a mandate: "Pastor our church, not the community."

"Dave," he said, "I've tried to guide my church into becoming community focused, but it seems every attempt has resulted in a cry to 'Circle the wagons and don't let anyone in or out.'"

This pastor isn't alone. He represents thousands of leaders who are trying to redefine their church's focus. They want to join the new breed of ambidextrous leaders who care for their flocks while occupying seats of influence with other community stakeholders. I call them For-Prophet Leaders.

Non-For-Prophet Leaders dream of a utopian church protected by a moat that encircles their fortress and keeps their sheep—and their tithes—safe from the encroachment of society. They define community engagement as, "Come join what we're doing."

One Good Idea

As an officer of the Chrysler Corporation, John Damoose enjoyed a distinguished twenty-three-year career in the automobile industry: ten years with Ford Motors, and the remaining with Chrysler. At Chrysler, John was Lee Iacocca's vice president of marketing and head of all three of Chrysler's car and truck brands. As such, he played a major role in leading one of the greatest turnarounds in corporate history.

Years later, John became president of the Christian Broadcasting Network and was my boss while directing Operation Blessing. John is one of the finest leaders I've ever had the privilege to serve under. During those formative years, I was driven to create new ideas constantly, resulting in frequent shifts to vision, goals, and strategy that left my team

> If you aren't willing to pay the price, you must adjust your expectations.

exhausted and ready to hang me in effigy. One day John summoned me to his office to share a lesson that would shape my life and ministry from that day forward.

Pulling out a blank piece paper from his desk John said (and I'm paraphrasing), "Lee Iacocca, chairman and CEO of Chrysler, and his team explored solutions to the company's seemingly inevitable slide towards bankruptcy. Iacocca, one of the greatest visionaries of all time, was looking for big ideas." As I listened, John scribbled down one word and said to me,

"This was the one big idea." Squinting to make out the faded ink, I read, "Minivan."

Sure enough, that was one big idea. The minivan replaced the station wagon as the large passenger car of choice in the United States. Its carlike handling, spacious and flexible seating, fuel economy, and cargo space led to the Chrysler comeback.

John continued with his advice about my leadership of Operation Blessing. "I admire your passion for creativity, but what is the *one big idea* for Operation Blessing?" I jotted down two words: "The church." And that began the church-lead community outreaches that would one day become the catalyst for launching Convoy of Hope. It was indeed a defining moment and helped to shape my focus of ministry that now includes CityServe International.

God's one big idea is the *church!* Have you ever pushed the pause button and pondered how your church is God's hope for healing broken lives and restoring crumbling communities? There's no Plan B!

For-Prophet Leaders

For-Prophet Leaders embrace the vision of the prophet Isaiah. He prophesied that God would make Jerusalem the center of His worldwide rule through a royal Savior who would destroy her oppressor (Babylon). Isaiah's prophecy is as relevant today as it was nearly three thousand years ago: "Your [church] will rebuild the ancient ruins and will raise up the age-old foundations; you will be called Repairer of Broken Walls, Restorer of Streets with Dwellings" (Isaiah 58:12).

God is raising up the "age-old foundations": neighborhood churches led by For-Prophet Pastors who are guiding their communities in spiritual, physical, social, and mental restoration. Isaiah's prophecy remains a perfect vision for imperfect times.

Transitioning from Non-For-Prophet to For-Prophet Leadership

How does a pastor lead a church from Non-For-Prophet to For-Prophet ministry? To address that question let me give you seven building blocks. Each is adaptable and scalable for any size church or community.

Research

Jesus said, "Don't you have a saying, 'It's still four months until harvest?' I tell you, open your eyes and look at the fields! They are ripe for harvest" (John 4:35). In a similar way, He might tell each of us, "Look at your community." Study a demographic survey made by your city management. Go on a listening tour to local governments, nonprofits, civic groups, and businesses. Educate yourself about your community and assess the most pressing needs while gathering an inventory of expertise and resources.

Relationships

Influence in a community always moves at the speed of relationships. There are no shortcuts to spending quality time with pastors and other community leaders. I'll be the first to admit this isn't always easy, as I learned through this experience.

While in Philadelphia casting vision to a group of pastors for hosting a Convoy of Hope outreach, one leader asked during the Q & A: "Convoy is working in some of the most dangerous areas in America. Have you ever had an altercation?" I thought for a moment and replied, "Just one, but fortunately we were able to separate the two pastors." The pastors chuckled, but the challenge of uniting pastors of diverse ethnicities and denominational affiliations isn't always a laughing matter. At times, kingdom diplomacy will feel like you're wrestling a cloud or dancing with porcupines, but persistence will pay off . . . and you won't want to move forward without these purposeful relationships.

It's been said, "If everyone agrees, then everyone isn't thinking." Nearly everyone welcomes a diversity of viewpoints unless they conflict with their own. Sharing the differing views of a team can lead to disunity and gridlock, but here's an exercise to help you guide your team towar productivity despite differing ideas:

1. Draw a large box that everyone can see. Fill the box with the ideas everyone shares.
2. Listen, listen, and listen until everyone has shared what is important to them. Place all these ideas inside the box.
3. Now ask, "Which of these ideas can we all agree on?"
4. Work with your team to narrow the list down to the essential ideas and draw another box around what you can agree on.
5. Develop an action plan or memo of understanding based on where you can start with the consensus of ideas.
6. As you achieve success and unity, widen the parameters of the box to include additional ideas and action points.

Representation

For-Prophet pastors are Kingdom diplomats; they're building the big "K" not the little "k." They actively search for ways to elevate other leaders and their ministries. This avoids the "crabs in a bucket" scenario of pulling others down in order to rise to the top.

Results

Position your church-based compassion programs to be feature- and outcome-based entities. *Feature-based* describes the program and what it does. *Outcome-based* describes the benefits of the program and desired expectations. For example:

Because of your child participating in our after-school tutoring program, they'll have improved test scores, class attendance, self-esteem, social skills, and future college and job prospects.

Resources

While serving in Washington, DC, for more than a decade I had a front-row seat to the billions of dollars appropriated every year by governments, corporations, foundations, and private donors for programs like those your church has in place or would like to start. By not competing for these resources, you allow entities that aren't faith-based and/or not as effective as your ministry to receive the funds and to become the recommended social service provider.

Recognition

For-Prophet Leaders are probably the best positioned in a community to bring honor to stakeholders who work tirelessly to improve the lives of their fellow citizens. Shouldn't the church lead the way in recognizing government officials, job providers, police, healthcare providers, firefighters, emergency responders, teachers, and other unsung heroes?

Replication

Many donors experience giving fatigue from constantly standing in front of a firing squad of compelling causes, all appealing for funding. World-class experts like Bill High, CEO of Signatry, say that donors are now looking for proven models, not causes as much.

At the end of the day, success begets a lot of grandchildren. There's nothing like God's favor to bring unity, fresh resources, and multiplication of successful vision and initiatives.

A friend once asked corporate executive Chuck Bengochea, "How do you prepare for your competition?" Chuck replied, "Well, I know if I'm making the greatest products in the world and offering the best service, then the competition becomes irrelevant to me."

As For-Prophet Leaders, if we're committed to bringing the best possible models of compassion to our communities, then the competition is irrelevant because we're occupying a seat at the King's table and setting forth proven solutions to brokenness.

Henry Ford said, "Whether you believe you can do a thing or not, you're right." As you read and digest *CityServe*, you may wonder whether you can transition to becoming a For-Prophet Leader. I know you can! When Jesus proclaimed, "I will build my church; and all the powers of hell shall not prevail against it" (Matthew 16:18, TLB), He was counting on your For-Prophet Leadership.

2

Neighborhood to the Nations

Wendell Vinson

Pastor, do you have a minute?" a woman asked. We were between services, and I was hosting a guest speaker representing an international compassion ministry, so one minute was about all I had. "Pastor, there's so much need in our city; it just doesn't seem like we're doing enough." To be honest, her comment irritated me a little, but I tried not to appear defensive. Perhaps this was another prodding of the Holy Spirit to engage the local church more effectively in healing social brokenness in our community, but I was already stretched thin and hoping someone else would figure out how to do that.

During that time of introspection, I couldn't shake free from three observations: (1) The church in most communities lacks a cohesive strategy for working together to respond to social brokenness. (2) God has positioned the church as the infrastructure to bring healing to its city, but it seems outside groups are extracting more from it than resourcing it. (3) The church needs to change significantly in the way it helps people sitting in the pews to build relationships with hurting people both locally and globally.

To address these challenges, I knew we couldn't continue to outsource compassion to people serving globally unless we were willing to reach out in compassion to our own city. From these observations, the Lord gave us the vision for CityServe and the strategy we now call "From the Neighborhood to the Nations."

White Blood Cells

Rich Stern, former CEO of World Vision, met with our CityServe board of directors and shared this convicting word picture: "God has designed our bodies so that when there's a wound or infection all the white blood cells move toward that infection to fight it off and bring healing. The church should do the same." Rich elaborated by telling us that when there's an infection or wound in our community the church should move in unity to bring healing and wholeness. Yet too often we ignore it or, worse, run from it. While Rich was sharing this powerful illustration, my thoughts raced towards the entrenched needs in our community and the absence of the faith community.

Across America, if you look closely, whether in urban centers or rural settings, you'll find a neighborhood church on nearly every major street corner. That church, no matter how humble it may seem, represents God's infrastructure and agency of hope for its community. Too often though, these neighborhood churches are underresourced to address the scope of needs surrounding them and don't know where to turn for help. They feel outgunned. It's as though they have a first-aid kit to work with in the middle of a war zone when they need a triage unit. They need backup and reinforcement, but no one's coming to the rescue!

At the same time, in most regions of our country there are large churches, even megachurches, that are thriving, adding new people each week, and growing in influence. Frequently, these churches aren't located in the most blighted parts of our communities. As a pastor of one of these larger churches, I feel confident in saying to my colleagues who also pastor large churches that if every megachurch in our country doubled in size today, it would do little to bring healing to the most troubled parts of our communities. There are numerous reasons for this, but a major one is that the poor will never visit our churches because they lack mobility to get there. Their world is in another zip code.

But what might happen if the megachurches got underneath and lifted the neighborhood churches in these underresourced and socially fragile areas? What if we took to heart the admonition from Jesus in Luke 12:48, "From everyone who has been given much, much will be demanded"? This challenge includes both individuals and groups of people gathered in churches. Ask yourself: What might happen if instead of plucking people from neighborhood churches, larger churches raised the tide of all these boats? What if we encouraged these local pastors, served them, and widened their church's capacity to become the go-to place for help and healing? In the words of A. W. Tozer, "A scared world needs a fearless church."

Outsourcing Compassion

I'm all for credible parachurch organizations that are doing effective charitable service around the globe, but all their good work will never take the place of the transformative ministry of Jesus through His church to local neighborhoods. Nor can we be satisfied with episodic compassion events that, candidly, do more to make the participants feel good than lift people out of systemic poverty.

At Canyon Hills church, we decided to invest a lot of our leadership and financial capacity into strengthening smaller churches throughout our region. Yes, the decision to move this direction versus expanding our main campus tested our margins and commitment, but it extended the reach of Canyon Hills beyond anything else we had ever done. Now our team is investing daily to strengthen pastors and leaders of smaller churches in difficult neighborhoods. We don't want to be over them but under them to enable them to more effectively minister to people in their neighborhoods. In most cases, pastors just need a trusted leader and friend to dream with them for student ministry to reach hundreds of children and youth or for a ministry to nurture single moms and impoverished widows struggling to make ends meet. So much potential is released when a pastor feels confident they aren't alone because another church is standing with them. Spurring on larger churches to help raise healthy churches in one of the neediest areas of our community is another way God is supernaturally using CityServe.

One of these small rural churches in Wasco, California, had fallen on hard times and closed for several months. This little town, like many, had been severely impacted economically through the recession and eventually this neighborhood church closed its doors.

> What they discovered is that operating in the compassion of Jesus makes soul-winning easy.

Then a young leader, Emmanuel Hernandez, accepted the assignment of relaunching the church in this impoverished neighborhood. He gathered a team and, with the support of CityServe, began meaningful compassion engagement to hurting people in the neighborhood. The team distributed food, clothing, furniture, household supplies, and even dog food! They made friends and shared the gospel. One by one, family by family, people started attending the church. Now, baptism celebrations are regular events each month and discipleship classes accommodate the new believers. As new people came to the church, they were immediately immersed in a culture of community compassion and engagement and, as a result, became effective soul winners. What they discovered is that operating in the compassion of Jesus makes soul winning easy.

Compassion Is Scalable

Sometimes we church leaders hesitate to respond to the needs around us because our focus is on what we *don't* have instead of what we *do* have. For example, although our resources were extremely limited, out of obedience to the James 1:27 call to "visit orphans and widows in their trouble" (NKJV), we started caring for the widows in our church and community. Years later, we had a thriving senior-living community on our campus serving widows and seniors all over Bakersfield.

Our initiatives to serve the poor began by giving away small amounts of food and household goods; now our programs operate out of a 165,000-square-foot, former Montgomery Ward shopping center in the heart of the city. This building, which was a dilapidated eyesore, is now a symbol of community renewal. At CityServe, we believe we can rescue, restore, and repurpose old buildings like this into Dream Centers and CityServe warehouses: "Your people will rebuild the ancient ruins and will raise up the age-old foundations; you will be called Repairer of Broken Walls, Restorer of Streets with Dwellings" (Isaiah 58:12).

God's love and compassion have no bounds, but His strategies are scalable! Start where you're at, with what you have, and God will bring the increase!

Becoming "Bless-able"

You may think I'm being trite when I say, "What God's people need most is God's blessing." Frankly, it used to sound cliché to me as well until the principle of "bless-able-ness" transformed my thinking, priorities, and definition of success. How do we become "bless-able"? The good news is that God has already provided the formula for His blessings in the Bible. Scripture repeatedly tells us that when we advocate and care for the hungry, the poor, the orphan and widow, the addicted, imprisoned, vulnerable, exploited, and unreached, God's blessing will be upon us. You can get inspired by the latest gurus of leadership and read the best-selling books on church growth, but if you aren't modeling servant leadership by responding tangibly to the cries of your community, you'll never experience the full "bless-able-ness" of God. "The generous will themselves be blessed, for they share their food with the poor" (Proverbs 22:9).

CityServe SoCal

In partnership with CityServe, the SoCal Network of the Assemblies of God is at the forefront of empowering churches for compassion evangelism. The SoCal Network leaders recognize that community engagement is the number one indicator of church health and growth, so together we've launched CityServe SoCal. We believe CityServe will be a model of compassion outreach for the United States and around the globe. SoCal Network superintendent, Rich Guerra, had a vision for a "Compassion Galaxy" that would equip and resource churches to lead the way in communities dealing with issues of food security, addiction, job readiness, foster care and adoption, and many more. Rich shared this vision with his assistant superintendent, John Johnson. These two leaders, their team, Dave Donaldson, and I set out to establish a robust supply network. This network includes:

HUBs. These medium to large warehouses are filled with donated product that's distributed through Points of Distribution (PODs) or neighborhood churches. The HUBs also function as places to train and resource PODs in compassion models and best practices.

PODs. These are neighborhood churches that are equipped to take donated products into the homes of needy families. Products include food, home furnishings, cleaning supplies, backpacks, school supplies, etc.

Training. This is a vital part of the Compassion Galaxy that Rich envisioned. CityServe hosts training sessions both online and at regional conferences. In addition, CityServe SoCal is linked with Vanguard University to host regional symposiums for compassion models with plans to offer a nonprofit leadership certification in the future.

Throughout this *CityServe* book, you'll be inspired by the stories from pastors who are leading HUBs and PODs. You'll understand how donated products aren't just a handout; they're tools for neighborhood churches to cultivate meaningful relationships with their neighbors.

From the Neighborhood to the Nations

CityServe and the SoCal Network believe that as we empower the local church to care for its community, it will emerge emboldened, envisioned, and more generous towards supporting compassion evangelism projects around the globe.

Whether you're a pastor, a business leader, or a worker in a cubicle at your office, as a Christ-follower you're part of the most compelling Spirit-led

> "The generous will themselves be blessed, for they share their food with the poor" (Proverbs 22:9).

Neighborhood to the Nations strategy ever designed: "But you will receive power when the Holy Spirit comes on you; and you will be my witnesses in Jerusalem, and in all Judea and Samaria, and to the ends of the earth" (Acts 1:8).

Right now, perhaps more than at any time in history, we have an amazing opportunity as the church to become known for demonstrating the kindness, unity, and compassion of Jesus. Our culture is stuck in an angry, toxic, polarized quagmire that only fuels division and dark hopelessness. Yet, like the first-century church, the conditions are perfect for today's church to rise and lead a mighty force for good, from the Neighborhood to the Nations!

3

It's Time for a Game Change!

Scott Wilson

All pastors and church leaders worth their salt say they care about disadvantaged and disenfranchised people. In many cases, however, their actual ministry strategy is designed primarily to increase the number of people attending weekend services. The result is that many of us invest relatively little time and few resources to touch the lives of "the least of these"—the very ones who flocked to Jesus.

One thing scares me: someday soon we're all going to stand before Jesus and give account for how we served or ignored the outsiders in our community. If that doesn't motivate you as a Christian, it should motivate you as a Christian leader who will be held accountable for how you lead God's people.

Some church leaders are afraid that becoming a compassion-driven church may make them vulnerable to the criticism they've become "liberal" and they've "ignored the gospel." That's misplaced fear. Effectively meeting the needs of people in the community opens many new doors to tell people about the redeeming love of Christ. But caring for people isn't just a means to the end of evangelism; it has inherent value of its own. Jesus loved, fed, healed, and restored people whether they trusted in Him or not. That's the measure of His grace, and it's one of the marks of a transformed church.

Imagine people driving by your church and saying, "Yeah, that church is incredible. It's making a huge difference in people's lives in our community!" I used to think people said that about our church . . . until I started listening to them.

After a staff meeting four years ago, our team had lunch at a restaurant down the road from our church. The mayor of our city was sitting near us. After we finished eating and got ready to leave, the mayor came over and said, "Pastor, I wonder if I could talk to you for a few minutes." I sat down with him at his table, and he said solemnly, "Pastor Scott, there's a problem . . . a big problem." I responded immediately, "What do you mean? Tell me what it is."

Without hesitating, he said, "You and your church have a bad reputation in our community."

I was stunned and asked him to explain what he meant: "Mr. Mayor, I don't understand. Please tell me what you're talking about."

He explained, "You're the biggest church, and in fact, the biggest organization in our community, but you have the reputation for doing your own thing. You're not really part of our community at all."

I tried not to be defensive as I explained, "Everything we do is designed to help this community. I wake up every morning thinking and praying about how we can make a difference in the lives of people." To be sure he heard me, I repeated myself: "I'm serious Mr. Mayor. It really bothers me that you would say such a thing because everything I do is for this city."

He smiled knowingly, "That's the problem, Pastor Scott. You're always doing things *for* us, but you don't do much *with* us. There's a difference . . . a *big* difference."

As I walked out of the restaurant, I knew this wasn't a complaint I could easily dismiss. The mayor had pointed out a profound misunderstanding in the way we were trying to live out our mission. In passage after passage in the gospels, Jesus spent time with outcasts of every type: despised prostitutes, hated tax collectors, the blind, the lame, and convicted criminals. Jesus didn't see them as projects to be fixed, but as people to be loved. There's a monumental difference between creating services to help people and becoming one of them.

That afternoon God also reminded me of the passage that's been the foundation for our church. When Jesus began His ministry and gave His first message, He read from the prophet Isaiah. As Jesus stood in the synagogue, He quoted:

"The Spirit of the Lord is on me,
because he has anointed me
to proclaim good news to the poor.
He has sent me to proclaim freedom for the prisoners
and recovery of sight for the blind,
to set the oppressed free,
to proclaim the year of the Lord's favor." (Luke 4:18–19)

He doesn't divide the world into dualistic spheres of *sacred* and *secular*. He cares for people where they are and uses us to meet their needs. We never fail to communicate the wonderful gospel message of transforming grace, but this message is received most readily if we also fulfill His mission of caring for "the least of these." In fact, in Isaiah's prophecy, the people who are recipients of God's grace become His partners. The prophet says, "They will be called oaks of righteousness, a planting of the LORD for the display of his splendor" (Isaiah 61:3). That's why we call our church The Oaks Fellowship.

God used the mayor's words to challenge me, inspire me, and redirect the efforts of our church. Our leaders prayed and planned, and within a week God led us to rethink everything about our church: our identity, our calling, and our strategy. Before my meeting with the mayor, if anyone had asked if we had a compassionate church, I'd have pointed to our support groups for addicts and hurting people, our food pantry, benevolence ministries, our assistance for struggling churches in other countries, and on and on. But suddenly we realized all of these were *for*, not *with*. We held a hand out to these people, but we didn't embrace them—we didn't identify with them and become one of them. Now, we've become committed to make compassion who we are, not just part of what we do. Caring for people is no longer a department of our church; it's become the soul of our church. True compassion couldn't remain a niche; it had to become the new norm.

We Redefined Success

For years our church defined success by the strength of our programs and the increase in our numbers. After my meeting with the mayor, we began to think differently. We redefined success as helping any of the gatekeepers—organizations already working to meet the needs in the community—accomplish their goals, whether we got any notice or not. We gradually shifted our vision from the success of our church to the crying needs of people around us. If we can help feed the hungry, provide shelter for the homeless, mentor kids, give blood, and dozens of other worthwhile functions, we realized we were fulfilling God's calling in Isaiah 61 and Luke 4. We wanted to be like Jesus and serve with no strings attached.

We wanted to be like Jesus and serve with no strings attached.

To facilitate the work of the nonprofits in our area, we invited all of them to come to a Sunday worship service. The leaders of all thirty-eight nonprofits came to the platform with signs describing the desperate needs they were meeting in the community. I told our congregation, "These organizations and agencies touch the lives of hurting people in our area. This is the body of Christ in action, and we have the privilege to be partners with them." Our people gave them a standing ovation and a generous love offering. We ended the service early so our people could go into the lobby to meet the leaders of these organizations and find out how they could get involved.

When the local food pantry wanted to make a big push to restock their shelves, we worked with a local grocery store that offered to match five dollar donations of food. We told our people about the partnership, and the partnership of the three organizations saw a fantastic response. The grocery store received a prestigious award for their participation, our people saw their efforts multiplied so they were able to provide for more people, and the food pantry was thrilled with the increased participation. All three organizations experienced a significant win.

To be honest, it took a while to earn the trust of some of the educators and business executives in the area. They assumed we still "had an angle." A principal suspected that we were offering to help mentor kids because we wanted to recruit them for the charter school that meets in our building, and some business leaders thought we'd pounce on people with a gospel message if we served at their events. Gradually, they realized they could trust us, and we became true partners.

One of the most significant benefits from our care strategy is that the reputation of our church has dramatically changed. I was shocked when the mayor told me that our community had a negative view of us, but after only a year of selflessly reaching out to care for people, the view of our church was reversed. The mayor asked me to speak for the Chamber of Commerce, and we gave a copy of my book, *Act Normal*, to every person who attended. The mayor wanted me to talk about what our church is doing to care for hurting people, and he wanted me to enlist the involvement of business leaders to become partners. As we've developed a "with" attitude, the mayor and other leaders have noticed, and we've earned their trust.

This new connection with leaders in our community has opened dozens of doors we never could have walked through only a year before. For instance, a year ago, we developed a strategy to connect with high school students and their parents through a strategy called "Friday Night Lights." Our goal was to connect with these families by encouraging our church members to attend their football games and support our local teams. The principals, however, were suspicious of us, and some of them were genuinely belligerent. This year, the same principals are calling me to ask if we can come to their schools again this year with our program.

As we redefine success as partnerships and selfless service, everybody wins.

We Provided Resources for Our Community Gatekeepers

As we thought about our community, we realized there are five types of organizations that serve as gatekeepers to serve people: schools, churches, government, nonprofit organizations, and the Chamber of Commerce. We asked a gifted and compassionate person in our church, Andrea Lathrop, to take initiative with each of these gatekeepers. We asked her to be our ambassador and liaison to each organization. She began attending meetings of these gatekeepers, introducing herself and offering the church's help. She gave her contact information to school principals, teachers, elected officials, business leaders, pastors, and the heads of the local nonprofit organizations. At first, they weren't sure The Oaks wanted to support their efforts with no strings attached. We had to prove ourselves.

Whatever the need, we tried to provide the resources to meet it. After a while, they realized our church is a trustworthy partner, willing to serve gladly and tirelessly, and our reputation began to change. Of course, our church couldn't provide everything the gatekeepers needed for every event. When we stopped competing, we realized we could earn their trust, become genuine partners, and really make a difference.

> They realized our church is a trustworthy partner, willing to serve gladly and tirelessly, and our reputation began to change.

We asked a consultant, Monty Hipp of the C4 group, to meet with our staff, board, and lay leaders, and together we studied our community and looked closely at how God had used our church in the past. When we conducted a demographic study of the area, the results astounded us. Among many interesting results, we found:

- over five thousand children waiting for placement in foster care
- over two thousand kids needing to be mentored through Big Brothers Big Sisters, Boys and Girls Clubs, or school programs
- over sixteen thousand people in our area living below the poverty line, and six thousand of them are children

So, we got to work. Our church hosts Parents' Night Out for foster parents every month, and we hold the foster care annual meeting for our area. We regularly let our people know of the opportunities and needs associated with these kids. When God prompts a couple to get involved, we're ready to help them.

On Father's Day this past year, one of the dads in this group tweeted, "Spending Father's Day with the fatherless and loving every minute of it." These couples take their own kids along to share their love and friendship, so the whole family participates in caring for those who are less fortunate. As these parents care for disadvantaged children, they're modeling grace and love as their kids join them.

Part of our strategy is marshalling efforts to help senior adults by cleaning up their homes, yards, and apartments; involving parents in children's ministry; providing pastoral care for the elderly and those in the hospital and nursing homes; offering benevolence to those who are struggling financially; sharing counseling resources for people with emotional, relational, and spiritual difficulties; maintaining support groups for those suffering from addiction, grief, divorce, and other problems; and meeting many other needs.

Team leaders give measurable quarterly goals for their ministries, and I ask them to explain how these quarterly goals fit into the annual projections. It may seem like administrative overkill to set goals this often, but we've found that it's important to the health of our teams and the effectiveness of our partnerships. In addition, people who might be big donors and those who are considering taking leadership of these teams need to know that their dollars and sweat are going into efforts that are changing lives.

As our care strategy developed, we realized we needed systematic teaching and training for leaders, so we created an online ninety-day course called "Building a Bridge between the Church and the Community." We make this training available to pastors and team leaders who want to develop a care strategy for their church. You can sign up for the course and connect to a certified ministry coach through minstrycoach.tv.

Today,

- 52 percent of all foster kids in our county go to our church
- 700 kids are in our after-school program every day, with daily chapel, Bible study, and tutoring
- 5,600 kids are in the charter school, with 1,200 of them in our church building every weekday

We Decided to Make a Difference

If we want to make a difference, we must get out of our church buildings and be with the hurting, the lost, the poor, the proud, the up-and-comers, and the down-and-outers—just like Jesus did. For this to happen, pastors must model it. We need to carve out time to coach a Little League team, mentor a student, or play on a community flag football team. Telling stories about the wonderful things that happened ten or twenty years ago won't cut it. Our stories of touching people need to be fresh. It starts with the leader being committed to being *with* people instead of doing things *for* them.

Caring for hurting people always comes at a cost. It's far easier to sit in our offices and give directions than to give our time, our energy, and our hearts to people who may not care or may demand far more than we can give. With God's help, we can become known as people who love not only in word but in deed. For that to happen, compassion can't just be a department in the church; it must be the very essence of what the church is about.

4

Earning Influence
in Your Community

Gene Roncone

Our church in Aurora, Colorado, was right in the middle of a building program when the 2009 recession hit. What looked to be a triumph turned to disaster. We lost our financing, unemployment disrupted giving, the hospital that was buying land from us went under, and we were forced to move out of our existing building and start meeting in a local school. Attendance plummeted from 1,000 to 240 people. Our dreams for the future seemed shattered.

But God was taking us on a journey to learn what community influence really is—and how different it is than we thought.

Phase One: Brokenness

Aurora sits right outside Denver and covers nearly twice the landmass. Today, its growing economy is fueled by the medical industry and new construction. Sadly, in my first eight years as pastor of Highpoint Church, my motive was to grow a large church. We built great programs and were one of the strongest churches in the nation in our denomination in giving to foreign missions. Ironically, while strongly supporting overseas missions, I didn't even know many of the neighborhoods in my own city. Outside of financing in-house ministries, we were spending very little on missions in the United States and nothing in our own city.

We wouldn't have thought of ourselves as prideful. We had programs coming out of our ears, but we were absent in the community. Our idea of serving was to hold an event at the church and expect people to come. When our church building was boarded up and we moved into a school, God began taking us through Phase One of becoming influential. It's called brokenness.

Phase Two: Discovery

This painful season of brokenness caused me to think differently, and for reasons I can't fully explain, I decided to work out of the MLK Library in our urban corridor on Thursdays of each week. I don't know why I was drawn to this neglected part of town except I wanted to get a feel for the city. Something tugged my heart in that direction. My board probably thought I was crazy—and sometimes I did, too.

The library sat on infamous Colfax Avenue, which runs through five municipalities in and around Denver, including Aurora. Colfax Avenue has been called the "longest, wickedest street in America." Once the main lodging corridor for Colorado's ski industry, it now sat in the dark shadow of crime, drugs, and violence. I learned that there were seven hundred homeless children in the public school system in this area. By "homeless," I mean they were sleeping on a couch, in the back of a car, in a sleazy motel, or in another transient situation, and had no idea where they would stay the next week. That statistic was mind-boggling to me.

Spending one day a week at the inner-city library wasn't comfortable. The bathrooms smelled horribly. They were the only place that homeless people had access to water, so it was common to see a homeless man in his underwear bathing with a washcloth in front of the sink. It was also common to see unmentionable substances and creatures on the toilet seats. Still, I was determined to stay . . . and to learn.

On Thursdays, I drove over there, chose a seat in the Ethiopian coffee shop area with its storefront-style windows looking out at Fletcher Plaza, where all the homeless people were laying around, opened my laptop, and began meeting with community leaders, city council members, government workers, pastors, teachers, principals, and nonprofit leaders—a new appointment every hour. Upstairs from the library are the neighborhood services division for the city of Aurora, so I was now in regular contact with city officials and staff. I took notes on all my interviews. My goal was to understand each person's heart for the city.

I befriended people I had never met before. One homeless man, Howard, let me follow him around, and showed me where he slept and how he kept warm at night. As I walked the streets in that area where our church began eighty-five years earlier, I saw the poverty, crime, homelessness, prostitution, and gang involvement that I never knew existed. Often I slipped into alleyways and buildings to weep in brokenness and shame. This was my city, and I hadn't known it well enough to see these needs.

> When our church building was boarded up and we moved into a school, God began taking us through Phase One of becoming influential. It's called brokenness.

God gave me favor with the people I met, and after a year I had an even better sense than most city leaders of what the city needed. Everybody tends to look at their own piece of the puzzle and not at what others are doing. One nonprofit leader told me, "I'm the only food pantry down here," and I heard myself answering, "No, there are twenty others." I realized God was giving me and our church strategic insight into what we should be doing. He was giving us a citywide view.

Phase Three: Service

We began to put that knowledge to work and spent the next year vetting and serving existing organizations who needed help. We subordinated ourselves to them and made ourselves problem-solvers in the city. This bought us a lot of street credibility with movers and shakers in Aurora, though that wasn't our motivation.

During this time, I met several times with every city council member and offered them assistance when I discovered needs they felt unable to address. I made Highpoint their go-to church for solving problems. We mobilized hundreds of volunteers and started giving money to others, even as our own dreams for a new building—or even our old building—lay in shambles. I coined a phrase that became part of our culture: "This is our city and each of us must become part of the solution."

We adopted the largest and poorest elementary school in the city, helping kids with clothing, food, and other needs so the teachers could focus on teaching. We gave the school thousands of dollars and sent many volunteers to help. The school was under review by the school board because of their low test scores. Two years later they had the highest increase in test scores in the entire school district.

The school's principal invited me to her office and informed me that many fifth-graders had never been camping because they couldn't afford to go—even though we lived next to a world-class camping area, the Rocky Mountains. She asked if we could help and our people gave thirteen thousand dollars to send every fifth-grader on a camping trip two years in a row.

We bought, fitted, and gave more than two thousand new winter coats to elementary students, and did the same with one thousand pairs of brand-new winter boots. We bought and donated more than three thousand books to keep students reading over the school break.

We began our annual "Love Aurora" initiative where hundreds of Highpoint volunteers serve other organizations—babysitting kids at counseling centers so moms can get counseling, funding science and chemistry assemblies in our local schools, and much more. Our "Love Aurora" podcast spotlighted amazing organizations and people who were making Aurora a better place to live.

In my office, I hung a seven-foot map that displayed every Denver neighborhood and started to think like an army general about the city. God spoke to me about the importance of praying downtown. We needed boots on the ground and God's guidance on what to do next. I had my eye on an empty storefront, and the owner offered to lease it to us for four hundred dollars for sixty days. We covered the windows and turned it into a day-and-night prayer room. Highpoint people drove there and prayed for different aspects of the neighborhood. We prayed for all community leaders. At night we heard sirens, gangs, and screaming from the streets. It was getting real for us.

Phase Four: Collaboration

Without trying to make it happen, Highpoint now had a seat at the table among community leaders. I had learned from conversations and observation of city leaders that true collaboration is when two parties bring equal money, resources, manpower, and creativity to the table to solve a problem. Many churches, I'm sad to say, either don't want to bring money to the table or they want to dictate all the terms. That approach is dead on arrival. Instead, I became addicted to collaboration because I saw how effective it was.

Highpoint began collaborating with the Aurora Police Department's gang intervention efforts, and I was asked to chair an important committee and work closely with the police chief. City leaders also asked me to serve as the secretary of the board for "Aurora Warms the Night," an organization that gets the homeless off the streets when temperatures dip below twenty degrees.

City leaders asked me to join "Leadership Aurora," a cohort of thirty leaders whom the city educates on every aspect of the city and the people behind key organizations.

The Aurora Chamber of Commerce became one of our most active partners and recommended us to businesses looking to invest dollars in community compassion projects. Currently we receive ten to twenty thousand dollars a year from Aurora businesses to help the neediest part of town.

Our relationship with the Aurora City Council has flourished. The council has come to me individually and corporately to request prayer and insight into community problems. Last year they were deeply divided over an issue and asked me to pray they would find consensus. They also voted to donate city funds to our boots-for-kids giveaway. In thirty years of ministry, I've never heard of a city council in a city of nearly four hundred thousand people giving money to a church. I covet the relationship and their trust.

> Our church now enjoys what I never envisioned before our crisis: true leadership and influence in our city.

In most cities there's tension between the mental health community and faith-based organizations, but Aurora Mental Health, the largest nonprofit in the city with nearly seven hundred employees, is our most valued partner. We've joined together on many effective projects. They donate a large amount of office space to us, so we can have a second administrative presence in a building in the heart of the urban corridor and a block from Crawford Elementary.

Phase Five: Leadership

Our church now enjoys what I never envisioned before our crisis: true leadership and influence in our city. Looking back, I see that God had us on a journey to become a trusted and valuable partner in community compassion efforts.

This hit home when we refinanced our building and I sent an e-mail to several community leaders asking if they would write a letter of recommendation to our lender on our behalf. I expected a handful to reply but was blown away at how many wrote letters telling the bank how valuable we were to the community. Our board wept together as one city leader wrote, "I have found there are several different kinds of churches in our city. Some exist in a state of self-preservation with an inward focus. Others have effective programs and leave a large footprint in reaching out to their community. Then there are those that carry others along in their wake by not only reaching out to the community but collaborating and mobilizing other organizations to do so. Highpoint is one of those churches." The lender said their executives told them to give us the lowest rate possible because they had never seen a church so valued by nonbelieving leaders.

These "successes" are not mementos of pride. God knows I never want to return to the arrogance that once isolated us from our city. I mention it as evidence that, contrary to popular belief, the church is still needed and valued by communities. We just need to start fighting the right battles.

Hindrances to Community Leadership

Many churches never make it to a place of collaboration and leadership because of a few common hindrances:

Selfishness. Churches tend to focus narrowly on their own survival and needs. They want to partner only if it grows their church or gives them valuable PR. Many pastors don't embrace a good idea unless they thought of it or are leading the effort. They may give thousands of dollars to denominationally approved projects, but nothing to local public schools, cities, or community organizations.

Arrogance. Churches tend to bring nothing but strong opinions to the table. They often offer quick, uninformed, simplistic advice about how school boards should run schools, cities should treat churches, and many other issues. After being on so many city task teams, it dawned on me that the church of Jesus Christ has lots of opinions but doesn't bring much money, volunteers, or collaborative skills to the table. That's why no one wants or needs them.

Spiritual impatience. If Christian leaders can't see measurable and immediate spiritual fruit, they lose heart and give up. They don't see that good works lay the groundwork for sharing the gospel.

Financial myopia. Most churches don't have a plan to finance their community involvement. The ones that can afford it would never consider donating money and lending volunteers to what seems like a "nonspiritual problem." My own church was so overly committed financially to foreign missions and our own in-house ministries that we had little financial margin to help our community. We slowly changed that by raising the profile and value of local efforts in our missions giving.

Elevating the Church's Role in the Community

Churches must value their role in the community. I've spent much time reviewing my notes from meetings with civic leaders and have identified five strategic and sacred roles only the church can play in today's communities:

• *Elevate the human spirit.* The church does this by appealing to the best, instead of the worst, that people can accomplish together.

- **Mobilize resources.** The church can quickly mobilize people and resources to overcome difficult problems, respond to emergencies, and meet complex needs.
- **Promote justice.** The church can serve as a moral compass to help our communities navigate through the dark side of politics, materialism, power, selfishness, and sin.
- **Meet unique needs.** The church can fill gaps that government, education, and political organizations aren't structured to fill.
- **Facilitate spiritual growth.** The church can resource people's spiritual needs by creating an environment for spiritual growth and discovery.

If you feel the tug, as we did, to become influential in your city, let me share this brief advice:

- **Influence requires grace-centered collaboration.** Your influence will never be greater than the relationships you have with those from different philosophical, political, and theological perspectives. I developed a lot of valuable relationships with "liberals," people I probably wouldn't have wanted to talk to before. Some are now among my best friends.
- **Learn the unique culture and needs of your community with the same dedication, patience, and sacrifice that a missionary does in a foreign nation.** What is your community's history? What do key stakeholders say they need? What and where are microcultures in your city?
- **Invest money and volunteers in things that are important to the city and its leadership.** If you don't have room in your budget, make room. Focus your creative energy, finances, manpower, and prayers on the "God-void" places where darkness seems prevalent and people are suffering. God will bless you for

it. If you aren't actively serving those God-void places, then serve someone who is.

• **Be a learner, not a dictator.** Recently, the governor of Colorado came to Aurora to address the region's mayors, and his office asked me to give the invocation. I ended up at the head table where several mayors quizzed me about our urban efforts. They then shared how disappointed they were with young pastors who were so focused on social justice that they had become antagonistic toward city leaders. These young pastors had passion, but no appreciation for partnership. Some didn't even understand the basic logistics of how cities work. For example, homelessness and other issues are usually not addressed through cities but counties. Fiery words spoken at a city council meeting weren't going to help with issues the city wasn't structured to address. Listening goes a lot further toward creating partnership than do passionate words spoken in ignorance or arrogance.

Today, Highpoint's main campus sanctuary is full, and we've gone from worrying that the church won't survive, to thriving financially and planting the Highpoint @ Colfax campus. Incidentally, our office downtown is right across the street from the MLK Library, where the journey of influence began for us.

We've learned that influence can't be given—it must be earned. Then it becomes a sacred trust. I believe God has a similar journey for your congregation as you listen to His heart for your community.

5

The Church—A Refuge for Hispanics

Dan de León

An interview with pastor and national Hispanic leader, Dan de León.

Q: Why should churches focus on the Hispanic community?

De León: The Hispanic population represents the United States' largest and youngest minority group. One out of four children in the United States is Hispanic. And 90 percent of Latino children in the country are US citizens. By the year 2050, one out of three children and over 30 percent of the US population will be of Hispanic heritage. These young children today will constitute a significant segment of the country's future. We need to reach them and win them to the Lord.

Hispanics are moving up in society, striving for better jobs. It won't be long before it's hard to find Hispanics who will work for car washes and gardening services. The first generation who had those jobs are growing old, and their kids aren't interested in those jobs. They'll have jobs as well-educated lawyers and business people who move into mainstream society and affect the political arena. Today, there are a few Hispanics in Washington, DC, but more will be coming.

Right now, most Hispanic families face serious challenges. Two-thirds of them live at or near the poverty level. Working to help these families has evolved from being an important service to an imperative for the competitiveness of our nation—and our churches.

Q: What are the biggest challenges and opportunities for the church in reaching Hispanic people?
De León: People often misunderstand the Hispanic community. They think all Hispanics are the same, and they're not. They also think they don't want to become Americans and don't want to mix in American culture. That's totally wrong. Some also say that Hispanics aren't hardworking people, but nobody can work harder. For instance, my son lives south of Atlanta. He started a construction business. People started hiring him saying, "With the last name of de León, that means he's a good worker." That's what our people do. They work hard.

> In terms of opportunities, most Hispanics come from a Christian background. They may not practice Christianity the way we do, but they have no problem talking about God freely.

In terms of opportunities, most Hispanics come from a Christian background. They may not practice Christianity the way we do, but they have no problem talking about God freely. Three weeks ago I watched a show on Spanish TV where a team of judges were evaluating children's talent performances. All three judges said, "Don't forget that the talent you have comes from God, and you should give Him honor every time you sing." Among our people, talking about God, Jesus, and church isn't a problem. You don't dare say those things in American culture. They'd probably kick you out!

Hispanics want to become part of mainstream society, so

the church needs to be the place where they find refuge, education, and motivation to become part of our American culture. Opportunities are there as never before.

Q: How can churches be culturally sensitive and relevant to Hispanic people?
De León: Culturally, there are major differences within the Hispanic population. People from Argentina are European in culture. Their parents are from Italy, Spain, France, and other countries. People from Mexico are Indian in culture. When you try to mix Argentinians with Mexicans, you're going to have some challenges. It isn't the language that makes a difference. Anyone can learn Spanish or English. You can learn the language, but you must live the culture.

Let's say you're an American pastor trying to reach the Hispanic community. You try to do it yourself because you speak a little Spanish. The people will listen to you, but the first time you imply that all Hispanic culture is the same, they'll look at you and say, "No, it's not!" The fiestas they have will be different, and the food they eat will be different. You can't relate to every Hispanic in the same manner. You must learn about their backgrounds and cultures if you want to relate to them in a personal way.

I've been the pastor of this church for forty-one years and had to learn this the hard way. We have eighteen nations represented in our church. If I go to their parties now, I can relate to the different cultures. I understand them.

I do think you won't grow your congregation just by reaching out to these people. You must be one of them. If an Anglo pastor is smart, he'll hire a Hispanic pastor who can speak their language, relate to their cultures, and gain their confidence that way.

Q: How do you minister differently to the first, second, and third generations of Hispanics?

De León: The first generation who comes to the United States will only speak Spanish, will live in a neighborhood they can relate to, and will have their own stores, restaurants, banks, and doctors. This is true of other immigrants, for example the Asians in Orange County, where you find a huge community of Vietnamese and Cambodians who have their own stores and don't speak English. So, the first-generation Hispanic culture is strongly Latino.

The second generation is bilingual and bicultural. They speak Spanish at home and English at school. They identify with both cultures. They still travel to their countries of origin to see their relatives. Their Latino culture is strong, but they also celebrate being in America.

By the third generation, they are fully immersed in the American culture. Their mind-set is not Spanish or Latino—they have no idea what that means. If the DACA (Deferred Action for Childhood Arrivals) children were returned to their countries of origin, they would be in a nation they don't understand at all. That's no longer their culture or people. Now they eat American food, go to American doctors and lawyers, and attend American schools. They still relate to some of their cultural traditions and food, but basically they are American in culture and language.

As Hispanic pastors, we must understand this. In our churches, the first generation wants services in Spanish with a Latino music style. The teaching must follow a Latino model. But we also need services for the second, third, and fourth generations. Those services must be completely in English, along with the music, teaching, and Sunday School.

For twenty years, our denominational region of churches has been intentionally opening English-speaking Latino churches. In our district, we have seventy Hispanic churches that are

English-speaking. These people maintain strong links with their Hispanic roots. Though they are American in culture and speak English, they don't want to leave their people. They still want to stay close to their parents and grandparents and have family celebrations with them, but they want to attend church in English, the language they are comfortable speaking now.

At Templo Calvario, we have Spanish and English services. When we get together as pastors, we try to be sensitive toward both sides. For example, if we are suggesting titles for a new series and one title sounds good in Spanish but makes no sense in English, then we have to come up with a title that makes sense in both languages. We also take care to be relevant to the Hispanic community in the illustrations we use. For example, if we were to talk about Babe Ruth, Hispanic people would ask, "Who is Babe Ruth?" Instead, we use the illustration of a soccer star from Mexico to make the same point.

For many years, this was a bilingual church and I was doing all the ministry in Spanish and English. It got to the point where we needed someone who lived that culture and language every day. So, seven years ago we decided to have one pastor in charge of Spanish-speaking ministries and one in charge of English-speaking ministries. These guys are not only teaching pastors, they are pastors of the ministries, designing the programs, developing their own teams, and being creative for their particular "church." They speak on Sunday mornings, maybe twice a month. The other two Sundays I speak or somebody else does. But those pastors are the main pastors. We encourage people to go to them for weddings, funerals, counseling, guidance, etc. It's complicated, but it works. The older folks want me to marry and bury their people, and of course I do that. The younger set is now used to the other guys and asks them to help on those occasions.

Churches need to open their doors and invite Hispanics to become part of their congregations. These are not the days of "white flight." This is a new day. These are the days of the multiethnic, multicultural congregations. The potential for having churches that reflect what heaven will be like is here today.

Q: How do you address the fears and uncertainties of immigrants?

De León: There's definitely a fear among the first generation and the DACA children. It's a problem. Two Sundays ago, our Spanish pastor said, "I want to congratulate this kid who just got his residency." Everybody applauded, yelled, and got excited. The Anglo church said, "What's this?" They don't understand the struggles kids go through to get their residency. Our own Spanish pastor struggled for eighteen years and spent over eighty thousand dollars to get his residency. Four times a judge told him he had thirty days to go back to Mexico. It scared the daylights out of him and his wife. His children were born here. Each time he got another lawyer, and it cost him more money, but eventually he got his papers.

These people live that life daily. At work they're always afraid someone will come in and ask to see their papers. So, they're always trying to get residency and the documentation they need, but in the process they live with the fear that a judge will tell them they have thirty days to go back to their countries of origin.

We offer seminars by different organizations to advise the illegal immigrants about the residency process. We have lawyers they can go to. We do whatever we can to assist them. Our job is to preach the gospel to anybody and everybody; we don't care about their social status or legal status. We just care about them as people who need Christ. We always tell them from the pulpit, "Get your papers taken care of. Become a bona fide American." We encourage that because we know they are here undocumented, and they don't want to leave. They're working here, their kids are here, and they've bought houses here—but they need to do what is right.

Q: Many in your church and community are poor. How do you challenge them to have a vision beyond themselves to give and serve the least and lost from your neighborhood to the nations?

De León: We have a food bank, and we feed the poor. In the Hispanic community, their jobs are often menial, and they don't make much money, but they make sure their kids get educated so they qualify for better jobs.

We encourage the people from the pulpit all the time, get your kids to go to school. I'm very blunt: "You don't want your kids out there gardening. There's nothing wrong with that because it's a job. But you want your kid working in an office making twenty-five bucks an hour rather than ten bucks an hour." They hear and accept that. We're very encouraged by their initiative.

> One outstanding thing about our people is that once they give their heart to the Lord, they are committed all the way. It isn't unusual to have them attend church three, four, or five times a week.

I teach them all to give 10 percent of their income and offerings on top of that for missions and programs. You can never outgive God. Put God to the test. A lot of these people started by gardening and cleaning houses. Today they own two or three houses, apartment complexes, all kinds of stuff. They're supposed to be the little people who have no money, but they do. They surprise us.

One outstanding thing about our people is that once they give their heart to the Lord, they are committed all the way. It isn't unusual to have them attend church three, four, or five times a week. They invite their friends and relatives to church. They accept the responsibility of evangelizing the world. This is one reason why I believe that the best hope for bringing revival to America may be through the Hispanics. That may sound presumptuous, but the numbers speak for themselves.

They are also very sensitive to the needy in our communities. Those who have suffered or have come from a needy background are more apt to reach out to the broken, neglected, and hungry people of our cities. The wonderful thing is that once they give their heart to Christ and are discipled in the church, the Lord starts blessing them and they become powerful instruments in His hand to change their communities.

Q: Why do you feel CityServe can become a significant help to Templo Calvario in reaching Hispanic people?
De León: We'll always have the poor and needy Hispanic, Anglo, or whoever. Here in Southern California we have a huge problem with the homeless. We must be available to help them. CityServe is a tremendous opportunity for us to become even more involved in the community and to reach out to the poor and needy. In this country, we'll continue to face the challenge of unemployed and homeless people. It's getting harder to buy a house in places like Orange County. Hispanics often live with two or three families in a two-bedroom apartment.

I like CityServe because they're thinking how to help churches serve their communities—not just after hurricanes, tornadoes, and floods—but through the day-to-day challenges of life. It's a city approach. I look forward to working actively with CityServe. We can have these HUBs, huge warehouses, where we store donated products from businesses and use them to bless the community. I see CityServe as the bridge between the needy and the church. If the church has access to the provisions in these warehouses and is aware of the needs in the community, it can use the products like a bridge to bring God to the community. It's an ideal response.

6

Compassion, It's Just "Funner"!

Rick Bezet and Darren DeLaune

One of the great overlooked benefits of serving in compassion ministry is how it lifts shame off our souls. When I speak of shame, I'm referring to feelings of regret from making self-centered decisions versus Jesus-centered and others-centered decisions.

Shame is one of the biggest weights on people in the church—to the point of being a silent epidemic. Ask the average Christian if they believe God loves them, and they'll almost always say yes. Ask if they believe God has forgiven them, and again, almost always yes. But if you stay in that conversation longer, ultimately they'll confess, "I don't know if God can ever forgive me for a couple of things I've done." Regrets surface as they wonder about a failed marriage, failed teen years, secret sins from the past, missed opportunities to help others, and the list goes on.

Compassion destroys shame and regret faster than anything I've seen. I think it's because when a person shows compassion, the overdilated "me" is less in focus since now the focus is on rescuing others and behaving like Jesus. He served others, wept for others, and prayed for others out of a heart filled with compassion. When we do those things, we step into the reality of behaving and loving like Jesus. For many, that's when they feel the Holy Spirit more than at any other time. There's simply no room for lingering regrets in a heart flowing with God's compassion.

Here are just a few examples of how God uses compassion in our lives and churches:

- James 1:27 states that by serving widows and orphans we can keep from "being polluted by the world."
- Acts 2:44–45 says part of the reason the Early Church grew so rapidly was because of their generosity: "All the believers were together and had everything in common. They sold property and possessions to give to anyone who had need."
- James 2:14–17 clearly claims that good deeds authenticate our faith in Jesus.
- Matthew 5:14–16 records Jesus' teaching that "good deeds" can be the thing that flicks on our "light" switch to a dark world and brings glory to our Heavenly Father.

When people are dealing with despair, I know if I can get them to help somebody with a need, God can use this experience to heal their own despair. It's a lesson for all of us. Instead of just preaching to people and yelling on social media, why don't we walk down the street to the woman's house who has cancer and can't cook for her kids, and bring them lasagna and a salad? Why don't we cut the grass for the man who lost his leg and is a God-hater? Then call me and let me know how the despair is doing.

People say a strength of our church is that it's relational. Though we're large, we function relationally like a small church. I credit a lot of that to our compassion ministry. When a church gets compassion correct, it feeds everything else: vision, giving, youth, adults, prodigals, waywardness, and even the pastor. Compassion clarifies our view and gets us all on the same page. Not to mention that it's just "funner" (yes, it's a word—I use it all the time).

When everybody is out there serving, it's way more enjoyable and meaningful. People love accomplishing things together they couldn't do alone. If you help someone or feed someone by yourself, that's a great moment. But if you and a bunch of friends and people from church all serve and feed people in your city at the same time, and when you get done you gather to talk about it, that's a whole different feeling. It's exponentially more fulfilling.

Being compassionate as a group also helps to remove bickering and frustrations. When we're serving with compassion, petty arguments seem small. People feel like, "Let's argue later. There's a homeless dinner tonight, and I've got to go help."

What Not to Do in Compassion Ministry

Here's some hard-won advice from my longtime friend and senior executive pastor, Darren DeLaune, on what not do to when building relationships in needy areas.

• *Don't stay in your zip code.* Ride around your town for an hour and let God break your heart. Jesus often ministered from a heart of compassion, and compassion came from "seeing the crowds" (Matthew 9) in the various cities He visited.

My wife taught me this. "If you want a heart of compassion for someone, you have to walk in their shoes." The first step to starting a compassion ministry isn't to form a committee or even to open a checkbook. The first step is to have your leaders go places they've never been, see things they've never seen, and let God break their hearts along the way.

• *Don't announce you're going to be a compassionate church.* Just be one. Let other people put adjectives on what you're doing and who you are.

• *Don't do it alone.* Our Little Rock Dream Center has more than eighty churches and many other businesses partnering with us. This is huge. Don't go in as "Your Church" promoting "Your Ministry." Go in as a community partner and try to promote others. Our Dream Center doesn't have services on Sunday mornings because there are other churches in that area. We want to open doors and support relationships, not to have a competitive mentality.

• ***Don't try to do too much at once.*** In the beginning, we tried to do everything: education, feeding program, homeless ministry, and more . . . all at one time! We didn't have the capacity or experience to make it work. Instead, we had to back up and ask, "What's one thing we know we can succeed at?" For us it was feeding kids after school.

Now our Dream Center offers programs for the homeless and children, a women's home, warehouse donations, and so on. But success starts with doing one thing well. It will help you find traction with everything that follows.

• ***Don't support compassion ministry with special offerings.*** Make it a permanent part of your budget. Designated funds say to the church and community that your compassion ministry is more than a missional thing you do once a year. It's who you are. At New Life, we took 2 percent of our budget and designated it toward our Dream Center. The ministry isn't supported by raising money from the congregation. Now many other churches and organizations give to the Dream Center as well. That leads to the next point.

• ***Don't make it your church's thing.*** Our Dream Center is a separate 501(c)(3) mainly because we wanted it to be the Arkansas Dream Center, not New Life's downtown campus. Did it start with us and was it totally connected to us? Yes, but wisdom has taught us not to limit who we can reach by making it strictly a church ministry. As a nonprofit, we can get lost people involved with our people, so they get to know Jesus. The Dream Center enjoys a wide spectrum of support from other ministries.

What Is a Compassionate Church?

As Darren mentioned, the Arkansas Dream Center in Little Rock is now a full-fledged member of that community, and we're exploring ways to integrate the CityServe model all over Arkansas. People accept, love, and trust the work we do. We've purchased other buildings and a warehouse in that area and refurbished them. We're seeing kids learn the gospel, graduate from high school, and become the first in their families to earn a college degree.

Each of our seventeen campuses now has a similar type of ministry reaching the needs of their communities. They differ by community because compassion ministry is not one-size-fits-all, but each is centered around loving, supporting, and serving those who live there. I'm happy and humbled to say that in our state we are a go-to ministry for referrals, even from state agencies. They say, "People need help with this or that. Let's go to the Dream Center."

To be a compassionate church means more than just adopting the label and having an annual sermon on compassion. It means compassion is pervasive in much of what you say in your church offices, in your living rooms, in your outreaches, in your staff, and in your budget. Once it's everywhere—then you're a compassionate church.

As compassion pervades your campus and your conversations and your spiritual atmosphere, you'll find people living freer, forgetting their shame, and becoming relationally stronger as they serve others—together. Compassion is just "funner"!

7

The Compassion Galaxy

Rich Guerra

R ich grew up in Los Angeles and has always been passionate about reaching people for Jesus and helping those in need. Prior to becoming the superintendent of the Assemblies of God Southern California Network, which represents over 480 churches, he pastored in Las Vegas, a mile from the Strip, and the Central Valley of California. While serving in Visalia, California, the community honored Rich for his leadership and for creating solutions to the city's needs. Here is an interview with Rich about what led him to help launch CityServe SoCal.

Q: What are some church-based compassion ministries you've championed over the years?
Guerra: While I was pastoring in Visalia, several defining moments changed my thinking and passion of pastoring. As I drove to church one Sunday morning, I was excited about speaking to our congregation of more than two thousand people. Yet as I passed church after church in the town, God spoke to me and said the following words: "We're not winning, we're losing." He made me realize it wasn't about just our church, but about all the churches and unreached people in the community. I started praying for other churches and for God to help me see those people who had never been touched by the gospel.

The second defining moment happened while I was preaching one Sunday morning. I saw a young woman who had been faithfully attending church. Her husband also attended faithfully, but only one of them would come each Sunday. When I asked her why both didn't come at the same time, she said they had a special needs child and one of them had to stay home on Sunday while the other attended church. I asked her what would happen if we had a special class for her son, so they could attend at the same time. She responded that they had been wanting to get involved in ministry and that would give them the opportunity to do so. We started a class with one teacher per special needs student, and that class planted the seed for what is now called The Miracle League of Visalia, which is a baseball field built specifically for special needs children. Now, close to two hundred children participate every weekend during the baseball season.

Once again, God was challenging me about reaching out to the community—not just about growing my church. I needed to discover the needs of people and ask Him to help me know how to meet those needs.

The leaders in our community came to realize we were a church that wanted to help needy people. When the superintendent of the schools asked us to adopt twenty-five needy families in one of their schools for Christmas, we agreed to that and eventually adopted close to three hundred families. Every child, age birth through eighteen years, received gifts of shoes, clothes, and an age-appropriate toy. We also provided a box of food for every family.

I finally understood what Luke meant when he wrote that although Jesus was in a synagogue full of people, He noticed a women who had been crippled for eighteen years (Luke 13:10–12). Was I willing to see people in my community who were crippled emotionally, physically, or spiritually? Not only did Jesus see her,

He spoke to her. He called her a "daughter of Abraham" (Luke 13:16). Jesus saw the potential of who she could become, not just who she was. Finally, Jesus reached out to the woman, and she was healed. She left that day thanking and praising God.

Q: You've cast the vision for a "Galaxy of Compassion." What is it?

Guerra: As I've had the opportunity as the Southern California Network superintendent to speak at a different Assemblies of God church practically every Sunday, I noticed one common denominator in all the healthy churches: they were doing acts of compassion for their communities. So many of our churches began as outward-focused ministries, but have become inward-focused. God gave me the vision for the Compassion Galaxy that would enable all our churches to be healthy and vibrant. I asked myself, *How could we help every church in our Network do acts of compassion in their community?* Regardless of their size, location, and resources, there are compassion needs all around them. That was the seed idea for the Compassion Galaxy, which CityServe is part of.

> We want to help every church in our network be prepared to do acts of compassion in their communities.

Q: How can churches in Southern California participate?

Guerra: For a church to be a compassionate church, three things need to happen:

• *The church must depend on God.* Many churches feel they don't have the people or the resources to help in their community, but with God all things are possible.

• *The church must focus on Jesus.* A common tendency is for a church to compare itself to another church or program rather than keep its focus on Jesus. Each church must ask itself what Jesus would see and do for the people in its community. Jesus was a master at stopping what He was doing to help a person in need.

• *The church must understand who the needy are in its community.* The church must move outside its four walls to find the needy and reach out to them. Who lives in your community? What are the greatest needs in your community?

When you've laid that foundation, then compassion is a natural outflow of your church. CityServe can train a pastor and the church members how to identify needs within their community and understand what acts of compassion will meet those needs. CityServe will then supply the resources necessary to help with those needs. It might be food, clothing, or furniture. Once the training is complete, a church is prepared to reach out in compassionate love to its community. We want to help every church in our network be prepared to do acts of compassion in their communities.

Q: As a leader, what have been two or three of your biggest challenges and solutions?
Guerra: One of the biggest challenges I've faced is that I assumed people were as passionate about certain things as I am. I quickly discovered they were not. I've always been passionate about reaching the lost and helping those in need. I just assumed people who came to church week after week shared that same passion.

One time after a service, I was greeting people in the lobby who were saying what a wonderful service it was and how excited they were about all those who had given their lives to Christ that morning. I noticed a gentleman waiting to talk with me after the other people had left. Somehow, I knew he wasn't going to compliment me about my sermon. In fact, he came up to me with a stern look on his face, and said, "I'm tired of you talking about reaching the lost every week. What about me? What about my needs?"

I was stunned. All I could say was, "I'm sorry. I just assumed that because you've been a member of this church for the past thirty years that you have the same passion I do. Obviously I was wrong." I began to think, *How can I instill that passion in other people?*

One of the biggest challenges of a leader is to communicate a God-inspired vision so it becomes the passion of the people listening. It's been my experience that most people and churches resist change, especially when it comes to a new vision. They tend to glorify the past instead of moving forward with the new and fresh things God wants to do. They're convinced that if they could go back to a time when things were good for them, then everything would be okay. Scripture is clear: God doesn't live in the past! He has something fresh for today and unbelievable for tomorrow. While I'm thankful for our traditions, tradition is to be remembered and appreciated, not relived.

Secondly, people resist change when they're experiencing too much pain in the present. Many young leaders are so passionate about reaching the lost that they forget about the people in their churches who are going through much personal pain. Maybe it's the pain of a former pastor who hurt or betrayed them, and that hasn't healed. Until people heal from painful wounds, it will be difficult for them to embrace change.

Finally, I've found people resist change when they're uncertain about the future. "If we change, what are we going to look like in the future?" Many people would rather stay the same than change to something they're not sure of.

Q: You've challenged leaders to live disciplined lives. You've said, "You can't expect uphill results with downhill habits." Please elaborate.

Guerra: I'm often asked what's the secret to my success. I don't consider myself successful—I hope that I'm just faithful. But if I've had any success, it's because of my personal discipline:

> I pray a little bit every day.
> I read a little bit every day.
> I exercise a little bit every day, and
> I try to do an act of kindness every day.

If you discipline yourself to do these things every day, you'll see results. Our problem is we skip days and then we binge. You'll never see results without daily discipline over time. Practice doesn't make perfect; it makes permanent.

> You'll never see results without daily discipline over time. Practice doesn't make perfect; it makes permanent.

Q: You've said there are times you go for it on the fourth down and other times you punt. Can you elaborate on that concept?

Guerra: A good football team knows when to go for it on fourth down and when to punt and get a better field position.

Sometimes we need to punt because the people aren't ready to receive the vision and apply it in their lives. How do you know when they're ready? I live by the phrase: "People tend to support what they've helped to create." When God gives me a vision, I know if I can get people to help me create it, they'll support it. Then it's time to go for it. Even though the odds seem to be against you, you know God is telling you to go for it.

Q: Is there anything else you'd like to share with pastors considering church-based compassion ministry as a priority for their communities?

Guerra: One day Jesus sent the disciples in a boat to go to the other side of the lake. While going to the other side, a violent storm erupted, and the disciples feared for their lives. Suddenly, they saw Jesus walking on the water, and Peter said, "Lord, if it's you, tell me to come to you on the water" (Matthew 14:28).

For a church to be a church of compassion, somebody must be willing to step out of the boat and walk toward Jesus. It's scary, it's risky, and it's uncertain—but if Jesus tells you to come, you're going to make it.

As long as Peter kept his eyes on Jesus, he was fine, but when he saw the wind and the storm he started to sink. Even then, Jesus reached down and lifted Peter up, and they climbed into the boat together.

My challenge to those reading this book is to get out of the boat and keep your eyes on Jesus. He will lift you up, and together you will walk on water.

8

Becoming Compassionate Leaders

Cary Summers

From a natural point of view, Museum of the Bible in Washington, DC, wasn't going to happen easily—and we knew it. Worse yet, so did our lawyers.

We hoped to occupy a building within blocks of the US Capitol, in a high-restriction zone governed by layers upon layers of permitting, regulations, and the oversight of numerous special government agencies. Some agencies were concerned about how our building would look. Others, we were told, wouldn't be sympathetic to us because we were a Bible museum.

Not only that, but we were seeking to create the third-largest museum in DC, at 430,000 square feet. This would be a major undertaking.

"There are seven major subcommittees you have to appear before, all with different jurisdictions," our lawyers told us grimly. "Any one of them could kill this project."

"That's why we hired you—to help us battle that out," we said.

But I knew the battle didn't belong to our lawyers or to me as the museum's president. It belonged to the Lord. If there was going to be a Museum of the Bible in DC, God would have to make a way.

This wasn't my first rodeo. I had learned much about leadership in forty years of service with companies like Bass Pro Shops,

Abercrombie and Fitch, Silver Dollar City, and Nazareth Village in Israel. In each, I had held a senior, or the senior, role. But the best example of leadership I know isn't from last year, the last decade, or even the last century but from 2,500 years ago.

Nehemiah faced one of the of the most complicated and most documented leadership challenges ever when God called him to oversee rebuilding the wall around Jerusalem. At the time, Nehemiah lived a thousand miles from Jerusalem and served as the cupbearer to the most powerful king of the day. Warlords in the area around Jerusalem certainly didn't want anyone rebuilding the wall because it would diminish their control over the people. So why would Nehemiah leave a legacy position, travel a far distance to take on a dangerous task no person had asked him to do, and incur personal sacrifice for a group of people he didn't know?

The answer is compassionate leadership. Compassionate leaders are those who take on the responsibility of serving their cities and communities in a selfless way that leaves things better when they're gone. For these leaders, the principles embedded in Nehemiah's actions remain timeless and will make or break their organization today.

Here are five attributes of compassionate leaders.

• *Compassionate leaders listen and are concerned for the condition of others.* Nehemiah heard the report of conditions in Jerusalem and then asked for details (Nehemiah 1:1–4). We all hear reports about the conditions of our communities, but compassionate leaders go further and spend time asking great questions and gathering information.

I saw this done well by the CEO of Coca-Cola, Douglas Ivester. Doug was a friend of mine even before he held that spot at Coca-Cola, and when I was in Atlanta I would drop by the high-rise headquarters of that famous beverage company to enjoy a little time with him. I often marveled as people from various departments came into his office and he'd say, "How's your daughter? Did your grandmother come out of surgery okay?"

One time I asked him, "Doug, how in the world do you know all this stuff about individual people? This is one of largest companies in the world!" He responded, "Every day when I get in that elevator, I remember that people love to work for people who have concern for them, not the corporation. So, I make it a habit to learn about the people working in these towers."

Doug had a real desire to know people, and he found out it was good business. His answer has a deep-rooted application to the church and nonprofit worlds of today. Having sat on committees at churches for forty years, I've observed that one of the hardest things for any pastor to do is to ask good questions of people. Good questions invite good answers. Great questions invite great answers. Great questions show compassion and concern for people, and humility and openness to hearing an honest answer about the organization.

> Compassionate leaders are those who take on the responsibility of serving their cities and communities in a selfless way that leaves things better when they're gone.

The first step is to let people know you care. It's asking, "How are you doing?" not just "How are we doing?" In many businesses, most of a leader's conversations with employees is spent trying to find information about the company or organization, not about the person. Even in churches, leaders too often sidestep compassion for individuals in favor of organizational assessments.

Secondly, when conversation turns to the shared mission of the organization, too many church and nonprofit leaders simply don't want to hear bad news. "Why is our enrollment in kids' ministry down? How are we doing in teaching people the gospel? Is our foster-care ministry making an impact?" I'm convinced that many leaders don't ask those questions because they know the answers and don't want other people to confirm them!

In Nehemiah's day, people were considered a commodity—their lives and deaths didn't matter to leaders. Yet the COO of the most powerful king on earth at that time asked great questions rooted in compassion for people. We all need to become better at asking, "How are you doing?" and "How are we really doing?"

• *Compassionate leaders act on feelings of compassion.* If a leader has concern for others and can learn to really listen, this leads to demonstrated compassion. Nehemiah didn't just experience feelings of compassion and then walk away from the challenge. He acted on his felt compassion, as all great leaders do.

At Museum of the Bible, we work behind the scenes daily with pastors of large churches and leaders of large ministries. We see the good, the bad, and the ugly. The very best leaders I interact with have a broken heart for people. You hear it in their voices, their tones, and the kinds of questions they ask.

Rick Warren, founder of Saddleback Church, is on our board. A number of times I've watched him in conversations where compassion wells up in his heart and he says to someone, "You know what? I sense you need a hug right now." With the person's permission, he gives them a big bear hug. I've seen men and women start crying on the spot and say, "How did you know I needed that!" Rick can sense it in his spirit. Yet his compassionate response is so rare!

I asked him how he knew when someone had a deep need like that. He told me that because he had talked with so many hurting people, and experienced the suicide of his own son, he has developed a brokenness of heart. He understands what heartache and tragedy look like in other people—and he acts on it.

Jesus is our ultimate model. He often acted because He was moved with compassion. Compassionate action only comes from people whose hearts are broken by the conditions of those around them.

• *Compassionate leaders wear other people's shoes.* Nehemiah didn't distance himself from the problem. Rather, he put his heart and his feet right in the middle of it.

Having visited the Middle East over one hundred times in the last thirty-five years, I've learned to set aside my Western sensibilities and truly listen to the people of the Middle East. Westerners tend to have a drive-thru McDonald's mentality: "Let me come in, fix something, give you some money, and then I'm out of here. Blessings."

In the Middle East, far more than here in the United States, life is all about multigenerational relationships. They take a long view of life, history, and traditions that seem like a waste of time to the fast-food mentality of Americans. One day during my travels there I heard some people arguing, and I went over to listen to them. I thought it must be about a current issue, but they were arguing about the Crusades!

Our typical fast-food mentality can hinder our endeavors in inner-city ministries. We've all seen groups of white, middle-class people swoop into a neighborhood, do a day of service, and then leave. This is a type of intrusion into the area of need rather than an infusion. We fail to see beneficial long-term effects because we're not willing to take off our shoes and put on their shoes.

Compassionate leadership means making a significant effort to understand other people's reality instead of affirming your own perceptions.

• *Compassionate leaders don't rush to conclusions.* One of the great enemies of good leadership is how much we think we know. We process what we hear through our knowledge bank and draw a quick conclusion. We act too quickly: "I don't have time. Here's my decision. Next."

Nehemiah was the opposite. He spent three days in Jerusalem walking around the wall at night, accompanied by a few good men and his horse (Nehemiah 2:11–17). He'd already collected the building materials and the blessing of the king. Why waste three days walking around the wall at night? Chuck Swindoll wrote in the book *Hand Me Another Brick* that this is where God put the steel into Nehemiah's bones. It didn't happen quickly or with fanfare, but in quietness with God and in gathering information about the situation.

Do we take time when nobody is around, and it's just us and God, to ask Him to put His wisdom, His steel into us? If not, we spend all our lives making quick decisions that for the most part are ours, not God's. The only way to avoid making rushed (and often wrong) decisions is to understand and appreciate the silence and the waiting when it's just you and God.

In the museum world, we have things called "roadblocks." Those are objects, exhibits, or kiosks we put in the pathway so people must slow down. Without these roadblock, many visitors would tend to cruise through the museum at high speed rather than stopping and enjoying what's there.

As we had our own walk through the process of gaining approval for Museum of the Bible, we didn't rush either. It wouldn't have helped. Rather, we were on our faces seeking God's guidance and blessing. We were willing to wait in the quiet.

• *Compassionate leaders rely upon God and recognize His power.* During the approval process for the Museum, we relied on a simple fact: It was God's idea and His project. We were privileged to help carry it out, but the museum wasn't ours. So, we didn't worry about it. We let God give us inspiration when we encountered obstacles. Sure enough, at every turn He kept showing us what to do and what questions to ask.

Even in the most daunting meetings, we never came in with fear. Rather, we had an excitement about what God would do next. At the end of all those meetings and working with all those agencies, the result absolutely stunned our top-of-the-industry law firm: Not only did we receive approval from every agency, but there was never a dissenting vote. We had 100 percent approval across the board!

"We don't get that kind of support on a traditional office building," our lawyers said. "It's unheard of!"

"God has gone before us," we replied. "He changed hearts."

Our lawyer team believed us because, in their words, "You're not that smart." They were right. That's how Museum of the Bible, which is bigger than even the National Aerospace Museum, was built in half the time of a normal museum and opened to the public in November 2017.

In the process I watched as God used all my experience before then—in the sporting goods world, retail, theme parks, and more—to help me walk through the challenges. People who know me say everything in my life was in preparation for this. In that small way, I felt like Nehemiah whose skill building and experiences in the king's palace proved invaluable when he accepted the challenge to rebuild Jerusalem's wall.

Whatever task you're in, God will draw on your experiences and use your life for His glory—especially as you seek to become a compassionate leader.

9

The Moment for a Movement

Doug Wead

Doug Wead is a historian, a Fox News contributor, and a *New York Times* best-selling author of over thirty books. He has served four American presidents. He is a co-founder and original board member of Mercy Corps, which has distributed more than two billion dollars of food and medicine around the world.

Q: As a member of Dream City Church* in Phoenix for several years, what impressed you most about Pastor Tommy Barnett and his church-based compassion ministry?

Wead: When I lived in Arizona, I would speak for Tommy Barnett from time to time. I knew his dad in Kansas City. I always liked Tommy. He was young, good-looking, dressed nice, drove fancy cars, and was a great evangelist. He was contemporary. Then he became pastor of a church in Iowa and started getting all kinds of criticism from other ministers. They said, "I could have a big church, too, if I ran a bunch of buses with kids from the inner city. But you can't run a church like that. None of them are paying tithe. I could have big attendance if I had Johnny Cash once a year at the fairgrounds and averaged that out in my attendance. His doctrine is wrong and extreme."

I thought to myself, *Listen to yourselves! Why don't you guys do all those things?* What Tommy was doing seemed practical to me, so I defended him.

Q: How did you come to see the importance of compassion ministries?

Wead: This became a priority for me after reading through the Bible every year. After three years I thought, *What's missing? What do I find in the Bible that I'm not practicing or finding practiced in Christianity?* It was overwhelmingly clear in verse after verse that it was feeding the poor. For example, after Peter and Paul decided to minister to different groups of people (Peter to the Jews and Paul to the Gentiles), they went their separate ways. Paul's parting words at the time were, "We should continue to remember the poor, the very thing I had been eager to do all along" (Galatians 2:10). It was so clear to me that this concept was scripturally based.

I had learned from my father to be an independent thinker. I didn't need the affirmation of my peers. I felt confident in what the Bible had to say. So, I started several nonprofits and took a trip around the world to look for places with the greatest needs. I went to India, Africa, . . . a wide variety of places. It was tragic. I came back and said, "This is outrageous!" So, I started raising money.

When the Cambodian famine began, I knew from having traveled around the world how terrible it was going to be and what heartache would result. So, I jumped on a plane and went to Thailand because I couldn't get into Cambodia. The night I came back, a congressman had arranged for me to have dinner with the Reagans at their house in Pacific Palisades. That week they were announcing he would run for president. Pat and Shirley Boone were also there. The only thing on my mind was Cambodia. Over dinner we talked about what we could do in Cambodia. Shirley Boone was very moved by my stories and introduced me to her son-in-law who had started Mercy Corps.

That led me to ask the person representing the Carters if they would let us have a reception in the East Room of the White House, and the first Charity Awards Dinner was launched. The next year Reagan was president and Nancy said, "You started that thing at my house. Why don't you come do it again?" Now we were bipartisan, so we were on a roll. Mercy Corps became our ministry arm.

Q: As a person with a front-row seat to the American political system, what can you tell us about church leaders and their engagement in the process?
Wead: It's been disappointing. I guess it's a lack of experience. I've arranged for many, many religious leaders to meet with presidents, and it seems the leaders are more concerned with getting a story to tell their congregation on Sunday than making a real impact. It's like a sermon illustration in the making. Some have had a real impact, but it's not common. Their first goal is to build their church, increase its numbers, increase its income.

> **If the church would just meet the needs of people in their community, they would build the church.**

If a pastor is afraid of stepping into new activities, the congregation can almost smell and feel his fear. In other churches the people labor under guilt: "Why aren't you bringing people to the church? Why aren't you helping to build my church?" If the church would just meet the needs of people in their community, they would build the church. Every audience is full of people with financial, marital, and relationship problems with their boss, family members, and coworkers. Those are the basic needs everybody has, and the Bible addresses those needs. If preachers preached to meet those needs, then people would bring friends to hear. Instead they get sermons on how to organize, why to be here on time, which service to go to—technique and formula.

Q: As a historian, do you see any similarities in our country currently to the disillusionment and confusion of the post-Vietnam War era that set the stage for the Jesus Movement?

Wead: Yes, I think so. I saw how the Jesus Movement took off, and I see some of the same similarities today: great divisiveness, disillusionment with government, and the media overplaying its hand. You also see the rigged corporate economy and the free enterprise system that allows monopolies to make money off war.

Similarly, this is the moment for the church to awaken and lead the way to bring meaning, civility, and solutions to the uncertainty and brokenness in our communities. The church will meet resistance in any attempt to engage with its wider community, and such resistance will not only be born out of ignorance, it will be born out of deliberate and malicious intent. Yet, we have also this injunction from Romans 14:16, "Do not let what you know is good be spoken of as evil."

So, we must get this straight. People will hate the church and will resist and purposely misrepresent its good deeds and works in the community, but we must forge ahead to help our nation. There are several guiding principles that might help you in your journey outside the walls of the church:

• *Be prepared for opposition.* Have videos, press releases, and comments ready to communicate your program clearly.

• *Stay happy and positive.* Smile. Jesus said, "By this everyone will know that you are my disciples, if you love one another" (John 13:35).

• *Stick to your original purpose.* If you're planning to help flood victims, don't get distracted into a discussion on abortion, gay marriage, or gun control. Stick to the chosen cause.

• **Step up and answer false accusations.** You can't control what people believe, but you can state your position and intention clearly. Give the public a chance to understand. Yes, Jesus was silent before Pilate, and there's a time for silence, but this is a time to speak up. "Do not let what you know is good be spoken of as evil."

Q: You speak of something called FOF and FOP. What are they, and how can they hinder leaders from achieving God's best for their lives and ministries?

Wead: FOF is fear of failure and FOP is fear of people. It's based on 1 Corinthians 3:21, 23: "All things are yours, . . . and you are of Christ, and Christ is of God." The fear of people can keep you from accomplishing what you want to. You don't have to be afraid of anybody.

I've met six presidents and worked for four of them. The solution to FOF is to die to yourself as the apostle Paul said. "For to me, to live is Christ and to die is gain" (Philippians 1:21). Jesus' constant sermon was very short: Fear not, only believe. "Do not let your hearts be troubled. You believe in God; believe also in me" (John 14:1). Pastor, leader . . . fear not, only believe, and do it!

*Dream City Church in Phoenix, Arizona, was previously First Assembly of God.

Part 2

THE NEIGHBORHOOD

As the local church directs its attention outward,
its focus shifts, its priorities shuffle,
and its purpose comes into clearer view.
Showing others God's love through
acts of kindness and compassion
builds a bridge of relationship,
making our testimony more relevant.

—Alton Garrison

10

Know Your Community before Fixing It

Bridget Dierks

It feels like our community is having a problem with poverty." I call these "street-corner assessments": You look around a community and draw conclusions based on what you see. Of course, our individual perspectives don't include very much information. That's why our data shouldn't be limited to our experiences.

I once heard a volunteer say, "The poverty rate must be going up. I feel like I see people in poverty everywhere I go." In truth, it was going down, but he was probably noticing low income people for the first time! That kind of perspective-shift happens all the time. We need a better approach if we're talking about creating programs that work.

Using a Data-Driven Method to Understanding Poverty

A desire for better outcomes led us at the Community Foundation of the Ozarks to seek a more data-driven approach to understanding poverty and to consider all aspects of poverty before trying to alleviate problems. Our efforts led us to create the Northwest Project in the poorest section of town in Springfield, Missouri. We've already learned much about how data helps define the problems—and how it can't help us avoid every surprise.

We began by looking at data related to poverty and saw that Springfield has a high poverty rate: 25 percent of the population makes less than twenty-three thousand dollars a year. At the same time, we have a strikingly low unemployment rate of about 3 percent. Our city is essentially fully employed, and yet poverty is high. What gives? The data indicates that many people are working low-wage jobs. They don't have access to health insurance, sick time, or vacation time, meaning they lose their jobs more frequently when they or their kids get sick, or they can't make it to work because of some other life event. This makes it harder to keep a job, let alone get a better one. People are often stuck at the same level for years.

We got our data from the census, and from a unique and helpful resource created by community leaders in Springfield every two years. It's called the Community Focus Report, and it examines thirteen areas of community need and engagement to bring to light things that are going well and not going well. It's a very data-driven document. We also have an active health department that tracks health data and monitors health outcomes and challenges in the city. I would encourage you to begin your data-driven compassion efforts by seeking out all available data on your community from a variety of sources. You may be surprised at what exists.

Data told us that Springfield's northwest section has more poverty than other parts of town, and so we focused our efforts there. We looked at more data to find out why the poverty rate was rising there, and we established a few theories. Among them was that people there tend to have uncompleted education and school debt to go with it. Usually they had to drop out due to health issues or family crises.

We also noted that Springfield is the only urban community in our region, and many rural families have migrated here. People who struggle financially in rural places move here and find mostly low-income jobs, and they no longer have the support system their family provided back home. When Grandma can't watch the child and Mom can't go to work, Mom has a hard time moving ahead.

With some clarity about what was happening, we decided to try to impact poverty connected to ten main issues. These include family stability, resolution of criminal background issues, health insurance, employability, and financial stability. The approach involves intensive, in-depth case management work with individuals, looking at their whole family budget, the opportunities for completing their degree, earning certifications to move into higher-quality jobs, and finding health insurance.

This encouraged us that data is indeed very useful when creating problem-solving approaches. On the other hand, broad data sets alone can't give you the granular view needed to effectively help people—which we soon learned.

Changing the Plan to Meet the Needs

Not all of our original approaches worked, and we soon found we had to adapt to truly meet the needs before us. For example, our original plan to help people get out of disastrous payday loans was to provide a loan pool from which they would borrow and to which they would pay back. It sounded good, but it was incomplete. Brilliant banker and community leader Todd Parnell pointed out that our process wouldn't impact their credit scores, and therefore wouldn't help them very much in the long term. Armed with that knowledge, we partnered with the CU Community Credit Union and helped our participants set up checking accounts, apply for their first traditional loans, and even purchase a home for the first time. This has proven incredibly important. Credit scores have improved, up to one hundred points a year. Linking our participants with a credit union became a major component of our program.

We also thought we would see more people who needed to resolve a criminal background, but we found that wasn't the case. From a legal perspective, family law issues were far more prevalent than actual crimes. Within the pool of people we were working with, criminal backgrounds weren't very common, so we redirected our efforts toward solving the problems that were there.

Another change came in our counseling endeavors. We knew that people in poverty tended to have higher rates of adverse childhood incidents—things like family eviction experienced as a child, abuse in the home, proximity to drug use and violence, and single parent (and related single income) families. We thought group programming that focused everybody on the future instead of the past would create healthy momentum. We soon discovered this wasn't a good solution. People are shaped by what they experience as children, and we found it much more effective to promote group counseling that allowed people to have in-depth discussions about their past and to share their unique perspectives in a safe environment.

> Not all of our original approaches worked, and we soon found we had to adapt to truly meet the needs before us.

We've also seen the high value of the cohort and ally system. Our program is very intensive for the first four months. Participants meet weekly for dinner, in groups of ten, and get deep into the guts of things. We observed that for the first month, participants keep the wall up somewhat and have an attitude of, "I can use a little help, but I'm okay." As trust builds and walls come down, they reach a tipping point as a group and start saying to each other, "I really do need help, and I'm going to help you as well." They have meaningful conversations about difficult topics related to their financial situations, which may involve the way they grew up, abuse in their homes, and more. These sincere discussions in the context of friendship help them think about how they arrived at their present situation and how to move forward. As they become honest about their challenges, they build a true community.

By adjusting our approaches to the data, we've honed our systems to achieve success in reaching our goals. Both broad data sets and data from the specific individuals and families who participated have proven invaluable. Already, in two years, fifty families have gone through the Northwest Project's program. They've earned more income, are moving out of debt, advocating for themselves for services, keeping cleaner and healthier homes to reduce asthma and other home-related illnesses, and are referring friends and family to our program.

The lesson is clear: Don't try to fix something without real knowledge of the problem and the community. Find out what knowledge is available in large data sets like the census provides, or in community surveys or studies. You can also gather invaluable information by spending time with the people you want to serve and hearing from their own mouths about their situations. The more we understand, the better equipped we will be to provide effective services to those who need it most.

11

Scalable Strategies for Smaller Churches and Communities

Steve Donaldson

"Our church is called Zacchaeus Tree. We lift people up, so they can see Jesus," declared the pastor of a small church and community.

Sometimes images of Andy Griffith and Mayberry form our perception of rural America. Unfortunately, realities of poverty and isolation are closer to the truth of what the average small-town community experiences today.

I carry in my pocket a bristleless toothbrush to remind me of a little girl our team met in a mobile home. They handed this little girl a toothbrush, and she clutched it to her chest and cried. They thought maybe she didn't like it for some reason. Then she darted into the bathroom and brought back a toothbrush with all the bristles worn off. All five children in her family had been sharing the same toothbrush. I carry that worn-out toothbrush with me, so I don't take for granted everything God has provided for me—which I want to provide for the rural communities I serve.

Current poverty rates in rural America exceed the poverty rates in urban communities, and there are significantly fewer social services available to address these needs, according to the National Advisory Committee on Rural Health and Human Services (NACRHHS). Persistent poverty counties have poverty rates of 20 percent or higher, and 88 percent of persistent poverty counties are rural.

The US Department of Agriculture notes that one in four children in rural America lives in poverty. And rural areas have more single-guardian households than urban areas. People in rural areas also struggle with unemployment, substance abuse, and domestic abuse. According to one study, a rural teen is more likely to misuse drugs and alcohol than an urban teen. Pew Research Center declared drug abuse to be the leading problem in rural America.

As Christians we know that statistics aren't the full picture, but we must ask ourselves: If the church vanished from these small towns, would anyone notice? Instead of asking, "How big is your church?" we should ask, "How is your church impacting its community?"

Understanding the Rural Culture

Several years back, I heard a lecture on small communities. The professor's research revealed what I have observed. In the past, there were three foundations of a small town: the family, public schools, and the local church. The community often centered around the local church. Over time, the family unit splintered, local churches lost much of their influence, and only public schools remained as a foundation in small towns. Despite this shift, the local church is still the best-equipped entity to facilitate healthy development within communities.

I'm reminded of the story when one of my friends purchased a pair of jeans, replete with designer holes and frays, for over a hundred dollars. His grandmother offered to wash his laundry while he was away, and after returning home, he found that Grandma had patched the holes and cut off the frays of his jeans. Grandma didn't understand the value of frayed jeans.

In a similar way, people outside of a small town often don't understand the community's local culture and its interpersonal relationships. Since the church is made up of its community and is

God's highest order inside a community, the local church can and must once again become a foundational entity in small-town life.

Becoming a Community Stakeholder

Rural church pastors often understand the vastness of the poverty around them. They may wonder—while struggling with their own limited resources—how they can minister to the needs of their community. Often, learning how to serve in these situations begins with a change in focus.

In his book *Crazy Love*, Francis Chan says, "Christians are like manure: Spread them out and they help everything grow better but keep them in one big pile and they stink horribly!" Hiding behind the four walls of the church building creates a church that is ineffective and inconsequential. However, when a church rolls up its sleeves, spreads out, and collaborates with the community, it unlocks a powerful force to address rural poverty.

Rural Compassion, the nonprofit organization we founded in 2003, targets communities of five thousand people or fewer, where you find the fewest social services available in America. A few years ago, we self-diagnosed that a lot of what churches were doing was episodic—one event, one time a year. Since Jesus identified "fruit that remains" as the goal of our work (see John 15 and 16), we knew we had to try something different. We found that when a church has ongoing engagement with the community it enhances the impact of episodic events.

We started thinking in terms of breaking cycles of poverty through connectivity with the main stakeholders in a community, like the superintendent of schools, principals, fire and police chiefs, social workers, business owners, and prominent families. We started sitting at the table without demanding to be at the center of the table. In a way, we were going back to a parish mentality, relating to other stakeholders in the community and owning local problems together.

Now Rural Compassion works in over one thousand communities, partnering with multiple churches of different denominations to train and coach their pastors to become communitarians. We train church leaders to spend up to one-third of their time working with community stakeholders. Collaboration between the church, schools, civic circles, and government is essential. One rural pastor tells this story of becoming what my brother David refers to as a "Christian Communitarian":

> I met with three law enforcement agency leaders, as well as the mayor, fire chief, justice court judge, soccer commissioner, directors of the counseling center, and the Chamber of Commerce. I also contacted hospice, the owners of the mortuary, hardware, and lumberyard businesses, and the building inspector. I attended multifaith ministers' meetings and made myself available to the hospital and the assisted-care facility. My wife partnered with the local schools. Through these contacts, we are seeing how the church can intentionally serve the community.

Serving the Community

Our goal at Rural Compassion is not to address poverty in an isolated way but to help the entire community become healthy and whole. We don't encourage churches to come into a community and announce, "We're going to start a food pantry, a clothing closet, and this and that." We want churches to relate to the community first, learn about the needs of the community, and then act. Many communities already have a food pantry to help their struggling neighbors. Once the church is aware of this, they can volunteer to help out at that food pantry rather than setting up a second one. If there are items like diapers and canned goods the pantry desperately needs but hasn't received through donations, the church can donate these items to lend a helping hand. This year Rural Compassion will give away over one hundred thousand pairs of new shoes through rural churches to children in the local schools. All these endeavors create intentional relationships that allow the church to collectively address the needs of poverty and ultimately share the love of Christ.

As rural churches begin to interact with their communities in ways like this, they immediately see significantly better results. One small city held a big harvest festival every fall. A church there decided to shut down their own harvest festival and help the city with theirs. One advantage of small towns is when you do something like that, everybody knows you sacrificed to serve the community. In fact, I would call that a big advantage of small towns: You live each day in the community and have regular interactions with people who live there. You see these same people at little league games, city parades, and the big events each year as well as at the grocery store and the gas station. Ministry isn't isolated from the rest of life, but woven into it.

One church volunteered to shovel the manure behind animals in the parade. They served their way into the hearts of the community.

Others become the best friend of the public school system and get involved on a regular basis to help schools reach their goals. We teach churches not to approach the schools with their own goals and dictate what success looks like, but to let the schools tell the church what they want to achieve. Churches have the power to pull in other groups in town to assist as well.

There are so many ways a church can become a community stakeholder, such as honoring public servants, offering classroom supplies for teachers, becoming a reading buddy in the schools, coaching sports teams, and undertaking community work projects. Why not host a Hero Day for local law enforcement? This can be a barbecue or breakfast where each officer receives a personalized

Bible with their name and badge number on it. Honor is the key with law enforcement. Each Bible serves as a trophy of appreciation to them personally.

Genuine appreciation is a fantastic tool. There are many other people in our communities who do wonderful things, yet no one notices them or praises them for their good work. The Bible commands us to give honor to whom honor is due. That includes the sanitation workers, the city clerks, and the mail delivery personnel. Let's not drill wells in Africa and neglect to give thanks—and maybe even a gift card—to the local people who keep our water clean.

This kind of ministry is so effective that I've started asking pastors to consider spending a third of their time in prayer and sermon preparation, a third dealing with church facilities, governance, and leadership development, and a third pastoring their town by working with community leaders and groups. If you can't do 33 percent, start with 5 percent—just do something. Exegete your community like you exegete Scripture. Assess the needs, strengths, and weaknesses. Become aware of everything around you. It's hard to bring solutions to problems you don't know exist. Working with the mayor, social workers, prominent leaders, and business people will cause you to do ministry differently.

As a church positions itself to become an important leader in serving its community and the dire needs of the people who live there, we begin to see those same communities become places where children and families flourish. Thanks to local pastors and church congregants with ambition to collaborate with their communities and local stakeholders, there's a fresh spirit stirring through rural American communities.

12

Getting Your Church Unstuck

Alton Garrison

I walked into the home of Mama Gregg, the oldest living charter member of First Assembly of God in North Little Rock where I served as pastor. Even before sitting down, I could feel the tension in the air. Mama Gregg was upset that the church was moving to a different location. She had grown weak and frail in her eighty-plus years, but she influenced around sixty older people in the church who had served and prayed for decades.

As I sat down to begin our conversation, she got straight to the point: "Are you going to stay with us or go to that new church?" she asked. By "new church," she meant the new location where a concrete slab had already been poured. She was essentially threatening a church split.

I said gently, "Mama Gregg, we're *all* going to the new location."

"No, we aren't," she fired back with more feistiness than I expected from a woman of her age and in her health. "The Glory resides at Twenty-Second and Franklin. If you go to that new church, when y'all get there, Icky-bod's gonna be writ on the door."

Icky-bod . . . was an old Arkansas saint's way of saying "Ichabod," which is Hebrew for "the glory has departed." I knew it was useless to argue with her, and I didn't want to wear either of us out trying. I thanked her as soon as I could and left.

When we got back into the car, the youth pastor who had been my silent partner on this visit asked, "Why didn't you try to convince her she was wrong, and you were right?"

"*You* try to convince an eighty-year-old charter member of this church!" I replied. As we drove back to the church, I wondered if any strategy, any prayer, any insight would bring us into unity again.

Truth be told, I was still surprised to be the pastor of a church. In November 1985, a member of First Assembly's board of deacons had called to ask if I would accept an invitation to interview with the board. That simple invitation brought drastic changes to my life and ministry.

> When church life focuses on small things, we lose sight of our bigger responsibility to the community.

First Assembly had a rich heritage of capable pastoral leadership, and I was a minister with absolutely no pastoral experience—none whatsoever! I had never dedicated a baby or baptized a believer. I had spoken at funerals but had never actually planned one. I had only officiated at one wedding but I'm not sure it counted since it was in a park and the marriage didn't last.

I doubt if the church would have considered someone with no pastoral experience except that the men of faith and vision on the board felt it was time for some "out-of-the-box" thinking. They'd been without a pastor for quite some time. The most recent pastor had been there just twelve months, and his predecessor had stayed just thirty-six months. I accepted the invitation to become pastor of the church, feeling the tug of God on my heart—and a fair amount of trepidation at what was ahead.

Though it was a good church with great people, it had been averaging between 450 to 600 in attendance for about thirty-five years. That's the definition of "stuck." I doubt they even realized it, but they had become comfortable with a status quo, maintenance mentality—more inward-focused than outward-focused, still strong in missions but with a global rather than a local emphasis. An easy rule of thumb: The longer a church is stuck, the more difficult it is to get it unstuck. A stuck church gets into survival mode and becomes risk averse and fiercely dedicated to the preferences and comfort of insiders with little thought given to reaching those on the outside. This is the opposite attitude to the Great Commission and the Great Commandment.

For example, one day the youth pastor overheard two men in the church talking. One said to the other, "I don't know if that other guy's going to stay with us or not. He's only been here ten years."

Ten years! As that comment illustrates, in a stuck church, vision shrinks, and the primary emphasis is placed on relationships within the existing body. Inevitably, the budget dries up; and these relationships devolve into arguments over silly things I call "policy manual" issues: carpet color and where you put the piano. One church I visited had a beautiful fellowship hall with a kitchen, but nobody could cook in it because people in the church didn't like the smells. That's "policy manual" culture.

When church life focuses on small things, we lose sight of our bigger responsibility to the community. Being stuck is a sad place to find ourselves, but it can happen to any of us.

Time for a New Vision

As little as I knew about being a pastor, I was convinced of one thing: We needed a new vision and an outward focus to help change the culture of the church; consequently, we began trying new things:

- We put together a ShareFest where one hundred churches in our city collaborated to do service projects. We had volunteers painting schools, cleaning parks, landscaping homes, and much more.

- Our own church helped remodel the Fire Department. We even built a room at our church where fire and police officers could come in and watch TV and enjoy coffee and dinner. Our staff lined up to greet them when they drove in, holding placards that read: "Welcome! We love you." That got the attention of our city.

- We served local schools however we could. One time we gave shoes to students in need.

- We taught our people to go to the mayor's office to ask how they could serve.

- I supported all these changes biblically in the pulpit. (If your changes are not biblical, you should not be making them. Just a hint!) I taught on the priesthood of all believers, saying, "Get involved. Don't be concerned only about your own preferences, problems, and needs. You're not just a plumber or a lawyer or a secretary. You do that to support your priesthood. Priests don't come to get blessed but to serve."

Leading a church into an outward focus is contagious. Most of the community outreach mentioned earlier occurred after I left! All this proved the effectiveness of what I call the Acts 2 Model. In Acts chapter 2, we find twelve significant factors to church health and strength (see next page for more information). Among those twelve factors, four in particular rise above the rest; and among those, the most important of all the factors is an outward focus and community engagement. This means that the most important predictor of church

---

Acts 2 Survey

With the help of research specialists and more than forty pilot churches, we designed the Acts 2 Survey, a one-year strategic process for Spirit-empowered churches to reach next-level effectiveness by identifying their church health, strengths, and challenges. The survey evaluates twelve health factors, each surveying at least one of the five functions revealed in Acts 2:42–47. Learn more at www.acts2journey.com about how the Acts 2 Survey can help your congregation.

---

health and growth in any circumstance is getting people to look beyond the church campus and engage the community in meaningful, powerful ways.

That is what began to happen at First Assembly. People caught the vision and experienced the power of taking the gospel and compassion of Christ to others. It became contagious, and the church began to grow not only in numbers but in internal health.

Patience Required

Another rule of thumb: Changing a church culture takes lots of patience. A deacon who was a dear friend challenged me early on in our efforts to serve the community. "Why do you want to fool with those fly-by-night people?" he asked. They're not going to stay with us. You're wasting your time." He meant the people coming to the church because they were drawn by our outward focus and community service. He was wrong. Those people stayed and became strong, stable Christians. That man became a great proponent of the changes once the results became clear.

Others within the church gave stronger resistance. Two years into my tenure, the vice chairman of the board walked into a board meeting. I knew something was bugging him.

"I think you've misunderstood something," he told me plainly. "We brought you here to preach. We're going to run this church." That was more than a pothole—it was a barrier. This man was a power broker if I ever met one. He was a large man, wore a Rolex on his arm, drove a Rolls Royce to church, and had succeeded in business. It was a four-hour meeting that night, and I challenged those men: "I'm willing to die for this church. Are you?" I used Scripture and my passion to make the case, but he still left upset.

A few weeks later, that man called me and said he had been unable to sleep the night of that meeting and was afraid he would die. Pacing the floor praying, he felt the Lord say, "Take your hand off that pastor and support what the church is doing." He did just that.

Then there was Mama Gregg. I prayed and prayed and finally felt like God gave me a solution to address the fears and concerns of those silver saints whose dollars and prayers and steadfastness had built First Assembly. One day I took fifty of them on a bus to the new property. On the concrete slab I had the builder trace an outline of their Sunday school room using chalk. I stood the people inside that chalk drawing and said, "I don't know where my office is in this new building. I can't tell you where the youth will meet. But I know where you will meet. Your class is right here." We then held hands and sang "Amazing Grace."

At the final service in the old facility, we were going to caravan three hundred cars from the old facility to the new property. It was a powerful time; but during the service portion at the old facility, Mama Gregg signaled to me that she wanted to address the congregation. My heart hit my shoes. *She's going to ruin the whole thing,* I thought. I didn't have a choice but to hand her the mic.

She walked slowly up to me, took the microphone from my hand, cleared her throat, and stood before all the people—with her decades of history and trusted voice.

"I have two things to say," she started and paused for a moment. Then she continued, "Always pay your tithes."

I'll take that one! I thought. *But Icky-bod's coming. I just know it.* I cringed as she continued speaking.

"Number two," she said, "always follow our pastor where he leads us."

I nearly fainted. She handed me the mic and sat back down. Relief flooded my body and soul, and the day ended up better than my best expectations. Mama Gregg apologized to me for her opposition after the ceremony was over, and the entire older group supported the church's move.

First Assembly got unstuck. God's blessings must be recognized as the primary reason, but a catalytic force was the strategic decision to become more involved in serving those in the community. As the local church directs its attention outward, its focus shifts, its priorities shuffle, and its purpose comes into clearer view. Showing others God's love through acts of kindness and compassion builds a bridge of relationship, making our testimony more relevant.

I pastored that church until 2001. Today, under longtime pastor Rod Loy, it runs eight thousand people on eight to ten campuses and gives $2.4 million a year to missions with a little more than $1 million to Assemblies of God World Missions per year for the last twelve years. It's a rather amazing testimony to the power of applying biblical principles and passion to church-based challenges.

Every church is on a journey, and that journey always calls us to serve Jesus and serve others. That's how you get "unstuck."

13

How an Ironman Made His Church Relevant

Chuck Bengochea

I was riding my bike in northern Georgia, many miles from home, praying and praising our Heavenly Father as I often did during my Ironman training rides. It's a favorite pastime to turn my bike into a "prayer closet" and get lost in worship of our King, Jesus Christ. But this day, out of the blue, God spoke to my heart more clearly than perhaps at any other time in my life.

Eighteen months earlier, my wife and I had felt the Holy Spirit moving us to explore other churches. We had attended the same church for more than ten years, but now it seemed He was moving us on. So, we began visiting different north Atlanta churches, including some nationally known megachurches. They were all amazing in their own ways, but none resonated with us. Ultimately, we realized we belonged back at our original church.

This circular saga left me perplexed because I felt certain that God had led us to visit these other churches. And yet here we were, back in our home congregation. I wanted to understand why God had done this. The process seemed a waste.

That's when He spoke to me while I was riding. His voice wasn't audible, such that others would have heard it, but His message was clear: "I took you on a tour of great evangelical churches to show you that they're letting me down!" He said. "They're busy preaching the gospel, but they aren't living it out."

I got to the house, went directly into my study, and wrote out what God had communicated to me. "Transforming Communities," was the title because that was the essence of His message: The church has a role and a responsibility to transform communities through love. That day Jeremiah 22:16 was imprinted on my heart: " 'He defended the cause of the poor and the needy, and so all went well. Is that not what it means to know me?' declares the LORD."

During the months following, I spent hours talking to local officials and parachurch leaders asking them what role my home church was playing in the community. Were we making a difference? If our church didn't exist, who would notice? The answer I got was unanimous: Our church wasn't affecting anyone beyond our own congregation. We weren't known for love or for pouring our hearts and resources into the community.

One night later, my wife and I were hosting a church training session in our home when, at the end of the event, the senior pastor and children's ministry pastor approached me and asked, "If you could run the church, how would you do it?"

My mind was still full of the "Transforming Communities" message so I responded, "Are you serious?"

"Yes," they said.

Opening my laptop computer to the twenty-six-page PowerPoint presentation I said, "This is exactly how I would do it."

"You've got to be kidding me," the pastor said. "You had this sitting there, ready for us?"

Now emboldened, I offered, "If you'll give me an open door to present it to the elders, I will."

They both nodded. Within days I stood before the elders and said, "Please don't shoot the messenger, but our church isn't making a difference in this community. We're doing a great job of preaching and ministering to our congregation but doing very little externally."

After taking them through the presentation I concluded with this question: "Do we want to be a church known for its love of the community—a church that spreads the gospel of Jesus Christ while ministering to the least of these?" I saw heads nodding. Their response was unanimous.

> I searched Scriptures and could find no secular-sacred division. If you're selling hams for the glory of God, as it says in Colossians and 1 Corinthians, that's sacred work.

That meeting was a turning point—and the beginning of a lot of hard work. Overall the congregation of two thousand people was supportive, but some isolated groups resisted. Initially I thought, *I'm just the messenger and can avoid getting into the weeds and making the changes,* but that cop-out ended when they asked me to join the elder board. At first I declined, but they persisted.

"We need a warrior who loves the Lord," they said. "We need someone to help us make these changes, someone whose instinct isn't to duck when the bullets fly, but to move forward. We think that's you."

They were right. Those traits had helped me carve a successful path in business and competing as an Ironman, but those strengths could become a weakness too. Still, I heard the call and had to say yes.

So, we're going to war, I thought. *I'm good with that.*

A year into my term as an elder, they asked me to be the chairman. By that time, the salvos were already flying.

A Businessman in the Church

As CEO of HoneyBaked Ham and in positions at Coca-Cola and General Electric, I had learned that leadership is caring deeply about everyone around you. I thought, *Why not approach this role on the elder board the same way?* I'm convinced that if you care more about other people's success than your own, you have a reasonable chance of getting everybody moving in the same direction.

But leading a cultural transition at our church proved difficult from the outset. People were set in their ways and resistant to change. This became vividly clear when we examined the mission and vision of the church. Before doing anything else, we needed clarity about who we were and what our primary purpose was as a church. At the time it was based on Colossians 1:28, to "present everyone fully mature in Christ." More than one eyebrow raised when I declared, "I don't think that's the right mission for us."

I believe deeply in mission and vision as plumb lines for where you go as an individual, a business, a nonprofit, or a church. Yet my well-meaning critique was met with this response: "That mission and vision stuff is businessman-speak," they said. "You're trying to bring business practices into the Holy Spirit's domain."

Admittedly, that made me furious. I searched Scriptures and could find no secular-sacred division. If you're selling hams for the glory of God, as it says in Colossians and 1 Corinthians, that's sacred work. "No, it's not 'businessman-speak.' It's about bringing clarity to the assignments God has given to us." Sensing we were at an impasse I recommended, "Let's fast and pray and seek God for agreement."

We did that, and the elders soon agreed to change the church's mission to, "We exist to glorify God by making disciples who love God passionately and love others unconditionally." That brief statement became the floodlight for our future.

Making Changes to Reflect Our New Mission

A lot of "pick and shovel" work came next. Before we could cast our gaze outward, several internal changes were the stepping-stones. We made changes to the church's governance and ministerial structure and established new principles for supporting missionaries. Then we opened the aperture to our community. The board wanted a community pastor who woke up every day calling schools, abuse shelters, foster care agencies, and other non-profits and asking, "How can we serve you?" But hiring a community pastor to provide leadership was foreign thinking to many. They were used to senior pastors, missions pastors, and teaching pastors . . . but a community pastor?

Next Convoy of Hope helped us organize a Day of Hope, bringing more than thirty local churches together to help solve issues in our community. Multiple thousands came, and it was a beautiful thing. We did that in subsequent years as well.

When the veil was lifted, we noticed there were many Spanish-speaking immigrants in our town. Day after day we saw them lining up as day laborers on street corners, waiting for someone to hire them. For our church, reaching out to the "Hispanic gap" appeared to be a bridge too far. Pushback included claims like, "They're here illegally." "They've broken the law."

"Okay," I said, "then I want everyone here who's ever looked at pornography or cheated somebody financially to leave the building. If they have broken the law, then why don't we let the Holy Spirit convict them?" The point is we're all sinners, and not one of us is worthy to throw the first stone at our brothers and sisters.

Ignoring the doubt peddlers, we hired a Hispanic pastor and started ministering to our Hispanic and Latino neighbors. Because of these changes and more to our community engagement, we went from having no presence in the public schools to becoming their most valued partner.

On the surface it wasn't a seismic shift, but we could feel the culture of the church changing. We began using a new scorecard to judge success and failure. We were no longer afraid of looking under the hood to ask, "How significant is our impact on people who don't attend our church?" "If we closed down tomorrow, would the city weep?"

This cultural shift hit home one day at a HoneyBaked Ham store when the mayor of our city walked in to make a purchase.

"Hey, Chuck," he said, "are you guys doing another Day of Hope this year?"

In that moment I knew people's perception was changing and that in our community we were becoming a catalyst not a cloister.

Years later, when my term of service on the elder board expired, a man who had served with me said, "You know, Chuck, God used you to be a prophet to us." His words moved me deeply because in my own eyes I wasn't a prophet, but a businessman serving as best I could in my church.

Pastor . . . leader . . . your church is called to be the heartbeat of its community. Where we have ceded too much ground, we must retake it. We do that by loving and serving others well, courageously turning our focus outward and setting a standard of excellence that all can aspire to. As an Ironman you will burn seven to eight hundred calories in an hour and only recover half of it. For 140 miles you face the growing plea of your body to stop, quit, rest, and replenish, but the finish line beckons louder with each stroke, pedal, and stride. With all my heart, I believe you are God's Ironman and Ironwoman for your community. "Let us not become weary in doing good, for at the proper time we will reap a harvest if we do not give up" (Galatians 6:9).

14

Starting a Dream Center in Your Community

Brian Steele

This is an interview with Brian Steele, executive director of the Phoenix Dream Center.

Q: Describe the Dream Center model for us.

Steele: To describe the Dream Center model, I need to share the driving motto of it all: "Find a need and fill it, find a hurt and heal it." Our model is to go into a community, find needs and fill them, and find hurts and heal them. Almost every Dream Center looks different as the needs of its city or region are different. The success of the model lies in the ability of each Dream Center to be a bridge between the predominantly faith community and the real-time needs of the people in the community around them.

Q: How could a pastor or leader start a Dream Center in their community? What is the process?

Steele: After helping nearly three hundred Dream Centers during their start-up phase, we've found that working with the Dream Center Network out of Los Angeles is the best first step. Some of this will include project readiness surveys and assistance with "counting the cost" of starting a Dream Center in the community.

Q: How do Dream Centers partner with churches?
Steele: Partnerships with local churches are not only critical to every Dream Center's success, they are also fundamentally a part of our mission of bridging the gap between the "seats and the streets." We've found that churches typically partner with local Dream Centers in one of three ways:

1. Financially, by donating out of special offerings, missions budgets, or through special project campaigns
2. In-kind, by donating food, clothing, services, household goods, or other items through donation drives
3. Providing volunteer support, by promoting both individual volunteer opportunities as well as short-term mission groups and even large-scale church workdays

Q: Many Dream Centers are church based. How does that work? Is it a separate nonprofit or under the church?
Steele: In most cases, but not all, each Dream Center is a separate 501(c)(3) entity. There are numerous reasons to do this, including but not limited to these:

1. Incorporating or separating the entities can mitigate some of the risk to the church and its assets that are associated with higher-risk endeavors Dream Centers often engage in: drug addiction overdose risks, mental and behavioral health risks, communicable disease and medical risks, and so on.
2. Most churches realize all too quickly that the costs associated with meeting the seemingly never-ending and absorbent needs of the community are immense and can rarely be covered by any one church as a department budget. Thus, being able to position the Dream Center as a community-owned

and community-supported entity becomes critical in fundraising and cost-sharing efforts.

3. Along those same lines, parachurch organizations like Dream Centers typically experience much higher success rates than churches in acquiring private foundation funds, government funds, insurance billing funds, private business funds, sports team funds, and more.

Q: Describe the models used by the Dream Centers to address needs of single moms.

> Our fear was that the evangelistic program would have a bunch of people who didn't care about Christ. We wondered, *We're a Christian organization. Are we taking Jesus out of the picture?*

Steele: It's become our overwhelming opinion and focus that prevention needs to be the dominant part of the conversation we have with all our support churches.

Teri Vogel, our Thrive program director, has established the basic goal of the Phoenix Dream Center's Thrive Foster Care Prevention and Reunification program: keep families together and intercept the situation before the parents are removed to a shelter and the kids moved to a foster care home. The typical situation works as follows:

1. A Department of Child Safety (DCS) caseworker receives a case in which a young family, typically a single mom, is on the verge of having her children removed, usually for neglect reasons of not enough food, no fridge, no beds, for example.

2. The DSC caseworker calls the Thrive program and asks us to do an intervention to help the family by providing any number of things such as case management, sober-living counseling, in-home respite care, beds, food, clothing, furniture, and other things that will help the family become compliant.

3. Thrive arranges the services and/or pulls the resources from our storage units, and delivers the services or items to the family.

4. The DCS caseworker monitors the compliance progress of the family and signs off at some point, releasing the family from the DCS system. This effectively keeps the family together, keeps the parents out of a shelter, and keeps the kids in school and out of foster care.

Q: Explain the two categories of programs you offer.

Steele: Category one is discipleship-based programs, which have a required religious component. The goal is to make better Christians. People in these programs must have a saving knowledge of Christ.

The other category, which is more evangelistic and addresses needs like human trafficking and foster care, allows non-Christians to be involved and cared for. In these situations, Christian components like church attendance or Bible study are voluntary. We did that primarily because of our human-trafficking program. We weren't going to force these girls to go to church. For those coming out of trafficking, some church services can be traumatic with the lights and noise and big crowds. None of that helps a fourteen-year-old girl who's been in severe trauma.

Another difference between the two categories is that government grants won't fund discipleship-based programs but they will fund evangelistic ones as long as the Christian component is voluntary. This was a knock-down, drag-out issue in some of my board meetings, but we had to see it as one program to win people and one program to grow people. Our fear was that the evangelistic program would have a bunch of people who didn't care about Christ. We wondered, *We're a Christian organization. Are we taking Jesus out of the picture?* The way I presented it was, "Think about the door to the church building. We don't stand at the door and ask people if they're a Christian, and stop them from coming in if they're not. So why do that for our healing and restoration programs? Why stand at the door and keep them out?"

My goal, especially regarding human trafficking, was to lower those barriers. Law enforcement is doing raids in the middle of the night and rescuing these girls. They're not going to sit there in a cop car in the middle of the night and ask the girls, "Are you a Christian or not?" If we had a purely discipleship-based approach, we'd have to have that conversation the next morning, and then decide whether to keep them or kick them out.

Ten years later, we don't see our programs being overtaken by non-Christians. Nearly all the girls have Bibles and go to Bible studies. It was a step of faith, and I was willing to be wrong, but what we've seen are peer dynamics taking place.

Q: How have you engaged the public sectors in your community, and how has that created opportunities for the Phoenix Dream Center?
Steele: We do a lot of fun things, like take the local police department pizza every month and say, "We love you guys." Most of our programs started through engagement with law enforcement. Our human-trafficking program started when I began doing ride alongs with the Phoenix Police Department. Weekend after weekend, they were arresting twelve- to fourteen-year-old girls and taking them to juvenile correction centers because there was nowhere else to take them. A police lieutenant said to me, "I'm begging

you to take these girls, if you can. I'm taking them all to juvenile detention."

So, we did. As a result, I serve as the chair of Governor Doug Ducey's Policy Committee and Victim Services Committee for Human Trafficking. I also chair the Victim Services Council for the Phoenix mayor's office. On the state level, I work with Cindy McCain and Gil Orrantia from Homeland Security and a university to find gaps in services and allocate service providers to fill them.

When it comes to partnering with government grants and programs, early on I made a strategic decision that no more than 15 percent of our revenue should come from a federal source. I knew the key to our survival was to diversify. Housing and Urban Development pulled forty million dollars out of Phoenix a few years ago and this decimated some programs that had to shut down. So, I decided we weren't taking more than 15 percent from one source.

Tommy Barnett always taught me that nobody gives like God's people. I believe that wholeheartedly. Our five million dollars cash budget every year is 60 percent from individuals, 25 percent from churches, and 15 percent from grants. I have a lot of major donors who help start projects, and I love getting a half-million-dollar check, but what I like better is when you tell me ten people are giving ten dollars a month. They're the ones who keep the lights on, the insurance paid, and let us move forward through summertime in Phoenix with our enormous electricity bills.

Early on, the Phoenix Dream Center was 100 percent funded by Dream City Church (formerly Phoenix First Assembly). This year it's 7 percent funded. I'm proud that we've diversified our funding so well, and I'm humbled because the program is funded by people giving online and writing checks and putting "Dream Center" on the memo line.

Q: What are practical steps to starting a Dream Center in my community? How do I know what area to help? How is your model scalable? Can you provide church-based examples for smaller communities?

Steele: A church can start with outreach to learn what the community needs. Participate in after-school programs. Learn how to get food and clothing to people. Most churches have a fridge, kitchen, or food bank. Eventually, churches learn what we learned: You must have a place to take people in. At first, you refer people to shelters, then you realize quickly that they're all full. The next step is the building-acquisition phase. At conferences we discuss the pros and cons of leasing or renting, and how to get a building donated to you.

In the last ten years, the real estate climate hasn't been good except for investors, but it's been great for municipalities getting stuff off their books. Probably a dozen Dream Centers started through dollar-a-year lease agreements with their cities. Cities can use tax write-offs, too, if you improve the property.

One church we know got their Dream Center started with after-school programs. In Tulsa, the Dream Center's amazing program for kids struggling with reading, writing, and arithmetic has literally changed graduation rates in that city. Then, once you get into therapeutic and rehabilitation programs, you're getting into heavy permitting, licensing, fees, and so on . . . but that's the next step.

Every situation is a little different, but engage the community, find the needs. It's the find-a-need-and-fill-it philosophy.

15

The Art of Neighboring—
A Church Movement

Dave Runyon and Jay Pathak

What would happen if every believer in your city attempted to build relationships with the eight households that are closest to them? In January 2009, a group of pastors began to pray and dream about the impact that we and our churches could make in our communities if we worked together. It started in Arvada, Colorado, when twenty-one churches united to start a neighboring movement. The movement has since spread and to date over 2,500 churches around the country are using the Art of Neighboring resources to impact their communities.

The catalyst for the movement occurred when we invited the mayor of Arvada, Bob Frie, to meet with local pastors to determine ways our churches could best serve the community. The mayor told our group of pastors something that was convicting, eye-opening, and transforming. He said, "There are a lot of issues that face our community, but the majority of them could be drastically reduced if we would just become a community of good neighbors." This simple, but powerful, statement struck us to the heart because the mayor was asking us to take the Great Commandment seriously and literally. We felt this was a call to rediscover the "Art of Neighboring."

A couple of months later, we met again to pray and discuss the mayor's statement, but we also invited the assistant city manager to join us. Based on her fifteen years of experience in local government and neighborhood issues, she said, "From the city's perspective, there isn't a lot of difference between the way Christians and non-Christians neighbor." This statement confirmed that we needed to work together and empower the people in our churches to be great neighbors.

> Our goal was to help believers become neighborhood catalysts who move themselves and others from strangers to acquaintances, and from acquaintances to relationships.

We developed a few resources and tools that helped our congregations take next steps to connect with their actual neighbors. Our goal was to help believers become neighborhood catalysts who move themselves and others from strangers to acquaintances, and from acquaintances to relationships. We identified three "neighborhood practices" that can help people take practical steps towards becoming a great neighbor.

• *Complete the block map.* This encourages people to learn and retain the names, jobs, dreams, struggles, and other details of the people who live in the eight houses closest to them. It's important to get people to fill out the block map themselves. This usually causes them to feel the impact of not knowing the names of their neighbors and leads to a clear moment where they realize the neighboring process begins with them.

• *Host a block party such as a neighborhood BBQ or potluck.* This creates an environment where relationships can be birthed and provides an opportunity for people to learn more about their neighbors.

• *Invite people to share a meal in your home.* This is where real relationships are formed. Block parties are great, but they rarely produce more than surface-level conversations. Having a person or a family over for a meal is a big deal and creates opportunities to connect in a meaningful way.

As pastors, we've discovered a multiplied impact when church leaders empower their congregations to become good neighbors to their geographic area of influence. Part of being a good neighbor is seeing the needs of other neighbors and hearing their stories. We can't just view neighbors as projects. We must be willing to be involved and do life with the people God has placed around us. When a family decides to press through discomfort and make the sacrifice of time to invest in their neighbor, this can transform the neighbor's life for the better. Sometimes engaging with neighbors means just spending more time in your front yard. Feel free to get creative and have fun while making meaningful relationships that open the door for powerful moments of ministry. When people take advantage of opportunities for engagement, they transition from being just acquaintances to deep friends.

If you're interested in learning more about "The Art of Neighboring," check out our book under the same title and the free resources online at www.artofneighboring.com.

16

Stay Put, Serve, Grow!

Jim Franklin

I grew up in rural Oklahoma, so participating in a citywide outreach to the poor in Los Angeles nearly twenty-five years ago was a major eye-opener for me. Thousands of people waited in line to get food. *How is it possible that people in a major city are in this kind of poverty?* I wondered. *Did this kind of need exist in my city?*

"My city" was Fresno, California, a few hours north and a world away from Los Angeles. Our church, Cornerstone, was in Fresno's inner city, and when I returned from LA, I led our church to organize a food give-away outreach. Five thousand people showed up! I was floored!

Obviously, if so many people needed food, one bag of groceries wasn't going to cut it. We had a small food pantry, as many churches do, but I had to imagine what it would take to do food ministry at the volume of the need. The answer seemed to be a warehouse.

Our prayers were answered for a warehouse near our church, and the seller even threw in a box truck. That was the beginning of Feeding Fresno, which fed close to a million people last year. We act as an outlet, supplying food for up to sixty different organizations including other churches, nonprofits, and universities.

Our church, which had three hundred in attendance when Feeding Fresno began, now draws close to three thousand. We occupy two city blocks and are a go-to ministry to help with city needs. We have a great relationship with city officials, the mayor, and the city council. They see us as part of the answer to community problems.

I believe there are keys to every city—including your city. One key in Fresno was addressing poverty, and the other was addressing youth violence. We've used both keys to unlock opportunities to share the gospel much more widely and with greater credibility.

Here is some advice from our years of compassion ministry.

Empower Your Own People and Other Organizations

We don't want to create volunteers—we want to create empowered people to reach their own neighborhoods. That's how ministry spreads, and it's much more effective that way. This is especially true when someone comes out of poverty, prostitution, drug addiction, gang violence, or some other difficult background. They're uniquely equipped to bring comfort to those stuck in the same lifestyles. We empower such people and put them in positions of leadership; we walk alongside them, and build systems and structures to help them carry out their ministries. Sometimes the people serving in our food give-away lines get in line themselves, because they have the same needs others do. That's empowering people to serve people.

We also empower other organizations by opening our hands and giving them what we receive. If we only fed people we encountered, our reach would be limited. But by helping other churches and nonprofits who have a heart to reach the needy as well, we multiply our reach, and God supplies more. We don't want to build a huge feeding ministry with our name attached; we want to serve our community through other agencies, group homes, churches, etc. As we give food away, amazingly our warehouse always fills back up.

On a practical level, here's what we do. Every Thursday afternoon we give food to twenty or so churches and nonprofits. Many of them are small and don't have a warehouse, but do have a food pantry of some type. Why Thursday? Because many churches want to have food give-away events at their locations on Saturdays. This helps them accomplish that.

Before they arrive, we tell them what we're giving away that day, and when their trucks and vans pull up to our warehouse, we have their specific truckload of stuff separated out and ready to load. Our volunteers do that for them, and they drive it back to their locations.

Choose Your Suppliers Carefully

Instead of going with donor sources, which limit our freedom to preach the gospel while giving away their donated food, we only work with organizations that allow us to share Jesus freely. We're not a food bank but a church. Our primary goal is to meet the spiritual needs of people, and within that to also meet physical needs as we're able.

That said, we've heard some criticism about engaging in a "social gospel" and creating a "welfare system." Churches need to understand that ministering to people's physical needs is not the same as diluting the gospel of Jesus Christ! Jesus was anointed to preach the gospel to the poor. We can't bypass the poor in favor of our other goals. Don't worry if people accuse you of practicing a social gospel when you release the poor, the oppressed, and those in bondage from what's keeping them down. Jesus is the answer to their physical and spiritual needs, and we must not neglect either one.

The balance is not to get so focused on providing for physical needs that you forget to keep the main thing, the main thing.

Go Slowly

How did we fill our ten-thousand-square-foot warehouse? Slowly. We hired a woman in our congregation who had a heart for this ministry. She had connections with food producers and the trucking industry. It was a God thing. Suddenly we had a few pallets of food, and we started organizing giveaways and giving to other churches. It didn't happen all at once.

One company heard about our ministry and loaned us a forklift on a permanent basis, even servicing it for us. A trucking company offered to pick up donated food for us and deliver it on their deadhead runs—when their trucks return home empty. Little by little we learned how to build a long-lasting food ministry.

Here's how it works in real life: a producer or donor will call and say, "We have six pallets of such-and-such product sitting on the dock. If you can get here by this afternoon, they're yours. Otherwise we'll have to get them off the dock. They're blocking us."

To keep on good terms with that supplier, you need the capacity to take all that product off their hands. You can't say, "We only want to take five pallets and leave the rest for you to deal with." They'll say, "Take it all or nothing." Worse, they might not call you again.

Food producers are in a high-volume, fast-paced business. When they have an overrun, discarded material, or an order that didn't come through, they can't sit and hold onto it. There's more stuff coming up behind it. Your job is to say, "Yes, we'll take it," whether it's five pallets or a whole truckload of canned goods or an item you don't know how to use right now. You relieve them of the burden, put it in your warehouse, and wait for them to call again.

Logistics are a big key. We're constantly on the phone looking for deadhead runs and other means to pick up donated food. It's not a passive ministry by any means.

You'll no doubt have opportunities to give away large amounts of produce. When an orange freeze destroyed an entire crop in the Central Valley of California a few years ago, we took nine truckloads of food and fed an entire city where the packing plants were located. God always has a plan for the material that's donated.

Befriend While Serving

We emphasize that recipients of food are our friends and guests. We never want them to feel like people in line waiting for a handout. We work hard to preserve their innate human dignity.

One way we do this is by setting up our own Wednesday food giveaway like a farmer's market. Instead of handing people a prepared box of food, we let them browse and select what they need.

Tackle Other Glaring Needs

Addressing youth violence is the other key to our city. We tackle this problem head-on in a creative and powerful way. Whenever a shooting takes place, we go to that very spot, usually within a week, and hold an outreach with bounce houses for kids, hot food, truckloads of grocery items from our warehouse, and a stage for presenting the gospel. This joyful block party is our way of showing the people who live in that area that the streets don't belong to violence but to community. This has given us street credibility with gangs who see that we're ministering to their loved ones. Many ex-gang members have found the Lord and now minister in those areas.

This has become such an important part of our outreach in the city that the police department has contracted with us so when a shooting takes place, they call our ministry teams to help de-escalate the violence.

Stay Where the Needs Are

Staying in your inner city rather than moving to the suburbs is a powerful statement of commitment to a community. When we outgrew our building, people said, "Now is the time to move to the suburbs. There's more affluence and land there." Instead, we made a conscious decision "to dance with the one who brung us"—so we moved further into the heart of our city.

Here's some strategic advice on that: Purchase as much property around your church as you can before you start building and renovating. This is because when you start pouring money into improving your facility and campus, it'll drive property values up and people will start moving in next to you. We saw this happen with new houses, apartment complexes, condominiums, and businesses all around us. When we took the lead, others followed.

Thankfully, we had bought as much land and property as we could afford beforehand, and as property values rose, so did the value of what we owned. Equally important, we could sell our properties to whom we wanted. In that way, we were in control of the development around us and could choose our neighbors. One great example is a charter school the district put in our neighborhood at a cost of eight million dollars. We helped the school in its first three years by renting them a building we owned at a reduced rate. We knew we needed a school to help the area grow and climb out of poverty. Now the school has its own facility. These types of things are taking place all around us.

This kind of practical, long-term thinking, led and guided by the Holy Spirit, will give you powerful results in your own city. Watch and see!

17

Think Creatively, Think Huge!

Mike Quinn

By the time I enlisted in the Army in 1972, I had lived in a riverbed as a homeless guy, gotten mixed up with the drugs of the day, and been in some extremely bad relationships. During that time, nobody ever talked to me about Jesus. I finally met a group of Christians in my army unit in Okinawa, Japan, who shared their faith with me and took me to their church. I became a Christ-follower shortly after.

Back in the United States, I married, attended a Christian college, and became involved in a little church in Ocean Beach. The Book of Ephesians captivated me with its missiology of the Early Church, and it drove me crazy that no church I knew of was actively doing more for their city. When some of us learned about a dump in Tijuana where people lived, we gathered food and clothing and began doing "dump ministry." There was no handbook for this. We literally made it up as we went.

In 1986, I came to Newbreak Church as pastor. It had thirteen people. We committed to some basic principles from the start: We would always (1) try to make things better, (2) keep our approach accessible, and (3) give away everything we could. We began organizing yard and home cleanup days for the many military families in the San Diego area. We felt a burden for schools near our campus, so we organized teacher appreciation lunches, held backpack drives, and donated school supplies. We even decorated and painted teachers' lounges—anything we could do to make them feel special.

As Newbreak experimented with outreach approaches and grew to multiple campuses, we learned about the power of creativity and doing things differently. Here are some ideas that worked for us.

Become the Go-To Place

A friend told me once, "I want to be the kind of church that if we closed our doors, the community would weep." Most times, if a church shuts down, nobody even knows. Local governments are zoning churches out of existence in some places and not just to increase tax revenue; they don't see the value a church brings to the community. Revolutionizing that negative perception is a big reason I get up in the morning.

Our Ocean Beach campus is only four years old and has already won awards from the town council and the Main Street Association for being the most outstanding partner in the community. We invite civic and school groups to hold public meetings, fund-raisers, football team meetings, military events, business meetings, and more in our buildings. We generally don't even charge them for it. We leverage our facilitates to create relationships and goodwill in the community.

We also tell city and school leaders, "If you have a family in need, please tell us, and we'll see if we can help solve it." Initially, they were suspicious: "What's the angle? What do you want?" We said, "We don't want anything but to bless families." In a short amount of time, they stopped asking why and just started calling us. We hear from teachers, parents, principals, and civic leaders who call and say, "We have this need. Can you help?" They know we always say yes.

Be Creative

We try a lot of innovative things to change people's perception of what church is. For several years, we've served police and fire departments by beautifying their stations and cleaning their cars inside and out. They can hardly believe it. It's like a shock-and-awe of kindness.

Last weekend we did a barefoot Sunday at church and everyone brought shoes to give to people in need through the San Diego Rescue Mission. As part of the giveaway, we washed people's feet, prayed for them, and blessed them with new shoes. It was superemotional and powerful.

> I believe that even small churches can spend a few thousand dollars a year on local outreach and do it effectively. It simply involves listening to the Lord and listening to people to hear their needs.

Some of our campuses have a Love Week or a Kindness Day where they bless strangers with random acts of kindness—giving bottles of water to parents at sports games, cleaning toilets and bathrooms, or buying lunch for everyone at every business in the town center (in collaboration with a local sandwich shop). We fund this out of our missions giving. I believe that even small churches can spend a few thousand dollars a year on local outreach and do it effectively. It simply involves listening to the Lord and listening to people to hear their needs.

Encourage Small Groups to Serve

One of our highest values is to get life-groups on a mission. Ninety-two percent of our Sunday morning attendees belong to a life-group. That number is so high because people don't just sit in living rooms or on back patios every week. They actively serve people. That's exciting and fulfilling.

Our threefold strategy is to begin the week with worship, connect to one another in a life-group, and become the church by serving inside and outside. That's the Ephesians model.

Give Authority Away

I push the leadership of our outreaches down to the organic level so they don't require staff oversight. We present the big strategy to our life-group leaders, then we give them the thumbs-up to lean into needs they see using their best ideas. We like to be decentralized because it empowers people and calls forth their good ideas. It's authentic, from the heart.

Shift Your Missions Budget

A lot of churches give a large portion of their budget to foreign missions, which is wonderful, but they aren't doing any local missions. It may sound radical, but I suggest that you cap increases to your foreign missions budget until your local missions budget is in balance. Raise money for projects at your local schools and parks, and for your city and its businesses. I consider this low-hanging fruit. There's tremendous need in these places. It's where people want to hear the gospel because often they're in a crisis and are looking for ultimate answers and long-term solutions. Be your community's best friend and reflect that in your missions budget.

Heal the Divides

Over the last few years, our county has experienced an influx of the second-largest population of refugees in the United States, outside of Detroit. They're from Africa and the Middle East, and there's a great deal of racial tension between them. For the most part, they are also poor and unfamiliar with Western culture.

Seeing this, we started a Dream Center-like ministry we call the Hope Center to serve the refugee community as well as the rest of the people in need located in East County. Our life-groups on all Newbreak campuses are beginning to engage with the Hope Center. In the first few months of this year, we fed 7,700 people and just installed a twenty-five thousand dollar commercial kitchen.

My heart is for smaller churches to grow and be "missionally viral" in their communities. I believe that even if you're struggling at the so-called weekend experience in your church, once you get people engaged in something like a Hope Center they'll connect, grow, and commit to your church's mission because it's real and it's happening in their community.

Think Huge!

We have a brilliant strategic thinker in our congregation named Darrel Larson who started a project called Give Clean Water. He works for a leading maker of water filters, and he asked an important question: What if we adopted the entire nation of Fiji and became the solution for their drinking water needs? Our church signed a memorandum of understanding with the Fijian Ministry of Health to help solve their potable water problem in a sustainable fashion. In just a few more years we will have successfully completed that project. Similar efforts are now underway in Liberia and West Africa. Several non-profits and the Assemblies of God have joined with us to make these projects happen.

If you want to find collaborators, do exciting work and have a lot of fun—think huge. Let people run with their big ideas. Tell them they can do it and put seed money behind them.

Keep an Eye on CityServe

CityServe started with a bang here in California, and it's only going to get bigger. Newbreak is excited to be in affiliation with CityServe in the San Diego region. CityServe acts as the conduit between large retailers and churches for donated items like beds, furniture, flatware, cups, microwaves, you name it. As churches build infrastructure and systems to handle these types of donations, they can serve their community in a truly new and powerful way.

Local churches in partnership with CityServe become the point of delivery for these donated items. If a church member hears about a neighbor who has been laid off, they can gather a group to retrieve helpful items at their church, deliver them to the neighbor's home, and set up things if needed. That's the ultimate outreach in my book. It allows small churches, and even small groups, to do things that were inconceivable before. I believe it will result in a major wave of new Christ-followers coming from refugee communities and neighborhoods of all kinds as people are deeply moved by the care and concern of Christians around them.

I hope this offers some ideas about serving creatively and taking risks to find what works. I can testify that the Holy Spirit will empower your efforts and the community will embrace your efforts.

18

How Donated Product Can Build Lasting Relationships

Rod Haro

I was sitting in the principal's office at a local school and couldn't help noticing she was polite but not exactly welcoming. You could feel resistance in the air, and the whole church-state separation argument seemed close to the surface. I had hoped to build bridges and offer help from our church for needy kids in the school, but she didn't seem interested. I left sensing we hadn't even formed a cordial relationship.

Not long after that, our church had the opportunity to give all 450 students in that school brand-new shoes, sized to their feet, with the principal's permission. The next time I sat in her office, it was a different story—she was definitely warmer and a little more welcoming. I told her, "Anytime you come across someone you think we could help, please call me." Her eyes lit up. A few days later my phone rang.

"Pastor, there's a single dad doing his best to raise four precious little girls," she began. "We did a house visit because there were some issues. All four girls are sleeping in one twin bed and the family has no washer, dryer, or extra clothes. Can you help?"

Within days we took that family four beds with bedding, a washer, a dryer, and clothing. The father was stunned. The principal was amazed. We prayed with the family before leaving, and two weeks ago that father—who said he appreciated our help but didn't want anything to do with a church—was in our men's ministry. I call that the power of CityServe to change lives.

For years our church ran a food ministry with a warehouse filled with food. Even though four to five hundred people came weekly to receive, we never saw them in church. They got food, left, and went to another food program to receive more. We formed no relationships with them; we simply maintained a food giveaway program. And because we were getting our food from government agencies, we couldn't give the recipients a Bible or invite them to church. That was a problem.

When CityServe began to emerge, I immediately saw the potential to revolutionize our marketplace evangelism and grow our churches. The difference with CityServe is it allows us to get into households that wouldn't ordinarily let us in. If you give someone a new table or couch, they're going to let you pray with them. Something of spiritual significance takes shape.

Our church has nine campuses, with the main campus drawing around 1,400 on a weekend. The other campuses are in rural communities of 10,000 or 15,000 people and run 75 to 250 each on Sundays. We plant churches all around the Central Valley of California to reach people who wouldn't come to one big church. Our goal is for each campus to be known as "that church"—the church that helps people, the church that makes partnerships with others, the church that has a buzz about it because it meets needs.

Since we started working with CityServe and operating a warehouse from our church, we've seen relationships and inroads formed with people and entities that didn't care to work with us in the past. For example, we always felt a burden to help law enforcement. Police officers go call to call, and see so much lack and human need. But we hadn't done much with the police department because they didn't see a use for what we offered. With CityServe, I was able to go to the chief of police and say, "If your

132 CityServe; Your Guide to Church-Based Compassion

officers see someone in a bad situation, contact us. Give us the opportunity to see what we can do."

The chief did just that. He called for help with a family who only had folding chairs in their house, so we stocked that house with furniture. I ran into the chief at my grandkids' little league game later and he said, "I've got to go see your warehouse, and see what you guys have there!"

Stories are coming in from all our campuses. We've trained our people to get stuff from the warehouse and give it to needy people around them. Every Tuesday is our staff meeting, and the campus pastors go into the warehouse to see what's available.

One pastor took a pallet of heaters to a trailer park where many elderly people lived. He took the heaters door-to-door and introduced himself as a local pastor. Most wanted a heater, and he talked to them and prayed with them. Then he noticed two ladies standing in a yard watering their plants. They were chuckling and smiling as he went to the next trailer. He thought it was because they had just received heaters. He didn't know the man in the next trailer was a notoriously cantankerous atheist who heckled any religious people who came to his door.

The trailer door opened, and our campus pastor introduced himself.

"I'm an atheist," the man announced.

"That's fine. I'm just finding out if people need heaters," the campus pastor said. "Our church is giving them away."

"You mean you'll still give one to *me*?" the man asked.

"Of course," the campus pastor replied.

"All right," the atheist said, "I'll take it."

The two ladies were flabbergasted that this cranky old man would even talk to the pastor, let alone receive a gift from a church.

Sometimes the things delivered to our warehouse are a bit of a puzzle. Furniture and diapers, everyone wants. But one time we received hundreds of stuffed animals. I thought, *What do we do with all these?* Nearby was a day care center that wasn't too keen on church or Christians. My wife went over there and introduced herself. Ignoring their skeptical reception, she said, "We have an abundance of stuffed animals that came into our warehouse. Could you use them?" The day care people softened and said, "Why, yes. We could use some of the big ones for kids to hug during therapy." It was like God gave us the solution before we even knew the need.

One guy in our church had his life spin out of control after his divorce. He moved away, got into crime and drugs, and was almost killed a couple of times. On top of being in a wheelchair, he was diagnosed with cancer. I hadn't seen him in years, but he moved back to the area and was popping into churches here and there, mostly to get sympathy. I saw him one day and learned he was in an apartment with no furniture. Because we had furniture in the CityServe warehouse, we gave him a dining set and a couch. You'd have thought we gave him a million dollars. He started weeping. "I know it's God. I know I should be back in church," he said.

He rededicated his life to the Lord, and every day without exception he's been working in the warehouse, sorting stuff and doing whatever he can. He's clean and living right. Recently, he's been working the soundboard on Sunday mornings. Every time I see the empty rack in our warehouse where that couch had been, I remember his story. Every empty space in our warehouse is a testimony of a changed life. It's CityServe making a difference.

The other day I was in the principal's office again, and she said, "Pastor, I need your business cards for the people we're helping." I noticed the *we* in that sentence. She was making it sound like our church and her school were in partnership now. "I'd like to give them your card," she continued, "because a lot of them need spiritual help, too."

That was as big an endorsement of our ministry as I ever expected from her. Six months earlier we had no relationship. Now, because we were serving people with a warehouse full of goods, we were becoming known as "that church." I'm confident the ministry we're doing now, empowered by CityServe, will continue to revolutionize our community relationships.

Food Waste

As many nonprofits and churches seek to address food insecurity in communities across the nation, we must give more consideration to another part of the solution: eliminating food waste. Here are some alarming statistics about food waste:

- Approximately 40 percent of the food produced in the United States goes to waste.
- The mountain of wasted food totals 63 million tons, of which 10.1 million tons never get harvested from farms and 52.4 million tons end up in landfills uneaten.
- The United States spends $218 billion per year (or 1.3 percent of GDP) growing, manufacturing, processing, distributing, and then disposing of food that never makes its way onto the table.
- Food is wasted at all levels of the food system. On the farm, low market prices, high labor costs, and a market that demands perfect-looking produce leads farmers to leave food unharvested in the field.
- Grocery stores and restaurants waste food because of over-ordering and trying to meet unrealistic consumer demands.

- Consumers waste food in their homes because of inefficient shopping and cooking practices, misunderstanding of date labels that leads to them waste perfectly safe past-date food, and lack of access to recovery mechanisms, like composting.
- At the same time we are wasting 40 percent of our food supply, one in seven Americans suffers from food insecurity.[1]

While food waste is a serious problem, it isn't without solutions that can effectively enable the food supply to spread to those in need. Already measures have been put in place at the federal government level, like the Good Samaritan Act, to provide tax incentives and liability protection to encourage food donations to charitable organizations. But more can be done.

We would encourage you to educate yourself on food waste and work towards effective solutions with your local government. "Keeping Food Out of the Landfill: Policy Ideas for States and Localities" by Harvard Law School Food Law and Policy Clinic is a great, free online resource to start with. A part of solving food insecurity in our communities may be found in acquiring and utilizing what is already available in more efficient ways.

Part 3

CHURCH-BASED COMPASSION MODELS

A place becomes a "hood" when neighbors move out.
It becomes a neighborhood when the neighbors
move back in. After repainting and outfitting
a dilapidated car wash with new equipment,
we held a grand reopening of the newly named
Auto Baptism. The car wash that used to be the
epicenter of crime ended up becoming
the catalyst for community-wide change.
People bought boarded-up houses to restore them,
and businesses started moving in
and upgrading their properties.
Together we put the neighbor back in the hood.

—Fitz Hill

19

Putting Neighbor Back in the "Hood"

Dr. Fitz Hill

The car wash sat on the most dangerous corner in Little Rock, not far from Arkansas Baptist College where I served as president. It was an eyesore and the site of thirty-six violent crimes in the past year alone. To no one's surprise, it was on the verge of shutting down—and no one would really care if it did. A burger joint sat on the same property, and an old drug addict lived there who panhandled and drifted around like a ghost of what the community had once been.

Everybody knew the car wash was the epicenter of violent crime in Little Rock. Someone was shot or stabbed there every couple of weeks. Everything about it was run-down and shabby, just like the community around it, though it hadn't always been that way.

So, I was surprised—very surprised—when I drove by that corner one day and the Holy Spirit spoke clearly to my heart, "Buy that car wash. It's the lead piece in what the Lord's going to do here."

Buy the car wash? I thought. *That's crazy! I'm a college president. What does this car wash have to do with restoring our campus and institution?*

It had been years since I ran a small business, but I knew I was hearing from the Lord. I had been seeking Him with fasting and prayer, and I couldn't deny He was answering—though in an unexpected way.

The more I pondered the idea, the more sense it made. Our

college had invited a number of people to come to campus as students or employees, but many refused because the surrounding area was too dangerous. The crime rate of an urban community is tied directly to the business community. When crime goes up, businesses flee and urban blight sets in. That's what had happened all around us. I got up my nerve to tell the college's board of directors that we needed to buy that car wash. Their response was: "We're not in the car wash business."

"Yes, but we won't be in the education business unless we buy this car wash, because it's keeping everybody out of this part of town," I said.

"What does it cost?" they asked.

"Around two hundred thousand dollars," I said, and steeled myself for their response. They looked at each other skeptically, but after deliberating for a while they offered a possible path forward.

"If you can raise the money, the college can buy it," they said.

So, I went to work and through grants and donations raised enough to purchase and renovate the property. Soon after we owned the property, I had to shut down the car wash after yet another violent crime. I decided it was time to give the burger joint on the property thirty days' notice to move out, so we could have a clean slate and a fresh start. Then we conducted a one hundred thousand dollar upgrade and got ready to reopen.

First Things First

This experience was just another unexpected challenge—and opportunity—in my journey in education and community transformation. Leading a college as president was never in my plans. I had spent nearly twenty years coaching college football as an assistant coach for the Arkansas Razorbacks, then as head coach at San Jose State University. When Arkansas Baptist College asked me to be their president, I told God, "I don't want this job, and I know You aren't sending me there to work. " He replied, "Oh, yes I am. I've prepared you for this with your service in Operation Desert Shield and Desert Storm as a transportation officer, and in all your years of coaching."

Out of sheer obedience, I said yes to the invitation. The campus was dilapidated and looked plain horrible. Homeless people were literally living in the basement. The buildings were in such poor shape that without improvements they were on their way to being condemned and demolished.

My first order of business was to listen to the Lord. There are principles here that I live by:

1. You can't hear the Lord just by listening to other people. Godly counsel is good, but leaders must practice hearing from God directly.
2. To do this, you must spend time praying and fasting. It's the only thing that clears out the clutter in our mind and heart.
3. You must be a clean vessel. You can't allow any areas of sin to persist in your life. Sin always gets in the way of hearing God's voice and in the way of effective leadership.
4. You must be willing to do whatever the Lord says, which often means venturing ahead on your own before people are excited to follow. That's the essence of godly leadership.

An Important Piece of the Community

Community transformation also requires an understanding of the culture of the people who live there. In the African-American community, a car wash is a central aspect of their lives, in the same way that barber and beauty shops are. People in the inner city keep their cars clean and looking nice. They also gather there and talk. When we bought the car wash, we bought an important piece of the community.

After repainting and outfitting it with new equipment, we held a grand reopening of the newly named Auto Baptism. We installed a lighted cross illuminating the roof to symbolize to the entire community that Jesus is "the light of the world." On the other side of the property, we opened a revamped restaurant.

Only then did I see the wisdom of the Holy Spirit's guidance. People began talking: "Have you seen the car wash? Baptist College is cleaning up the community." It made them feel good to see the sparkling new touches we had put on things. It even felt different there. I also hired the old guy who lived there to be the security guard, so nobody would break in and steal anything. It was part of investing in the least of these rather than running off "problem" people. We gave him eating privileges at the college campus, and at one point I got him into a rehab program.

> You must be willing to do whatever the Lord says, which often means venturing ahead on your own before people are excited to follow. That's the essence of godly leadership.

Things changed dramatically at Auto Baptism. Over a three-year span the number of violent crimes on our property dropped to zero—a stark difference from the thirty-six the year before we bought it. The refurbishments had created a momentum shift, and crime in the surrounding neighborhoods went down 70 percent! On the business side, we made our money back many times over. On some days, we had to empty out the quarter machines because they were so stuffed with quarters.

I watched how a car wash became the catalyst for community-wide change. People and businesses started coming in and upgrading their properties. They did something I call "putting the neighbor back in the 'hood.' " A place becomes a "hood" when the neighbors move out. It becomes a neighborhood when the neighbors move back in. All around our college, neighbors moved back in and bought boarded-up houses to restore them to use. Our college alone bought around one hundred properties. Together, we were putting the neighbor back in the hood.

People sometimes said I had vision, but the truth is I was simply following God's orders. God provided resources for everything that happened, not me. I ask leaders, and I ask you, are you pursuing your vision or God's vision? We must be tied into God's vision, because His vision comes with provision. When we do that, all the resources come—and we leaders look pretty good besides!

Today, I no longer serve as president of the college, but I'm still involved teaching as a tenured professor and helping recruit students. I also continue to serve the community through my roles on the state board of education, as an appointee of the governor, and as an outreach lay pastor along with my wife, Cynthia, at New Life Church in downtown Little Rock. A significant breakthrough came when we partnered with New Life's Little Rock Dream Center to address the needs as Rick Bezet and Darren DeLaune share in chapter 6.

Community transformation can happen a thousand different ways. I'm here to tell you, sometimes it starts with a car wash and obeying the voice of the Holy Spirit—even when He tells you to do something unexpected.

20

Connecting Life Coaches to Food Ministry

Joyce Dexter

In 2011, Lake City Church in Coeur d'Alene, Idaho, where I serve as food bank director, built a freestanding, 2,400-square-foot food bank on our church property. It's a nice facility, and we were giving away lots of food. But after a couple of years, I was discouraged. It didn't seem like we were helping people in a long-term way. We saw the same faces week after week, and their situations stayed the same. Our goal was that after a while these people would no longer need food assistance. But how could we accomplish that in a compassionate, dignified way?

I made it a matter of persistent prayer, and soon a plan unfolded in my head. I took it to our executive team and they liked the idea. I consulted with the director of the Union Gospel Mission, and he liked it as well.

The plan was to provide a life coach for each person who showed up to our weekly food giveaway, to suggest solutions for their future and create an off-ramp from needing food assistance, through the power of life change.

With our church's approval, I recruited life coaches, mostly retired business people who generously agreed to volunteer time to invest in people. We gave them additional training and made sure they were willing to have difficult conversations and not take people's responses at face value but to look for underlying problems. Our life coaches would serve on the front lines, greeting people when they walked in and saying, "We want to help you by walking alongside you. We're a short-term, crisis-needs food bank. You've been coming in for a few years now. What's going on in your life? What could change? Tell me your story. What's driving your need?"

The life coaches would then come up with a plan to get people moving forward. This could mean help with résumés, job searches, or interview skills. We would even help people buy nice clothes for job interviews. A budget counselor would counsel them on setting up budgets and personal finances. Every time that person returned, the life coach would look at their computer file and talk about what needed to happen next.

> It was scary to think of making such a change. We had not heard of food pantries holding recipients to these kinds of standards before. It would have been much easier to keep doing things the old way, but we cared too much to let people remain stuck.

It was scary to think of making such a change. We had not heard of food pantries holding recipients to these kinds of standards before. It would have been much easier to keep doing things the old way, but we cared too much to let people remain stuck.

So, I drafted a letter to inform people that on June 1 we were implementing a new system involving life coaches and participation in this aspect was required to receive food. The response from several recipients was extremely negative. "Forget this," they said, but in more impolite terms. "There are other food banks in town. We're not coming back to yours." We lost some volunteers, too, who went to serve at other food banks instead of ours because they wanted to give food without strings attached. One person even told me that I had an evil soul. In our first month of using life coaches, the number of families we served dropped from 700 to 250.

Then success stories began to roll in. One man came in and told a life coach that his wife had left him, cleaned out their bank account, and taken the house. He was living in his car. He had an amazing résumé for a homeless person. Our life coach helped him with some suggestions, and a few weeks later the man came in and announced, "I got a job!" Stories like that became common.

Our volunteer group also embraced the new approach. We built a dedicated, loyal group of eighty people who believe strongly in helping people this way. We now serve four hundred families a month, and we're drawing people who truly want a hand up.

To be candid, some people still come in wanting food with no desire to change. They fight us every time. I admire our life coaches because they take the flak. But they feel that their investment is worth it, and we treat everyone who comes through the door with dignity and respect.

We made other positive changes as well. For example, we modified the food bank to work on a point system and set it up like a grocery store. People walk the aisles and choose what they want. They use points like money. We place a higher point value on junk foods and give away healthier foods, like fresh produce, for free. We have more than a hundred items to choose from, and our inventory changes constantly.

We made this change to preserve people's dignity and freedom of choice, but also because when we gave boxes of preselected food away, we were getting a lot of unwanted items back in the donation box in our lobby!

We also continue to serve a continental breakfast and noon meal in the lobby of our church every Wednesday when the food bank is open. We try to use foods people can get from the food bank to show them how to prepare food in a healthy way. It's alarming to see a generation that doesn't know how to prepare food if it doesn't come from a box or a can.

Elderly people are the primary recipients of those meals, and a lot of them look forward to it as an outing because our volunteers love on them so much. One elderly man brings his wife and calls it their weekly date.

Today, we're proud not only of our food bank, but of our church's heart to reach out to the community, and the fact that we fund it all through cash gifts, in-kind donations, and volunteers, accepting no federal or state funding. We have more food in our food bank than the government food bank in our area, and we provide something better than food—life coaching from business experts who care about helping families and individuals make the best of their lives and abilities.

21

Partnering with Public Schools to Feed Hungry Kids

Randy Valimont

I didn't expect to get a dose of reality at our annual Christmas outreach, but reality walked in the door in the form of two boys, ages ten and twelve.

For twenty years we've bussed hundreds of children to our church on a Sunday near Christmas to give them gifts, feed them a meal, and tell them the gospel story. We turned the gymnasium at our main campus into a Christmas festival, and hundreds of volunteers drive buses, minister to kids, and serve food. It's a great time. Year after year, fifty or more kids give their hearts to Christ on that day. For many of them, the gift we give is the only one they receive that year.

This particular year, as the Christmas event was winding down and volunteers were putting kids on the right buses to take them home, two young boys didn't seem to have a place. After volunteers talked with them for a while, the boys finally revealed that they hadn't come on a bus. They had walked to our church from their house—six miles down a road with no sidewalks! They hadn't wanted to miss out on presents and on the prospect of a meal because they hadn't eaten anything else that weekend.

We could hardly believe that children in our community were going without food. I had assumed that city, state, and federal services kept that from happening. The fact that kids in our city were going hungry was a wake-up call to all of us. We had to do something.

Our staff started researching the need in Griffin, Georgia, and found that the poverty rate was an alarming 32 percent—almost twice the national average. One key statistic in any city is the number of children who qualify for a free lunch and breakfast. Half were concentrated in one public school. Many who received free breakfast and lunch on weekdays had no other meal during the week and didn't eat between Friday lunch and Monday breakfast. Many had younger siblings who weren't in school but were also hungry and suffering. These were more than statistics. We were staring at the very definition of food insecurity.

In a small way, we started taking food to kids in that particular school. Then other churches and nonprofits joined us to create the Spalding County Collaborative. Each one took responsibility for feeding kids in certain schools.

Three years later, our program has grown to feed 250 kids a week at a cost of twelve thousand dollars a year, and that's just our church's portion. We call it our backpack program. We purchase food from Kroger's or Sam's once a month, load it onto a church bus, and drive it to a local food pantry that gives us storage space. The food consists of shelf-stable items such as microwavable meals, Vienna sausages, granola bars, breakfast bars, chocolate milk, juice boxes, applesauce, and fruit bars.

On Wednesdays, the kids in our program bring to school the backpacks we gave them and leave them in the principal's office. On Thursday, about a dozen church volunteers pick up the backpacks and fill them with ten nonperishable items. Each backpack's contents are identical. On Friday, the kids pick up their backpacks from the principal's office, take them home, and have food for themselves and their families for the weekend. That happens every week.

We had been sending buses to pick up kids for church for more than twenty years, and we noticed an immediate synergy between our backpack program and our bus ministry. When we started giving away backpacks full of food, those kids started getting on our buses on Sunday mornings. We began running routes to parts of our city that hadn't previously been receptive to our buses, and our volunteers began to build relationships that hadn't existed before. We soon found that the neediest kids were the least likely to tell us about their needs until they got to know us. Most didn't want to shame their families.

We are sowing as much as we can into these kids—and already we see good results. Recently, a girl who started on our bus ministry at age five graduated from Georgia Tech. She's an engineer. The other day a young man came up to me and said, "Five years ago I was a bus kid and got on the bus for the last time. I graduated high school and went to college. I wanted to come back and say thank you. You guys loved me, and God gave me a purpose and plan."

Our church gives around $2.5 million a year to missions, and we've always done things for the community surrounding us, but when we began serving children who were hurting, people's hearts for missions went to a whole new level. More people are giving to missions outreaches now because they see what we're doing locally. Millennials, in particular, need to see where their dollar is going locally before they give to missions at all. Once people see what we do locally, they're more willing to give to help people they can't see.

We've built up such goodwill with our education system that principals and teachers fight for our help now. It all started that day when two boys couldn't resist the thought of a meal and a Christmas gift on Sunday morning. They didn't know it, but they opened our eyes to a whole new world of compassion.

22

Wait No More! A Church Model for Foster Care

Dr. Sharen Ford

Every child dreams of a happy home, and when a foster family provides one, the impact can be profound.

I believe that if all the people God has spoken to about becoming foster parents would obey that calling, the system wouldn't have a shortage of foster parents, and there would be far fewer cases of foster parents taking kids for selfish or even wicked motivations.

Thankfully, many Christians, and even whole churches, are responding to the call to help foster children in America. What can you, your small group, church, or neighborhood do to support foster families? Let me offer some practical guidance.

How to Help Foster Families

I'm greatly encouraged that in a number of churches, multiple families have come together to support foster care, either by becoming foster parents or by supporting those who do. I think of Project 1.27, which started out of Colorado Community Church with the goal of making sure there were no children waiting for homes in their state. Project 1.27 serves as a bridge between the Christian community and the foster care system, inspiring, recruiting, and resourcing churches and families to foster and adopt. To date they have cared for 800 kids and helped 340 of them to be adopted by Project 1.27 families. There are examples of this kind of church-based ministry in other states as well.

If you feel drawn to help meet this need, what are some steps you can take?

Step 1: Pray

The primary activity of any person or group wanting to support foster care is prayer. In the beginning, ask God to speak to your heart about what you can do. Ask Him to open your eyes to opportunities and people you can help. Ask Him to put you together with others who have the same heart to support foster kids and families.

Step 2: Look around You

Likely, there are foster families in your church. If you see children of color with an Anglo family, for example, it might be grandkids, adopted children, or family friends—or it might be foster kids. Broach the conversation with someone sitting next to you or plan a casual event for foster families to attend.

You'll probably find in your midst some foster families and "kinship families"—a grandma or aunt who is caring for a relative's children because of an unhealthy situation. Both offer situations where acknowledgment and support are desperately needed.

Step 3: Make Safe Environments

Shame keeps a lot of foster kids and kinship caregiver (nonparental) families undercover. They don't want to admit that something went wrong in their families. A safe environment is one where you don't lead with a lot of questions. Befriending or accepting someone doesn't require knowing their story or details about their background. And some kids might give you a real answer, speaking directly from their pain. They might become angry or sad or tell you information you don't know how to handle.

Don't put a spotlight on people in tough circumstances. Things will unfold when it's time. Your goal at this point is to provide acts of service, kindness, and safe relationships.

Another safety issue involves things like sensory disorders and attachment disorders. (Focus on the Family has a series of booklets about these topics.) Pastors, children's pastors, and volunteers should be knowledgeable about treating children with these disorders gently and appropriately.

Step 4: Start to Assist

Once you've found likeminded people, and perhaps some foster families in your church or neighborhood, look for opportunities to come alongside them.

One of the best examples of community commitment I've seen is the Catholic parishes in Colorado Springs, who are working with the Fostering Hope Foundation. Licensed child placement agencies contact the Fostering Hope Foundation to refer foster families in need of help and support. Families from the parishes and other churches are recruited and trained by the Foundation to support their assigned foster family. I hear story after story of foster parents who say, "I would have quit after taking that first foster child, if not for my support group."

What does "coming alongside" foster families mean? It might mean doing their laundry or mowing their lawn or taking their birth kids to baseball practice while the foster parents take the foster child to therapy. It might mean making dinner or doing whatever you can to lighten their load. Little things make all the difference.

In a church context, maybe it's about volunteering in the nursery or youth room. Why? Because the foster child may have separation anxiety or may not get along well with other kids, and this will cause their number to flash on the screen so often that the foster family is embarrassed. Or perhaps a former regular attendee now shows up only rarely, or always late, because it takes them so long to get ready. Saving seats for them might mean a lot. Be alert to such situations; talk to your pastor or children's pastor and let them know you and your group would like to help foster families. Others in the church can pitch in as well. I know an auto mechanic in Grand Junction who gives significant discounts to foster parents and an orthodontist who gives adoptive families a reduced rate. "Coming alongside" looks like whatever helps that foster family succeed.

Step 5: Make It a Community Thing

More and more churches and public entities hold backpack or suitcase drives for kids in the foster care system, so kids can change locations with greater dignity than clutching a plastic trash bag of possessions. Duffel bags with two wheels are inexpensive and can make a huge difference in a child's self-perception.

Some groups work together to give Christmas gifts specifically from each foster child's wish list. In one county, local businesses host a foster parent Christmas party to give foster parents a nice dinner and gift cards. It's their way of giving back to families who are supporting kids in their community.

One church makes brand-new quilts for every child who enters the foster care system. Why is this a big deal? Because foster kids live with "clothing insecurity," if I can coin a phrase. When children are removed from their house, it's often done quickly by a police officer and social worker. Even if there's time to retrieve clothing, sometimes it's not allowed because the adults in the home have been smoking illegal drugs, and the smoke permeates clothing, bedding, and stuffed toys. It's not uncommon for kids to enter the foster system with nothing but the clothes on their backs.

Upon arriving at the foster home, kids might receive one or two new outfits, but most of their clothes will probably come from a bin in the closet or garage with clothes left from previous kids. When foster kids leave a home, they leave the clothes as well. With that in mind, imagine someone handing you a quilt with your name embroidered on it . . . that you get to keep and take with you wherever you go. You can see how meaningful this would be to the child.

I encourage churches and nonprofits to partner together to multiply their efforts in projects like these. Think what your church denomination or association could do if it announced it was supporting all foster kids in your zip code with new clothing or backpacks or suitcases or some other creative way of caring.

Step 6: Consider Fostering a Child

I recommend researching Christian foster agencies in your community. Not every faith-based agency does domestic foster care. Some only do international adoptions and infant domestic adoptions. Do your homework. Contact my office at Focus on the Family, and we can provide a list of agencies to consider in your state. Or simply search for information yourself and start kicking the tires. Some states have no faith-based foster care agencies at all, so you will need to work through public child-welfare agencies. Be prayerful about it and ask God to supply a believer as your caseworker. Whatever your chosen pathway, the opportunities are plenty to support the success of foster families and foster children in your area. I pray that your church or group's Spirit-led solutions will affect the lives of many as you serve the least of these.

Guiding Principles for Raising a Foster Child
Dave and Kristy Donaldson

Here are some of the guiding principles that pastors can follow when advising families about raising a foster child. The process isn't always easy. These are the guidelines we used when we became foster parents to Barbara when she was sixteen.

- Instill significance and security by sharing with your foster child that "God blesses us with children through childbirth and through foster care and adoption." All our children are special gifts to our family from heaven.
- Set clear boundaries. While we abided by the rules and guidelines mandated by the US Children's Bureau, we also had rules and expectations as part of the Donaldson household. The best way to teach this was by a natural immersion into our family's routine: church on Sundays and Wednesdays, our son's baseball games, meeting our friends and neighbors, and helping with cooking and cleanup. Yes, there were confrontations with Barbara, but the most persuasive teacher was peer pressure from our biological children.
- Education must be a top priority. Although we tried to help Barbara finish high school with passing grades, she didn't seem to care. She faced the real possibility of being held back for a second senior year. We stayed up late with her to help her study, and she finally passed! Many foster children are so accustomed to failure, it becomes their expectation. Helping a foster child develop the disciplines to succeed is one of the most challenging but rewarding aspects of this journey.
- Meet your foster child at their level of maturity. Even though Barbara's biological age was sixteen, her social skills and cognitive abilities were closer to those of a much younger child.

Most of these kids lack the benefit of a normal childhood; therefore, you must raise them from their current maturation point with a consistency of unconditional love, patience, and affirmation. Barbara not only caught up with her age group cognitively and relationally, but she excelled, so that she graduated with honors from Evangel University.

- Give your biological children time and understanding to adjust to a "stranger" now sharing their parent's attention, occupying their space, and using their things.
- Pray and claim God's promises. One of the greatest promises from God's Word we claimed for ourselves while parenting our kids is: "I am the LORD, the God of all mankind. Is anything too hard for me? . . . I will give them singleness of heart and action, so that they will always fear me and that all will then go well for them and for their children after them" (Jeremiah 32:27, 39).

23

A Church's Health Care Ministry to an Aging Population

Tom Knox

At twenty-nine years of age, jobless, I moved into my mom's basement in New Jersey.

With nothing else to do, I drove down to visit my brother at Regent University. I hadn't heard of CBN, but seeing satellite dishes on campus, I introduced myself. "I see you have satellite dishes," I told the receptionist. "I used to do sales and programming for Dish Network."

They had an immediate need, so they hired me to run production teams and telethons, and to fill commercials. I had little experience in those areas, so whenever Pat Robertson showed up, I ran into the bathroom to hide.

Three years later I was a senior vice president at CBN. God gave me great favor. Pat eventually met me and approved of my hiring. It was a great experience. But God was not done transitioning me. As head of marketing, I had to study the demographics of the senior population as part of Pat's effort to build a senior living complex on the CBN campus. The consultant I worked with on that project told me one day, "You have a deep interest in this. I can tell that senior care resonates with you. You must read *Age Wave*, by Ken Dychtwald. I think it'll change your life."

I looked for the book in local book stores (in those pre-Internet days) but couldn't find it. I wanted that book so badly. A few nights later I couldn't sleep. It was 3:30 a.m. Unsettled, I prayed and wrestled with God over something undefined. Then I heard a voice in my heart say, "Get up and get out of bed." This had never happened to me before, so I obeyed and sat there wondering, "Am I supposed to pray or sit here or what?" After a while, I went back to bed. At 4:07 a.m. I heard the voice again: "Get up, get out of bed, and turn on the TV." I obeyed. C-SPAN was on and someone was interviewing a man. His name was Ken Dychtwald, author of *Age Wave*. He was talking about how seniors need solutions and baby boomers demand better options. He looked directly at the camera and said, "Someone's got to start a Senior Corps, like the Peace Corps." I said aloud, "That's me."

I had already seen my grandmother—an incredibly wonderful, smart, nurturing woman—have a terrible experience as an elderly person. As she aged, she got sick and moved into a nursing home rehabilitation facility. One day she was in bed pressing the button for someone to help her. Nobody came. She tried to get out of bed, fell on the floor, and was pinned next to the hospital bed for approximately thirteen hours. She had a mild heart attack while waiting there. That's where my aunt found her when she came to visit.

We immediately brought my grandmother home, and within three months my mother, a strong believer and tough Italian, was on the verge of a nervous breakdown from providing the necessary care, managing health services, and being up at night with my grandmother. I thought, *This is crazy. How can a woman who lived such a great, faith-filled life and had a strong family and some financial resources not find the right help?*

At the right time, I resigned from CBN. I had just enough money saved up to buy a little company that provided hospital beds, oxygen, and various health supplies to seniors. It was located in an old delivery warehouse with exposed pipes everywhere. The main vehicle was a converted ice cream truck. On my first day in those shabby conditions, I grabbed an order to deliver a walker and a box of adult diapers. My employee said, "What are you doing? You can't go to that neighborhood at this time of evening." I said, "I'm from New Jersey. I can do it." I jumped in the converted ice cream truck and took off.

She was right. The delivery location was basically a crack house. It looked condemned. Guys were loitering out front. It was getting dark . . . and I was scared. I thought of calling my wife. I thought of selling the business. *What have I done with my life?* I thought. *I'm in debt. I know CBN will take me back.*

Instead of driving away, I grabbed a pocketknife and stuffed it in my pocket, just in case. I took off my jacket and tie, which had been so out of place all day. I dialed 911 preemptively but didn't hit "send." As I approached the house I repeatedly yelled, "Health care worker." Inside, the building smelled disgusting. There were people everywhere. It felt like a horror movie. I announced the name on my delivery sheet, "Mama Jones!" and someone replied, "Third floor." Up the stairs I went, cautiously but quickly. Coming to the third floor I saw an open door and light streaming into the hall. The Bible Broadcasting Network was playing on a television inside the room. I walked in with my deliveries and the woman, Mama Jones, reacted as if I'd brought her a check for ten thousand dollars. She got up, hugged and kissed me, and said, "I'm all out of diapers." We talked and prayed together for the next thirty minutes.

Walking back to my van, I said to myself, *I'm all in.*

Two years later, after an invaluable season of learning, I sold that company and started Seniorcorp in my kids' bedroom, just like the man on C-SPAN had said. I began driving seniors around, giving them advice, going to their houses, and hiring caregivers for them. The things I observed, and the culture we created, helped us expand across the country to provide excellent, effective, and dignified service to the aging population, as well as outreach and ministry to the staff of caregivers, many of whom are single moms or working poor.

That's my story. Now I want to tell you how churches can help this great and necessary cause.

The Great Opportunity

The Age Wave is here and all of us in some way are learning to face the challenges and opportunities of serving the aging population and their family members. Citizens sixty-five and over increased in numbers from 35 million in 2000, to 49.2 million in 2016, according to the US Census Bureau.[2] Many adult children are caught in the "sandwich" of raising their own children while assisting and providing for their aging parents. They rely on employers to be flexible with work hours so they can accomplish this.

> Senior care ministry needs a committed leader with understanding of this population and maybe even expertise in the field.

The opportunity for churches to impact the aging population and their families has never been greater. But many churches seem strangely disconnected. Why?

Senior care isn't relevant. Building programs around children, teens, and young families is certainly a priority, but to be truly relevant with nearly one-third of the overall population (seniors and adult children who assist them), churches must serve the aging population.

It takes time and is harder than other types of compassion ministries. Both true. Serving seniors requires more personalized communication, since they often won't use e-mail, computers, tablets, and so on. Interacting with them means a lot of one-on-one personal contact—home visits, phone calls, and traditional services such as potlucks and game nights. For many in our fast-paced generation, this feels slow, uncomfortable, and like a move backwards. *It requires a heart for seniors and experience in helping them.* Senior care ministry needs a committed leader with understanding of this population and maybe even expertise in the field. A parish nurse or a church member with leadership traits who has dealt with aging parents or someone with long-term care experience are all excellent candidates. But available people are not always easy to find.

That said, the benefits of serving seniors are many—and so are the benefits to churches.

Healthy seniors help seniors. The opportunity for fellowship and companionship is great among able-bodied seniors and those who can use their help. This provides a sense of community and any number of ministry opportunities within a church's aging population. They just need to know how to connect with each other.

Loyalty and continuity in the congregation. The aging population resists moving between churches and making life changes. There will be increased loyalty and continuity in your church if you engage seniors and welcome them.

Financial support. The senior population may be a mixed economic group, but plenty of seniors and their adult children have financial resources to support your church—if they feel they are being blessed with time, resources, and ministry.

So how do churches begin to help in senior care? Let's look at four key areas that can transform your senior care approach.

A New Approach to Senior Care Ministry

Assign a leader. As mentioned, the best candidate may be a retired or semiretired nurse or social worker. They have institutional knowledge to make an immediate impact. If a professional isn't available to volunteer, look for a competent adult who has given care to aging parents. That experience builds compassion and some level of competence. Your goal is to find someone who will "own" this ministry to seniors.

Create simple opportunities for fellowship. The best ideas are the simplest ones. Here are five easy fellowship ideas most churches could do right away:

1. A monthly recognition lunch to honor a senior (or two) for their life and ministry, including the presentation of a computer-generated certificate.

2. A biweekly phone-in conference call with a short devotional and a time of prayer for needs.

3. Volunteer visits to seniors to provide a simple lunch, visits with children, sing-alongs, and conversation. These visits can be held in homes of shut-ins, at community centers, or at church.

4. Pet visits at church or at a home, with a small group of well-behaved pets.

5. Senior mentoring opportunities. Canvas your group of seniors to see who would be willing to consult with people in the church who are looking for information and wisdom in business or finances, sewing, cooking, prayer, parenting, ministry, and more. Seniors want to give back and will, if you give them avenues.

Provide resources. Churches are natural hubs for seniors who need help, and many people within churches can assist seniors in basic, nonprofessional ways to improve their lives. This includes those with handyman skills who can do limited repairs such as fixing a fence or a broken cabinet door or replacing light bulbs. Others, especially healthy seniors, may be willing to help with basic errands, driving, companionship, and meal preparation for needy seniors or their families.

Those who bring a lunch and spend time with seniors do a great service to their community. Half of good senior health care is social. When people are lonely and shut in, they stop taking medications and stop eating well, and that creates health problems, imbalances, and falls, which put them in the hospital, and problems escalate from there. The social aspect of care could easily be covered by people who are willing to share their time with a senior.

Churches are natural hubs for seniors who need help.

It would be valuable to maintain a list of two or three registered nurses who are willing to do a quick phone call with adult children who would like advice on navigating care needs. This is a wonderful ministry opportunity. These RNs should not do home visits or make advocacy phone calls but simply provide guidance once or twice per family. These will not be answers to clinical questions but tips on navigating the systems involved in senior care.

Churches can keep a list of people willing to volunteer and update it every ninety days or so. Safeguards and parameters should be established to avoid misunderstandings or blurred lines of responsibility.

The second type of resources comes from outside the church. A lot of pastors know there are needs within their congregations but don't know how to connect people to outside resources. I understand that some pastors get nervous when businesses offer services and ask the church to recommend them. It's wise to be cautious, but being overly cautious cuts people off from good care opportunities. Most of the time, people just need phone numbers for resources such as Meals on Wheels, transportation services, companion services, food delivery, someone to give them a bath, or care managers who work for an hourly fee. Seniors trust churches to guide them to resources. With a little effort, churches could find local, trusted services. Some resources are subsidized, and others are paid. Subsidized assistance can include Medicaid, the Veterans Administration, Ride-Share programs, and the area Agency on Aging. Paid services can include top home-care agencies, transportation and food delivery options, and a local geriatric case manager.

Expand Your Influence.

The single biggest crisis facing senior care is the massive shortage of caregivers. Most seniors want to age at home, but the more than nineteen thousand national agencies can't find enough compassionate and available personnel to help them do this. At Seniorcorp, we spend a huge amount of time finding, training, and keeping workers. The turnover rate is well over 100 percent. We're all fighting to keep the same people.

Caregiving doesn't involve medical procedures like giving injections or working with feeding tubes. It involves things like driving, making meals, doing light housekeeping, helping someone bathe, or get in and out of a chair. We call these ADL—activities of daily living. It's amazing how many people we train quickly feel comfortable moving into this area of employment.

A recent study showed that more than 80 percent of professional caregivers describe themselves as faith-based and regular worshippers. Yet there's a huge disconnect between recruiters and church members. Pastors are reluctant to share access and names with outside groups, to exhibit good stewardship. But this builds unnecessary barriers. It's the talk of the industry that the best caregivers are behind church walls. Studies show this is true, and conferences spend lots of time discussing it. So many potential workers are not aware that caregiving is a rewarding career because they don't hear about it. I understand that pastors must be careful, but churches must also take the lead to address the caregiver crisis in America.

Churches alone could solve the senior care labor crisis by changing their posture toward senior care providers. Maybe it means keeping a list of reputable agencies and training programs. Maybe it means hosting a lunch or job fair with representatives from local senior care organizations. The basic need is to bridge the gap, to give church members, including the unemployed, stay-at-home moms, retirees, and others access to training and immediate jobs. And it expands your church's influence well beyond your campus as these people begin to serve the neediest in your community.

I believe that if most pastors would connect people with training programs and available jobs, the senior care crisis would virtually disappear.

It's among the highest callings to help seniors, our mothers and fathers, finish strong. Like an unreached people group, the aging population and their overwhelmed families need others to minister to them. Seniors are open to the gospel, vulnerable, highly appreciative, and often living right in front of our eyes, waiting for us to give them the honor, kindness, and assistance they deserve.

24

Setting Up a Nonprofit for Your Church

Paul Thompson

I was the oldest child of a Baptist minister whose first parish church was in an extremely poor part of northern Minnesota. One night, after spending the day with a very poor family, I had a life-defining conversation with God. "I hate poverty," I told Him, "and I want to do something about it."

After college, I got a job as the executive director for a residential treatment center for delinquent kinds that was partly supported by a faith-based organization and partly by local and county funds. I began to observe other nonprofit leaders, few of whom were doing a good job of leading their organizations. Some were doing illegal things and defrauding people. For example, the faith-based organization that supported the residential center I worked for held telethons to raise funds and used kids from our center as examples of those who needed support. But we never got any money from those fund-raising efforts.

Provoked by this, I earned a master's degree from Pepperdine University in the management of nonprofits and researched what I called "the integrity gap" within the nonprofit sector. I compared what the various nonprofits' fund-raising literature said they did against what they really did. During this research I discovered one organization, World Vision, that stood head and shoulders above all others in their integrity. That was one reason I went to work for them for seventeen years.

I tell that backstory because leadership excellence has been my focus for decades. To this day I aspire to build more effective leaders in the nonprofit sector. Too many people believe that nonprofit organizations are run by ineffective leaders. Despite the example I just gave, it's generally not true. Some of the finest leaders I've met lead nonprofits. In fact, I've seen Fortune 500 CEOs step into the role of a nonprofit leader only to crash and burn because nonprofits are significantly more complex. Most for-profit companies generally have one mission: profit. Nonprofits have multiple objectives and their work is more nuanced.

Let me take you through some basic steps for a church considering starting a nonprofit. My goal is to enhance your success and leadership in your endeavor.

Why Start a Nonprofit?

Nonprofits and churches are both 501(c)(3) (the portion of the US Internal Revenue Code that allows for federal tax exemption of nonprofit organizations) entities and must meet the same requirements of the IRS. A church must pass a couple of other tests relative to its creed and in so doing is relieved of certain responsibilities. For example, a church doesn't have to file an IRS form 990 like other nonprofits.

So why would a church want to start a nonprofit? One major reason would be to partner with and receive funds from businesses or foundations whose legal structures may prevent them from supporting a Christian or sectarian organization that promotes a single creed. For example, suppose you're seeking funds from a foundation in your city to create an after-school program for poor children. Your goals and the foundation's goals are consistent but the foundation's guidelines prevent them from funding religious organizations or sectarian causes. Unless you have a way around that, you won't receive the funds.

A church in that situation may want to consider creating a subsidiary nonprofit entity that would agree not to proselytize. It would exist for nonsectarian purposes. The church itself could continue to evangelize according to its mission, but the subsidiary nonprofit could receive funds from organizations that cannot or do not want to support evangelism.

There are effective ways to ensure the subsidiary nonprofit stays consistent with the church's mission. For example, some of the board members for the subsidiary could also be on the board of the church if they understand and support the specific missions of each.

Does Our Church Really Need a Nonprofit?

Maybe—or maybe not. The first step in making that decision is to achieve extreme clarity on what you want to accomplish. What would be the mission of the nonprofit? Whom would it serve? What services would it provide that are different from those provided by the church? Where would goods or services be delivered? How would they be implemented? Does meeting the goal require the creation of a separate nonprofit? Getting at the core values, beliefs, and priorities of the proposed nonprofit is a basic step that is often neglected or not clearly understood by those considering it.

For example, suppose your church has a relationship with a food company that wants to donate a certain product, such as bagels. You want to set up a nonprofit to access that specific resource, but bagels alone will not provide a balanced meal for the people you want to serve. You would need donations of a wider variety of foods from other businesses to accomplish your goal of providing a balanced meal.

Or say you want to start an early childhood education center. While that's an important thing to do, if you haven't researched how to educate children at early ages effectively, you may end up being nothing more than a babysitting service.

The other initial question is, does the community need what you want to offer? Every discussion of nonprofit work begins with a thorough community needs-assessment. Ask people in your benevolences ministry what needs they see. Then get out there and interview other organizations to find out what problems are present and what organizations are meeting them. It's an honest and transforming dialogue, and you'll learn much.

Once a church has a clear and compelling mission and has identified a specific need, it may find there are good reasons to start a separate nonprofit. One such reason might be to protect the church from liability if something goes wrong. Say you want to create a senior care center adjacent to the church and plan to use some government funds in the form of bond money. If an employee in the center does something wrong to a resident, the family might file a lawsuit. If the center is run by a separate nonprofit, the church will be protected, assuming they're following all their fiduciary responsibilities such as having a legal board of directors.

Another good reason to create a separate nonprofit is to facilitate collaboration with other organizations. Historically, though there are any number of like-minded churches and nonprofits serving the same communities, usually they aren't partnering together. A nonprofit that can engage support from other nonprofits and churches in a dynamic, noncompetitive, community-serving way achieves a strength of collaboration that has the potential of being nothing short of profound.

Incorporation

The clearer the assessment of needs and the vision for meeting them, the faster and better things are likely to go in the steps that follow. This includes creating articles of incorporation that set out the tenets of the organization and its purpose. The secretary of state in each state requires these articles to grant nonprofit status. I call this the skeleton.

Bylaws are the muscles on the skeleton. They give more clarity about what kind of organization it is, its mission, number of board members, committees of the board, terms of service, and so on. You can only develop your bylaws after you have clarity and unanimity about what you want to do. They help you create the organizational support mechanisms that allow your endeavor to become a legal entity.

Articles and bylaws are primarily for the use of the board itself. Major donors or foundations occasionally want to look at them to do due diligence.

Most nonprofits enlist the services of a lawyer who is knowledgeable about nonprofit law in their state. You can also get templates for bylaws and articles off the Internet, and revise and adjust them to meet your needs. Then you file them with the IRS and your state's secretary of state.

Doing all of this and receiving approval to operate as a nonprofit in your state may take the better part of a year.

Boards

Part of incorporating involves creating a board structure and selecting board members. I do a lot of counseling for boards and have witnessed many disaster stories when the board is dysfunctional. On one extreme is the founder of a nonprofit who stacks the board with his close friends. In such instances the board is influenced inordinately by the founder, and they don't take their fiduciary responsibility of holding the executive accountable seriously.

On the other side of the spectrum are board members who only look at legal requirements, finances, and governance but aren't engaged in the program side of the organization and don't really care about it. They ask questions about the finances and governance but not about the impact of the organization and whether it's serving the community in a dynamic way.

I always encourage nonprofits to see each seat on the board as a precious, important commodity that should be well-cared for. You want every board member richly committed to the mission of the organization and vibrantly involved in nurturing it, based on their respective experience and abilities.

A good board also has strong governance in the way committees are structured. Each committee has a clear mission. There might be a governance committee, a finance committee, an audit committee, a program committee, a marketing committee, a fundraising committee, and so on. Each has a clear role and mission, and is functioning with energy and enthusiasm.

The classic three Ws of board governance are wealth (or access to it), wisdom (or unique knowledge and the ability to use it for the benefit of the organization), and work. This is one way of creating diversity on your board. Some nonprofits only look at wealth, and they throw a deep-pocketed, major donor on the board. That's a huge mistake. You want people on the board who have other reasons for being there, aside from financial wealth.

25

Creating a Community Development Corporation

Lee de León

In 1980, Templo Calvario Church in Santa Ana, California, launched a food bank that quickly began resourcing a network of sixty churches and nonprofit organizations near us. Soon we were serving three hundred families each week. Yet a survey we took after several years revealed that some families had been receiving food for as many as ten years. Either they were depending on our food bank to make it through the week, or we were just another stop on the rotation of food banks they visited weekly. Either way, we weren't helping them break free from the cycle of poverty.

Following that survey, with the blessing of our church elders, we took steps to establish a community development corporation (CDC) to go deeper with the families we served. We wanted to be part of long-term solutions for their lives and help them find financial stability. Today our CDC focuses on education (through a charter school and parent training), economic development (financial literacy, home ownership, and small business development), and other faith-based initiatives.

If your church is considering a CDC to meet needs in your community, here are a few things we've learned in our journey that might help you.

What Is a Community Development Corporation?

CDCs are a type of nonprofit organization that targets a specific neighborhood or city with the goal of revitalizing a blighted community, usually through economic development, education, and housing. CDCs go beyond the activities of typical nonprofits that address immediate needs to implement long-term solutions to restore broken communities. Some CDCs are faith-based, some are not.

Economic development can be anything from commercial real estate to small businesses to franchises to . . . you name it—basically anything that brings life to the economy of a neighborhood. Sometimes in blighted areas big chain markets have moved out along with smaller chain stores. This leaves large gaps in malls and business areas, which means people in the community must drive more than a few miles to buy groceries at a decent price. CDCs encourage development by training people and creating partnerships aimed at building businesses in a certain area. Creating jobs and encouraging business development are a big piece of what CDCs do.

Providing education is a more recent development. Historically, most CDCs weren't involved in education, but it seems more are venturing into that area now simply because they already have a presence in a community. Some are operating charter schools, which are public schools operated independently by a CDC, an entity the CDC creates, or by another nonprofit organization. In our case, we've been operating a charter school for fifteen years and are considering opening more. The charter school feels like a private school but because it's a public school, students don't pay to attend. Our CDC board manages it.

CDCs usually don't get involved in tutoring and after-school help. Those are handled by regular nonprofits.

Affordable housing is another pressing need and has been for many years. Some CDCs build apartment complexes, and federal funding often subsidizes the rent payments of those who live there. The CDC owns the building, and some own multiple apartments and housing complexes. For some of them it becomes a multimillion-dollar industry and a large aspect of their organization.

Many CDCs help people build or buy homes at a discounted rate. Our CDC isn't involved in providing housing. We choose to help people get into home ownership by providing classes on financial literacy and helping them gain the knowledge to start small businesses.

> If you get involved in things every leader in the city knows you shouldn't be involved in, it probably won't help anybody. Listen to your city and community leaders, and implement their wise advice.

In recent years I've watched as more and more people have become interested in CDCs, yet it isn't always the best path for a church or nonprofit. If your goal is to do after-school programs or a food pantry, you don't need to be a CDC. Any nonprofit will do. If you want to aim at the larger issues of housing and economic development, then you need a CDC. Why? Because housing and urban development puts you in a special category, which opens the door to funding that isn't available to regular nonprofits.

We suggest you do research to discover whether another CDC may already be operating in your community. Remember, it's easier to incorporate and launch a CDC than it is to sustain it and help it thrive, especially without a major commitment from individuals or a church to support it with dollars and hours. I've seen many CDCs launch and then disappear, never to be heard from again.

Making a CDC work takes work. Are you and your organization willing to commit to that responsibility?

How Do You Establish a CDC?

Here are some key steps for establishing a CDC in your community:

• *Determine if there's a need for a CDC in your city.* Many cities and communities have established CDCs that may be looking for volunteers or partner organizations. Join them! Save yourself the trouble of duplicating what already exists, and you may also find like-minded partners to add strength to your efforts.

• *"Pray walk" your streets.* This has become extremely important for me. For a few years I've set aside time every week to walk the streets of my city, observing and interceding for it. I do this alone because with others along it's too tempting to talk. During these times of prayer, I see the challenges and struggles that many face each day—the crowded apartments that house multiple families, the tattered vehicles that moms and dads drive to two or more jobs. As I walk and look, I bathe an area in prayer. Normally I don't have a specific focus. I'm just trying to capture what God is speaking to my heart. When I get back to my office, I take time to reflect on the walk and journal what I saw and sensed in my spirit.

• *Establish relationships with city and community leaders.* Many church and nonprofit leaders aren't good at having conversations with city leaders. Make this a priority. Find out from these civic leaders about the needs of your community. Share your idea for a CDC with them and get their input. You could even consider having them work with you. Don't bring them your fabulous idea and insist they get on board. Listen to their ideas first and be receptive to their critique of your plans. If you get involved in things every leader in the city knows you shouldn't be involved in, it probably won't help anybody. Listen to your city and community leaders, and implement their wise advice.

• *Think and plan together.* If you decide to move forward with a CDC rather than a standard nonprofit, gather like-minded people and groups to develop a simple one- to three-year strategic plan. You don't have to start with a major project like building one hundred units of housing. Start by revitalizing a couple of houses down the street. That's how most CDCs start—with small, manageable projects. Before you know it, the county will say they have dollars available to help, and so does the city, and then you're off and running.

Our CDC made the mistake of launching businesses too early, and we didn't have the capacity to carry out our responsibilities. By "capacity" I mean trained staff, connection with partners, and access to funding. Thirteen years later, the timing was right, and our capacity was greater, so we moved into that area with more confidence and experience and success.

> You don't have to start with a major project like building one hundred units of housing. Start by revitalizing a couple of houses down the street.

I tell people to act like a CDC before you become one. That will help you experience what it's like to be a CDC and select projects appropriate to your size and skills.

What Can Our CDC Do?

Again, start with manageable things and use what you have to your advantage. For example, most churches have classrooms and facilities of some kind. Ask a business professional or manager in your church to give the unemployed in your community soft skills training: how to dress for success, show up on time, communicate well with a boss and coworkers, and so on. These skills help people gain and sustain employment. Give the project a fancy name like Workforce Development Seminar and advertise it locally. Set up a computer and help participants conduct a job search afterward.

That's a simple, low-cost venture that most any group can do. If you're a little more adventurous, look around your community for homes that need to be fixed. Many senior citizens live in dilapidated homes. Perhaps you'll find an empty home on a certain block. You can ask the city if they'll work with you to move a single mom into it so it's no longer an eyesore. Offer to do all the necessary repairs and renovations to provide safe and comfortable housing for the mom and her family and to make the house an asset to the community again.

If you have a business expert in your midst, hold a workshop about how to launch a business. Walk participants through the preparation of a business plan. Teach them how to be an employer. We have one initiative for young, business-minded people who want mentors to help them achieve success in business and in life. We help to pair the participants with an appropriate mentor for their journey.

The final step to becoming an official CDC is to find an attorney who is willing to do pro bono work and help you file the necessary paper work to incorporate. Once that's complete you're ready to take the first, small steps toward providing long-term help to the community around you.

26

Family Centers: How to Establish One in Your Community

Jonas and Anne Beiler

The vision for the Family Center was born out of a tragedy. In 1975 our second daughter, Angela, just nineteen months old, was killed in a farming accident. In an instant our lives were in shambles, and Anne and I didn't know how to process the mountain of grief. We retreated into an isolated, fathomless, and painful place. I describe it as "our seven years of silence."

We convinced ourselves that time, business, and helping others would heal our wounds. Anne thought I was doing okay, and I thought she was doing okay. But the truth was that we were both dying inside. The feeling of dying while still living is a tragic situation. You do your best to keep the victory, but a thought or event can unleash the floodgate of heartbreaking emotions.

Finally, we decided to seek the support of a professional counselor who helped us to be open and honest about our grief. Just becoming aware of how parents suffer and heal differently helped us immensely. For example, it helped my ability to empathize with Anne when I learned how especially agonizing it is for a mother to lose a child she has carried in her womb for nine months, nursed, and nurtured. The bond between a mother and her child can only be fully grasped by a mother. It can take several months, or in some circumstances, years, for the father to develop that kind of a bond with his child so it's difficult for him to understand the depth of grief his wife is experiencing. The counseling sessions provided the breakthroughs we desperately needed. They revealed that truth itself is healing.

During our counseling process, the Lord birthed a passion inside me to help other couples address the pain and isolation a loss can cause in the marriage. Often I thought, *There must be a better way than suffering so long with this level of pain and distance from my wife.* So, Anne and I decided to start by helping couples in our home. We created the Angela Foundation. It was named in honor of our daughter and offered couples counseling services at no cost. Over time, the counseling ministry grew and so did our dreams to build a Family Center to house the ministry in Gap, Pennsylvania.

Gap is a fitting name for the town because it is here the Amish and non-Amish worlds collide. No one looks twice at the horse-drawn buggies that trot in what looks like an oversized bike lane. But, like most communities in the United States, there's a hidden brokenness of troubled marriages and family discord.

I wrote about this in my book *Think No Evil*, which dives into the tragic story of the Amish schoolhouse shooting.

Many Family Services under One Roof

In no way would I want to paint a picture that the Family Center was easy to start, because it wasn't. However, the Lord blessed the Center and at its peak over four thousand people used the facility over a one-month period. The decision and strategy behind the Family Center, which housed a network of services under one roof, grew out of these observations:

- Before the Family Center, clients roamed around town with their kids to receive all their needed services, which was both an inconvenience and a hardship for the families. This resulted in parents not taking advantage of the available help. We needed to remove as many excuses as possible for people to receive treatment by housing all the services in one location.

- Offering a variety of services in one place reduced the stigma attached to some of the more intimate care needs and minimized the anxiety or discomfort people felt when showing up for the services.

- Combining services under one roof created a powerful synergy of expertise and programs, which resulted in holistic healing for our clients. For example, elder care and day care could work together, so elderly people could hold and cuddle babies as emotional therapy. Our clients from the pregnancy center could be introduced to a counselor right down the hall. Or if a professional counselor diagnosed a client with an eating disorder, we could send the person to an in-house nutritionist.

- In Lancaster County, there were community programs and services that benefited from relocating into our Family Center because there was high foot traffic in our facility. For example, the community library moved into the Center, and its usage grew significantly. The county continued paying for the books and an employee to run the library.

- Placing a coffee shop in the Family Center not only provided a nice amenity for our clients and the library, but it also became a moneymaker for our enterprise. Obviously, coffee shops are commonplace in libraries, churches, and colleges today, but not when we opened the Family Center.

- The success of the coffee shop got me thinking about other social enterprises we could house in the Family Center. We soon introduced day care and elder care to the Center and discovered that when done right they are highly profitable.

- The idea, "If you build it, they will come," as depicted in the movie *Field of Dreams* is true. Harrisburg Community College asked to use our facility as a satellite campus. It was so satisfying to see our clients have access to a college education and attend classes at the Family Center.

Family Center's Mission and Programs

We opened the Family Center to help families thrive by providing a hub of interactive services that foster healthy relationships and model community cooperation. Our mission statement was "Serve people, strengthen families, and build community." Our ongoing team mantra was "Putting families first so they last."

We decided it wasn't good enough just to provide services. We needed to create interactions or partnerships between services and build a low-anxiety atmosphere where people could feel comfortable getting the services they needed.

The Family Center building was capable of housing these experts and services:

- Café and public library
- Pregnancy center
- Family doctor
- Nutritionist
- Chiropractor
- Thrift shop
- Food bank
- Day care/early learning center
- Homeschooling services
- Senior care
- Special needs children services
- Gymnasium/auditorium for sports events
- Auditorium for worship services

- Counseling center with services including:
  ◊ Group therapy
  ◊ Premarital counseling
  ◊ Marriage counseling
  ◊ Depression counseling
  ◊ Anger management
  ◊ Grief management
  ◊ Play therapy for children and adolescents

Building a Church-Based Family Center in Your Community

At the Family Center, the services we provided were managed and governed by ten different nonprofits and boards. This worked well, but the Center would have had even greater potential if it had functioned under the covering of a church with the financial and volunteer capacity to administer and resource the vision.

Here are the basic steps to building a Family Center in your community:

• *Develop a strategic plan* by defining the services you want to provide, creating a budget, determining essential employee and volunteer roles, allocation of office and service space, and other elements that arise during the planning process.

• *Form a funding proposal to seed the operations for at least one year.* There are a variety of funding streams available from private donors and foundations to government grants. Don't be afraid to seek the assistance of experts in marketing, fundraising, and grant writing.

• *Recruit a licensed professional counselor to oversee the services.* Having at least one credentialed professional with experience on-site will reinforce the Center's credibility.

• *Create a scalable plan.* As my friend Dave Donaldson likes to say, "Don't outkick your coverage." Envision what is manageable and then scale your programs accordingly. We spent several years establishing the Counseling Center and then added services over a period of ten years.

- *Cultivate synergism between your team of professionals* by meeting regularly to review the status of your clients and discuss ways the network of services can better serve them. We found great success with this approach of regular team interaction.

- *Ensure the center is on a sustainable path.* Even though a Family Center could be accountable to a governing church, the services should be under their own nonprofit organization with a board, budget, and plan to become self-sustainable. Looking back, this was my biggest miscalculation. While I tried to work with the nonprofits in the Center to wean them off the notion that "Jonas and Anne will pay for it," the dependency was so deeply rooted that the organizations didn't make the shift. In hindsight, it's imperative from the outset that your strategic plan includes a budget and fund-raising strategy that moves all the services to becoming self-sustainable. This will allow your Family Center to thrive and meet the community's needs for years to come.

> Envision what is manageable and then scale your programs accordingly.

- *Sign a memorandum of understanding (MOU).* Make sure you create a MOU that outlines your vision, values, financial policies, and any other special guidelines or requirements. Your nonprofit, governing church, and service providers should all agree on this document, and the individual parties should sign it. This will ensure commitment with your involved parties to the plan and strategy for creating a successful, sustainable, and scalable Family Center.

A Final Word to Pastors

As a professional counselor who has served in the same community for over twenty years, let me first say, "I love pastors . . . period." There's no substitute for the local church. That being said, I would encourage pastors to make sure their church is known for more than just telling people what they need to change, but offering a pathway to healing as well. That way the church doesn't add to people's already existing burden of denial, guilt, and despair. Every church, whether big or small, can provide services such as lay counseling.

After counseling thousands of people with every form of brokenness imaginable, I've witnessed the tragic void and disparity when someone doesn't have a church family who cares. Conversely, I've been blessed with a front-row seat to see the Holy Spirit work through His church to touch people's lives. Where else can you find built-in spiritual discipleship, close-knit family, and a continuum of care essential to spiritual and emotional health? Where else can a wounded couple like Anne and me be transformed into wounded healers? It's Jesus and His church, the ultimate Family Center.

27

Church-Based Counseling Ministry

Dr. Wayde Goodall

The church is a healing community where the broken, wounded, rejected, and bound can receive healing. The church is "the pillar and foundation of the truth" (1 Timothy 3:15). It is where we stand on the truth and hold up the truth of the abundant life in Jesus Christ. It is where people become healthy, set free, and grow into the person God created them to be. Lay counseling involves listening, praying, godly counsel, and hope. The body of Christ is meant to be a community of born-again believers who care for others.

The Church's Responsibility to Its Members and the Community

The Christian church is composed of people who've come to a personal relationship with Jesus Christ. They are "new" people because they're spiritually born-again and are "children of God" (John 1:12). They represent Jesus Christ and imitate Him. Jesus not only took on Himself all our transgressions but also demonstrated how to love, forgive, and help people. One of the goals of the church is to be a trusting and healing community.

I often say the church is much like a hospital full of sick people who are not only getting well but are becoming doctors, nurses, and leaders in that hospital. We all have flesh issues (acts of the sinful nature, including immorality, impure thoughts and deeds, anger, orgies, and drunkenness) that we deal with all our lives. As we grow in our Christian walk, we can develop strategies for addressing temptation, avoiding traps of the Enemy, and resisting sinful behavior, but the battle of the flesh against the Spirit (Galatians 5:16–24) will go on all our lives.

The Christian can develop skills to help people in need and bring healing to other members. The Christian community is a body in which believers can experience therapeutic (remedy intended to bring healing) treatment for life experiences and healing in all areas of their lives. This caring community, where Jesus Christ is present (Matthew 18:20), can be a tremendous source of health and hope to the larger community—the village, town, or city in which it resides.

This doesn't mean we avoid asking people outside the church such as professional counselors or doctors to assist us or someone we care about. When we find a qualified professional to assist a person in need, it is called referral. Individually, we should also seek the best trained people we can find when there are deep-seated challenges. Often there are people within the Christian community who can offer spiritual, emotional, relational, and, at times, even physical assistance and healing to people who are struggling.

Strategies for Ministering to People's Needs

The church can train people in the basic skills of counseling, such as:

- Understanding how to develop listening skills
- Knowing how to define or diagnose a person's core problem
- Knowing when and how to find another person (referral) who can offer professional help for those with in-depth needs

- Discerning and understanding how to help a person with their true spiritual needs, including spiritual deliverance issues, and helping people develop disciplines so they will become mature and stable

In fact, these qualities are required of all believers, not just pastors and leaders, and are urgently needed as people struggle with their past, present behaviors, guilt, shame, unforgiveness, stress, confusion, anxiety, satanic attacks, and a host of other issues.

Counseling involves a caring relationship in which one person seeks to help another deal more effectively with the stresses of life and painful experiences from the past or present. Counseling can occur in an office or clinic; it can also occur in restaurants, shopping centers, houses, work settings, and churches.

Lay or paraprofessional counseling is simply people caring for people. People in the body of Christ reach out to others in need by listening, understanding, offering wise advice and help, and thinking of ways to assist others in their need or in emotional or spiritual pain.

Some have asked, "Is lay counseling effective?" The answer is a resounding yes. The research in this area tells us that it can be most effective. In fact, it can often be more helpful than professional counseling because of the degree of empathy, compassion, and follow-through that caring people give. At times the professional who counsels for a living can be too busy to offer the same degree of empathy and compassion a friend can offer. Though we need the skills and expertise professional counselors and medical providers offer, we also know the power that love, trust, and understanding have on people who need help.

Churches that have an organized lay counseling program are reporting tremendous results of people receiving quality help. I call this type of counseling, "friend-to-friend counseling." These are some of its advantages:

- Friends are often the first to notice a situation that needs attention in a person's life.
- People often come to their friends first, even when they aren't certain their problem is a problem.
- Many people need personal counseling but can't afford the high cost of professional care.
- Pastors can often refer people to the lay counselor in the church rather than secular counselors or psychologists. (Note: Referral is a necessary part of counseling with some individuals. We should always refer people to those who can offer the best help for their problem.)
- Many Christians aren't willing to visit a secular counselor. However, they will counsel with a friend, a fellow Christian, a pastor, or a counselor in the church.
- Christians can intervene in crisis situations.
- Christians should be concerned with the needs of the whole person—emotional, behavioral, relational, spiritual, and physical.
- Christian counselors can regularly plan, promote, and conduct marriage and family enrichment experiences for the congregation.
- Pastors wouldn't be overloaded with counseling sessions if they had people in the church who could assist people with counseling and other needs.

Some limitations to this type of ministry exist in the areas of mental illness, in-depth counseling, legal issues, or medical issues. In those cases, we offer prayer, comfort, and assistance along with looking for a qualified expert to help people with those types of needs.

Christian counseling acknowledges that the principles of the Bible are true and effective. The truths found in the Scripture tell

Christians how to live their lives, have healthy marriages, forgive, get over past mistakes and sins, and help others who are in need. Christian counseling also demonstrates compassion and faith in a miracle-working God. The Bible gives us principles of life, supernatural wisdom, and insight. In addition, God gives believers unique spiritual gifts so they can help one another.

I believe that most Christians want to help people in need; however, they're afraid to become involved because they don't know what to do or they're too busy to care. Often in the Christian community, believers feel they aren't qualified to listen well or to help people sort out their issues. As a result, they ignore the people needing help and hope they'll get better. Most of the people don't get better; silently, they continue to desire help and hope for someone to listen to them, to offer understanding and wise advice.

Wounded, confused, and bound people desire to be healed. No one is happy when their life is falling apart or when they're addicted to something. People don't get married and plan on getting a divorce. Physical, emotional, and psychological sickness and pain are never part of a person's plan or dream for life. People are suffering all around us. The body of Christ carries one another's burdens and helps those in need. We're a family, we've been purchased for a price, and we care for people as Jesus did.

Part 4

THE NATIONS

In human terms the situation seemed hopeless.
God, I thought, *how do we awaken your church
to see the great need and perceive this amazing moment of
opportunity for sharing the love of Jesus with Muslim people?*
I heard the Lord say, "As you speak boldly
for these who cannot speak for themselves,
I will raise up a 'coalition of the willing.'"

—Wendell Vinson

28

CityServe SoCal and One = Two

John Johnson

This is an interview with John Johnson, the assistant superintendent of the Southern California Network of the Assemblies of God.

Q: Why do you think churches are having minimal impact on their communities?

Johnson: When I became pastor of a church, such as Covina Assembly of God, I would go into the community and ask people about our church. We had a huge building, but people in the community didn't even know what it was. We had resources, but the community didn't know about them. It was a travesty! I prayed for ways to connect with the community.

Q: What did you learn?

Johnson: I learned that while we're often well-meaning, we're using antiquated vehicles to reach our communities in a contemporary world with highly diverse settings. This occurs because we aren't listening to what the community says about their needs. We're addressing perceived needs, but no one actually wants the "product" we're "selling."

Q: What happened when you started listening to the community?

Johnson: Our church's compassion arm grew to have all kinds of ministry for the hungry, the homeless, prisoners, the elderly, orphans, recovering addicts, and more. We also invited other churches to join us for a day to serve our city. Together we completed projects the city of Covina would present to us including cleaning parks, painting buildings, and much more. All of this resulted from listening to our community!

Q: How did you and your wife model this compassion in your church and community?

Johnson: My wife and I have always tried to model for our congregation what we wanted to see them do, so over the course of fifteen years we fostered thirteen kids from the Southern California foster care system. The most significant thing I've ever done in the ministry was to be a foster dad.

Q: You're a good example of what I [Dave] call a "communitarian" because you've involved yourself in so many sectors in your community. What was the result of this approach?

Johnson: I feel God has ordained all of us to occupy a seat at the community table. When we became community centered, the mayor and all the councilmembers would come to our special outreach events and eventually became personal friends. Our church did things from back-to-school drives to Christmas toy giveaways for underprivileged children. People would come by the thousands because of the reputation we had earned serving the city. Los Angeles County and our state congressman acknowledged Covina for being a city that was making a difference. The director of our food bank was selected as the woman volunteer of the year by the state of California. She and her husband were flown up to Sacramento, where she received a certificate acknowledging her work.

Q: How does building a strong neighborhood strategy embolden the church for missions to the nations?

> We need to connect people, locally or globally, to the mission endeavors they are contributing towards.

Johnson: I love the phrase Wendell Vinson champions, "From the Neighborhood to the Nations." This is what excites me about the One=Two campaign. It appeals to the younger generation who are passionate about justice and causes. But, young people want to be able to experience the work. We need to connect people, locally or globally, to the missions endeavors they are contributing toward. I've used local missions to help grow foreign missions and the other way around. For example, I had people in my church who supported overseas missions and felt that satisfied their missions "itch." But I would challenge them about reaching their neighbors. So, we would take those people to see our impactful inner-city work, and it would encourage them, because if we can do this in our city, we can do it overseas as well. It's about discovering the view of missions that people have and guiding them into a holistic view of ministry.

Q: Could you elaborate further on CityServe's One=Two campaign and what excites you about it?

Johnson: As a pastor, it's extremely helpful when I can present local and global missions at the same time and receive one offering for both. I don't have to keep asking my congregation to give to missions. When you give to CityServe International, you touch the world. Think about the potential of One=Two! When a person gives a recurring gift of eighteen dollars, one part stays in the region to help the local church reach its neighbors and the other part goes to aid Syrian refugees in Lebanon, Jordan, and Turkey. It's a huge winner for the Kingdom! (For more information visit www.1Equals2.com)

Q: What about CityServe SoCal motivates you?

Johnson: CityServe will resource churches to carry out God's vision for their community. The goal of the SoCal Network and CityServe is to take away every excuse for a church not to reach their community for Christ. I would encourage pastors and churches to connect with CityServe and the One=Two campaign online and join forces to establish this model across the nation.

Q: You are championing a church-based movement to help the Syrian refugees. Why is this so important to you?

Johnson: The refugee crisis is the greatest humanitarian crisis to hit this world in my generation. We've learned that if a person is forced to become a refugee, they'll remain one for an average of seventeen years. Experts for the Assemblies of God say that if we're going to reach immigrants or refugees we have an eighteen-month window. Inside that short window, we have an opportunity to build a relationship with them and earn the right to share Jesus. I've never considered this crisis as a money problem but as a time problem. We're running out of time, not money. God has opened a window of opportunity in the heart of Islam for us. We've prayed and prayed for a door to reach Muslims, and God has provided one. We're going to reach Muslims through compassion—by giving a cup of cold water in Jesus' name and by loving unconditionally.

Q: Are there any biblical correlations to your vision for the refugees that stand out right now?

Johnson: I've been studying the story of the prodigal son, and God has been working on my heart. There's an often-overlooked truth in the story that can impact all that's going on with the United States and refugees, here and abroad. We can all identify with the role of the prodigal son, but we may never think about ourselves as the father. The father was out waiting before the son ever came back. God wants us to emulate His unconditional love, acceptance, and forgiveness for people and to prophetically know where to be standing when they return. That's one of the reasons I support World Vision. They've been serving in places like Lebanon and Jordan for decades and were prepared for the huge migration of refugees to these nations. Literally, millions of refugees that were previously living in regions closed to the gospel now dwell in no-man's-land, and the door has opened for us to be there.

Q: Any closing thoughts?

Johnson: If your church is in decline or plateaued, you can change your church's paradigm and move forward by engaging in compassion ministry "From the Neighborhood to the Nations."

29

Jesus, a Refugee

Dave Donaldson and Wendell Vinson

Agrandmother sat cross-legged on the ground as the tent's derelict plastic flapped in the wind. Draped by grandchildren and shielding a disabled son lying behind her, she recounted their desperate journey from Syria to Lebanon. When asked, "How did you make it?" a fierce look of determination swept across her weary, war-torn face. "Many times I wanted to stop and die along the road, but I kept saying to myself, 'I must have hope for my children,'" she shared. Noticing we were all about to produce a waterfall of tears, she squeezed her granddaughter, smiled, and said, "We made it and I'm grateful to God."

This woman is a victim of the worst humanitarian crisis of our time. Half of Syria's prewar population—more than eleven million people—have been killed or forced to flee their homes. More than 6.1 million people remain displaced within Syria. Some 1.8 million of these were newly displaced in 2017—approximately 6,550 people each day. They live in informal tented settlements, crowding with extended family or finding shelter in damaged or abandoned buildings. Some people have survived the horrors of multiple displacements, besiegement, hunger, and illness. All have fled to areas they thought were safe, only to find themselves caught up in a crossfire once again.[3]

Over two million Syrian refugees are living in Jordan and Lebanon, where they have resided for more than seven years. After visiting Jordan and Lebanon, my [Dave] first impression was one of amazement, because the region's two smallest countries were the ones accepting the largest number of people. Their mercy and hospitality are beyond description. Yet leaders in these countries concede their communities are at a breaking point due to the scarcity of resources and fragile infrastructure. This is usually the case when developing countries open their arms and borders. Such is the case with Turkey, where more than 3.3 million Syrian refugees have fled across their border, overwhelming urban communities and straining the already fragile system of health care and educational support.[4]

While I had a tangential connection to the refugee crisis through Convoy of Hope in Europe and from what I had seen in Jordan previously, this all changed when I heard Rich Stearns, former CEO of World Vision, speak at a large philanthropic gathering. Rich shared passionately about the plight of the Middle Eastern refugees and how churches in the United States were largely disengaged. He confided that the Lord needed to do "heart surgery" on him to remove the "scar tissue" of callousness and presuppositions. Quoting the late founder of World Vision, Bob Pierce, "Let my heart be broken by the things that break the heart of God," Rich said, "If I could add one word it would be *repeatedly.*"

A month later, Fred Smith, founder and president of The Gathering, invited me to join Steve Haas, World Vision's Catalyst, on a trip back to Jordan and Lebanon. I was delighted Steve was leading the trip because we've known each other since his Willow Creek Church days, and he has always impressed me as passionate, knowledgeable, and unrelenting in engaging the church in God-sized missions. I would soon discover that Rich and Steve represented a relatively small circle of influencers sounding the alarm for the church to awaken to the refugee challenge of the

Syrian crisis. On a subsequent trip, Steve and I brought Wendell Vinson, John Johnson from the AG SoCal Network, and Darrel Larson with Sawyer International Water Company along with us. On this trip, Wendell shared his vision for a "coalition of the willing."

A Coalition of the Willing

As Dave, John, Darrel, Steve, and I [Wendell] arrived at a refugee tent settlement in Lebanon's Beqaa Valley, within sight of the Syrian border, I was gripped with immense sadness at the sight of so many innocent children living in such terrible conditions. I tried not to think about the carnage their young eyes had seen and the unspeakable pain thrust upon them as innocent bystanders. Minutes before our arrival that day, I had received a text from my daughter in California, which included pictures of my two grandchildren smiling and laughing while enjoying their day. As we walked through the refugee settlement, the beautiful and curious children circled us, forcing me to make comparisons. These children are no different from my own grandchildren, yet their lives have been turned absolutely upside down with little hope in sight of things getting better.

In human terms, the situation seemed hopeless. I prayed silently as we walked, "God how do we awaken your church to see the great need and perceive this amazing moment of opportunity for sharing the love of Jesus?" I heard the Lord say, "As you speak boldly for these who cannot speak for themselves, I will raise up a 'coalition of the willing.'" Joining this coalition of the willing starts with understanding the crisis and what we can do about it.

What We Learned about the Crisis

- What is a refugee? "A refugee is someone who has been forced to flee their country because of persecution, war, or violence. A refugee has a well-founded fear of persecution for reasons of race, religion, nationality, political opinion, or membership in a certain social group. Most likely, they cannot return home or are afraid to do so. War and ethnic, tribal, and religious violence are leading causes of refugees fleeing their countries."[5]

- The Syrian refugee crisis started when antigovernment demonstrations began in March of 2011 as part of the Middle East's Arab Spring. But the peaceful protests quickly transformed following the Syrian government's violent crackdown as armed opposition groups began fighting back. Since then, some estimates account for over five hundred thousand persons killed because of this conflict.

- Most of the refugees want to return home. "About nine out of ten people being displaced want to return home when the situation is resolved."[6] Many will tell you they're thankful to be staying close to their home country and will even show you their house keys as a symbol of their hopeful return.

- Contrary to popular thought, most Syrian refugees don't live in sprawling camps. Most settle in urban communities or find low-wage jobs in rural areas.

- Roughly three-quarters of the refugees are women and children. They aren't terrorists, but are vulnerable people fleeing violence and the persons who perpetrate these acts of terror.

What Is God Up To?

With so much heartache, it's appropriate to ask, "What is God up to?" When I read Acts 17:26–27, it's clear God isn't surprised by human tragedy and can transform even this migration of the multitudes for his purpose and glory.

And He has made from one blood every nation of men to dwell on all the face of the earth, and has determined their preappointed times and the boundaries of their dwellings, so that they should seek the Lord, in the hope that they might grope for Him and find Him, though He is not far from each one of us." (NKJV)

Of the estimated 68.5 million refugees worldwide, multitudes come from nations that have been closed to the gospel of Jesus Christ for decades. Given the perilous nature of their present condition, many are open to anyone who will help their families survive. Reports indicate thousands who have shown an openness to the message and love of Jesus amid the wake of persecution. The churches we visited in Jordan and Lebanon are experiencing a spiritual awakening and are growing significantly. One church we visited, Resurrection Church in Beirut, has grown five-fold in recent years by offering an array of relief and development opportunities to the Syrian refugees who reside in their midst.

> Reports indicate thousands who have shown an openness to the message and love of Jesus amid the wake of persecution. The churches we visited in Jordan and Lebanon are experiencing a spiritual awakening and are growing significantly.

One church was experiencing so many conversions to Jesus that the government mandated they "Stop baptizing Muslims!" The pastor replied, "We only baptize Christians."

In the wake of this revival, there's an Enemy of these souls who is using his full arsenal to "steal and kill and destroy" (John 10:10).

What Is Satan Up To?

The Enemy's plan to steal, kill, and destroy the Syrian people is being carried out through a protracted conflict in the form of bombing, poisonous gas, and an unending list of horrific human rights violations.

But the Enemy's weapons also include less lethal attitudes of apathy and racism. At one service I [Dave] implored a congregation to wake up to what could very well be the greatest opportunity in history to show the Muslim world Jesus' message of compassion, love, and eternal hope. While sharing this, I noticed a commotion several rows back as a man stood facing me in the aisle with hands on hips and mouthed something like, "How dare you speak about political things in my church!" As he left the auditorium, his family followed, along with others from the congregation.

I responded by saying to the congregation, "The root of this crisis isn't political, but spiritual. Do we need any more proof of our mission to love them than that these people are made in God's image and Jesus died on the cross for their souls?"

Jesus, a Refugee

There was a family fleeing under the cover of night across the Nile and into Egypt. They were refugees escaping the persecution of a wicked king whose power was threatened. This family joined other caravans of families who were unloved and unwelcomed. The family I speak of was Mary and Joseph and Baby Jesus as recorded in Matthew 2. The first years of His life, Jesus and His parents lived as Middle East refugees. King Herod had ordered the execution of any boys two years or younger in Bethlehem and the vicinity. Like their modern-day displaced counterparts, Jesus and His parents had to flee from an evil tyrant, bent on violence and destruction.

Every church leader knows there's a limit to the times they can ask their congregation to support yet another compassion initiative without risking donor fatigue. CityServe has launched a reoccurring gift campaign called One=Two. The goal is to create an ongoing funding stream for the CityServe HUBs (warehouses) and a compassion fund to serve refugees. We believe this is fully aligned with the Great Commission . . . reaching out from the neighborhood to the nations.

For example, the compassion fund includes a partnership with the SoCal Network of the Assemblies of God and World Vision to support the refugees in Lebanon, Jordan, and Turkey with relief supplies and education for Syrian refugees' smallest family members. The goal is also to undergird the churches in this region—those shouldering the weight of caring for these beleaguered populations.

Pastors who've already hosted a One=Two campaign in their churches will be the first to tell you the simplicity of a monthly donation to transform their neighborhood and help refugees in other nations is elevating the vision, generosity, and impact of their churches. We also invite business leaders to host One=Two campaigns for their employees. (For more information visit www.1Equals2.com.)

Jesus said, "Whatever you did for one of the least of these [refugee] brothers and sisters of mine, you did for me" (Matthew 25:40).

Skipping ahead more than thirty years, Jesus proclaimed to His disciples, "For I was hungry and you gave me nothing to eat, I was thirsty and you gave me nothing to drink, I was a stranger and you did not invite me in, I needed clothes and you did not

clothe me, I was sick and in prison and you did not look after me"
(Matthew 25:42–43).

Jesus' comments left His disciples scratching their heads,
"Lord, when did we see you hungry or thirsty or a stranger or needing clothes or sick or in prison, and did not help you?" (Matthew
25:44). Could it be that Jesus was reflecting on a time when He
and His family were refugees in need of food, water, clothes, shelter and aid, but nobody cared? If so, cannot His words to His
disciples serve as a potent charge for us to serve refugees today?

What Will We Do about It?

This is a moment of unprecedented opportunity to spread the
gospel in places that traditionally have been closed to Jesus' message of love. It's a moment that calls for us to pray and to respond.
The Lord is using acts of compassion to open doors to the human
heart. "Because of the service by which you have proved yourselves, others will praise God for the obedience that accompanies
your confession of the gospel of Christ, and for your generosity in
sharing with them and with everyone else" (2 Corinthians 9:13).

30

The Church and the Refugee Crisis

Steve Haas

I had just stepped away from the conference podium after addressing a thoughtful gathering about the opportunity to share in providing real hope for the over 2.3 million Syrian refugees our organization touches. As I hadn't left the conference staging area, a small group gathered to engage further. It didn't take long for someone to confront me with a question I've heard many times before.

"I don't want to seem like I'm negating the needs you just shared," a tall and serious woman pressed softly. "I mean thirteen million displaced Syrians is certainly heartbreaking and worthy of compassionate prayer . . . but what about the needs here in the United States?"

Whether a justification for unwittingly shutting our ears due to fear of the perceived injustice beyond our border, or a sense of our own compassionate limits, isn't this a question we've all asked? Pressed by the needs around us and the related sense of insecurity and devastation, hasn't this crossed all our minds?

In the national dialogue, *stranger* and *foreigner* have become synonymous with the words *terrorist* and *unwanted*. In a nation that harbors a vaulted notion that we accept the global poor and are compassionate to the "huddled masses yearning to breathe free," increasingly there's talk of building fences and reducing immigration—while we're still standing in the narthex of a Christian church. Our faith's international resignation, isolationism, and reduced missional engagement seem to be driven more by a collective fear and partisan politics than strong faith and grounded theology.

So where does this leave the sincere Jesus follower? Does the Bible give guidance for what seems a hot topic in this increasing "salad bowl" of a nation, a description by some for the United States in the twenty-first century?

Stories of Immigrants

A humorist once stated that the church is the "only institution created for the benefit of the nonmember." With a haloed history of outreach to the outsider, it should come as no surprise that the Scriptures, the two-thousand-year-old playbook for the Christian community, is a detailed chronology of displaced people. From Abraham's journey from Harran to Jacob's wandering from home, to Joseph's being trafficked to Egypt, and Ruth's departure from Moab, the storied list of Old Testament immigrants is long and complex; the word *stranger* is mentioned over ninety times.

> Counting our first forebears, chronicled in the first chapters of the Bible's first book, God's care for those deemed outsiders makes it clear what our attitude should be toward those who are not "one of us."

The Scriptures speak of divine care and concern for those not like us, those not from "here." Counting our first forebears, chronicled in the first chapters of the Bible's first book, God's care for those deemed outsiders makes it clear what our attitude should be toward those who are not "one of us."

"Do not mistreat or oppress a foreigner, for you were foreigners in Egypt" (Exodus 22:21). As if to make sure the directive was understood, the writer of Leviticus draws out the meaning yet further: "When a foreigner resides among you in your land, do not mistreat them. The foreigner residing among you must be treated as your native-born. Love them as yourself, for you were foreigners in Egypt; I am the LORD your God." (Leviticus 19:33–34)

Make no mistake about it, with God there is to be no "us and them." Underlining that sentiment is this passage in the Book of Numbers:

"The community is to have the same rules for you and for the foreigner residing among you; this is a lasting ordinance for the generations to come. You and the foreigner shall be the same before the LORD." (Numbers 15:15–16)

Through Moses, God directed His people to respond sensitively to the sojourners in their land:

"When you are harvesting in your field and you overlook a sheaf, do not go back to get it. Leave it for the foreigner, the fatherless and the widow, so that the LORD your God may bless you in all the work of your hands." (Deuteronomy 24:19)

Now let me tell you about a man called Miled. He lives in Lebanon and has been in God's service for twenty-one years, but five years ago his ministry changed.

Syrian refugees started coming in increasing numbers over the nearby border, arriving with next to nothing and needing everything. This posed a dilemma for Miled and other Lebanese church leaders. You see, there's a well-founded animosity toward

Syrians in Lebanon—Syria's military occupied Lebanon for about thirty years—so the newcomers weren't welcome, especially as their numbers swelled above one million, a quarter of Lebanon's population.

Miled searched his heart and decided to see this as an opportunity from God, a chance to put the gospel message of love into action. He and his church embraced refugees unconditionally, providing food and other care. They also welcomed them to church services if they wanted to come.

One of the refugees who started showing up was a woman we'll call Fatima, a widow who escaped Syria after seeing her teen daughter shot in front of her. She and her two surviving children settled in a tent in Miled's community. She heard that the church was helping people, but at first she was reluctant to investigate. "I'd heard only bad things about Christians," she said.

Miled was different. He had no hidden motives. "Our only goal is to ease your burden," he told the Syrians. For Fatima, that meant helping her restart her career as a tailor while also assisting other mothers. A skilled seamstress, Fatima suggested organizing a sewing club for refugee women. Miled's church and a Lebanese aid organization, Lebanese Society for Education and Social Development (LSESD), partnered with World Vision to bring this idea to life. Today, Fatima trains ten women in the sewing group. They just landed a contract to make hundreds of school uniforms for local students.

Fatima and Miled have become friends, with Miled calling her "my sister." She now attends church regularly, eager to hear more about Jesus, who sacrificed Himself for all people. In time, she found something she couldn't have received anywhere else. "The pastor reinforced the idea that we must pray for our enemies. He taught me forgiveness of others," she said, explaining that she has forgiven her daughter's killers. "Now I have peace."

When you see Fatima, she radiates joy. "Anytime people come, they ask, 'Why are you so happy?' I tell them I have joy thanks to the church. Though I live in poor conditions, I'm happy—unlike in Syria, where I had three houses but wasn't happy."

What God Is Not . . . and Neither Should His Followers Be

Let's direct our focus now on what God is not. God is not defined by:

Us vs. them. Much of our stinking thinking comes from a not so subtle me-centric theological construct that likens my life and spiritual journey of greater worth and divine attention than that of someone else. Often this heresy is buttressed by a nationalistic fervor, thinly veiled by one's economic or social superiority. According to the apostle Paul, this was one of the primary obstacles that tripped up the Israelites, and we can easily find ourselves stumbling here as well. In Romans 9, Paul enumerated the blessing of the Israelites with a rousing list of heaven-sent accommodations, graced supremely from the hand of God.

Theirs is the adoption to sonship; theirs the divine glory, the covenants, the receiving of the law, the temple worship and the promises. Theirs are the patriarchs, and from them is traced the human ancestry of the Messiah, who is God over all, forever praised! (Romans 9:4–5)

But rather than turn their blessings outward for others, serving as a pass-through of compassionate response as God had commanded them to be, they intensified their grip on what they possessed and directed their gaze increasingly inward. "Us vs. them" became their rogue faith's unofficial rally cry. Eventually, the horizon line of God's goodness became the top of their own trench. *Local vs. international.* Our God is a sovereign God over all His global domain. As such He harbors no favorite human subjects, whether they claim a Christian title or are antagonistic to His kingdom agenda. For many Jesus followers, this is hard to swallow as an acceptance of faith itself speaks to a dividing line between those who accept God's gracious favor and those who reject it. Regardless, the Scripture is clear that all God's human creation shares His *Imago Dei* (image of God), simply by the fact that He created them.

Christian leader and writer John Stott states that it's an injustice to exclude weaker or marginalized members of society as it "denies the very roots of the creation story as affirming each person as made in the image of God and worthy of dignity and respect."

Who God Is

Sovereign. The Psalmist said, "The earth is the LORD's and everything in it, the world and all who live in it" (Psalm 24:1). The Dutch Prime Minister Abraham Kuyper stood on biblical authority when he stated, "There is not a square inch in the whole domain of our human existence over which Christ, who is Sovereign over all, does not cry, Mine!" If this world is His, then it isn't ours. All of God's good gifts are simply held in trust to be employed for the entire human race. Jesus is Lord over all of creation and as that truth sinks in, we might as well get used to the fact that He uses the movement of people to accomplish His purposes.

God has never turned away from death marches, ethnic cleansings, or forced displacements in countries like South Sudan, Syria, Myanmar, Somalia, or Iraq. He registers every name of the nearly sixty-six million homeless persons who have fled for safety's sake from untenable living environments. He can use these events to transform life as we know it for His just and righteous cause.

After all, we serve a God who received the most dehumanizing form of capital punishment possible—death on a cross—and transformed that perceived death into an open offer and symbol of spiritual liberation and everlasting life.

Who We Are

When describing our mission in the world, someone once coined the phrase, "ambassadors without portfolio"—an apt phrase for an official representative not assigned to a specific location. Anytime we nationalize our faith, mix our theology with any political ideology, our faith becomes infinitely smaller in scope as we marginalize our reason for being. Jesus didn't come to institute a country club with a high-minded membership, alert to outside interference. He came to marshal His creation for a revolution of love and justice, against which the "gates of hell" cannot prevail. The only requirement for membership in this band of brothers and sisters has always been a commitment to follow Jesus and to surrender our rights to Him.

> If this world is His, then it isn't ours. All of God's good gifts are simply held in trust to be employed for the entire human race.

Faith over Fear

Our way is clear, and the time is now. For many years, millions of Jesus' people have uttered intercessions to God on behalf of those who've never experienced the love and mercy of Christ. Presently, in historic numbers, millions of traumatized human beings have been displaced and languish in refugee camps, tent settlements, the open air, or on the streets of our own country, desperate for some semblance of the very thing Jesus told His disciples to do:

"I was hungry and you gave me something to eat,
I was thirsty and you gave me something to drink,
I was a stranger and you invited me in,
I needed clothes and you clothed me,
I was sick and you looked after me,
I was in prison and you came to visit me." (Matthew 25:35–36)

It's as if in trying to make His assignment clear, Jesus has chosen to illustrate again this favorite portion of Scripture in overcoming the resident prejudice, personal unease, or communal stigma in reaching to touch the outsider within our country or beyond our borders. The question ultimately comes to the person seeking to be obedient to Jesus' call: Do we see a stranger, an outsider, or as Mother Teresa described them, "Jesus in His most distressing disguise"?

31

Mad about Compassion

Doug Green

When Jesus encountered a man with leprosy, He was moved. Read Mark 1:41 in your Bible and decide how He was moved: Was He moved with indignation or compassion? In the opening phrase of this Greek sentence, you must decide: *indignant* or *compassionate*?

Almost every English translation of the Bible chooses to say some version of: "He was moved with compassion."

But in the New International Version, the translation committee broke tradition with the majority of the others and chose: *"Jesus was indignant."*

When you look up the first-century use of the Greek word, it can go either way. Translators are forced to make a choice: Was He compassionate or was He outraged, angry, incensed—indignant?

I contend Jesus was both *indignant* and *compassionate*. Let me explain.

Jesus Was Indignant

In much the same way that Jesus wept and was deeply moved—a form of indignation—at the tomb of Lazarus, Jesus is blazing mad at the power of evil today, incensed at all that's unclean and destructive in our world. In fact, when it comes to the Enemy who steals, kills, and destroys, Jesus is ticked! He hates sin and the destructive consequences of sickness and suffering. This isn't how it was supposed to be.

Good news! Jesus did something wonderful with His righteous indignation. He said to the leper, "Be clean!" With authority, He barked out the command, and the sting of disease was defeated. Instantly! The physical toll and the social isolation were over. *It is finished.* The leper's skin was promptly healed because Jesus was mad enough to do something *supernatural* about it!

Just like our Savior, our anger with human suffering drives us to a place of compassion. For example, who gives their life to end human trafficking unless they're totally vexed about little girls being bought and sold as slaves for a thug's profit? Who feeds and educates the poor? The person who is outraged by the cruel hand of poverty! When someone is furious about orphans living in gutters, they build a home and give the kids a chance. Substance-abuse ministries are sustained by those who abhor the destructive consequences of addiction—something they often know firsthand.

Our *righteous anger* drives us to *righteous action.*

Jesus Was Moved by Compassion

His actions spoke loud and clear. The rest of verse 41 shows us He did something nobody was supposed to do: He reached out His hand and touched a man with leprosy. He didn't just say, "Be clean!" He reached out His hand. His deed matched His words.

Compassion is costly. Not everybody is happy to see justice. Helping others, surprisingly, isn't always a welcome adjustment. Righteous change stirs the pot, but once you start, there's no turning back. So, what fuels your mission of compassion on those tough days? Your righteous anger with human suffering—over and over again!

So . . . *indignant* or *compassionate?*

Like Jesus, be both and do both, for the "lepers" of this world need somebody mad enough to do something *supernatural* about it!

32

Millennials Making a Difference

Danita Bye

When nonprofit leaders discuss the millennial generation, we either hear glowing praise or intense frustra-
tion, rarely anything in between. Dennis Thum, the chaplain
at the University of Sioux Falls, gave me this analogy. "I think
of it as a camel. When you interact with the first hump, you
see impressive, emerging leaders who give you great hope for
the future of the world. Then when you talk with those from
the second hump, you see young people who appear to be lost,
without hope."

Look at the popular "stats and facts" you'll find on Google
when you search for anything relating to millennials:

- Born between 1980 and the mid-2000s they'll comprise
  more than 50 percent of the workforce by 2020.[7]
- The 2017 Bloomberg article "A Quarter of Millennials
  Who Live at Home Don't Work—or Study" reveals that
  approximately 33 percent of 18–34-year-olds live at
  home or in college dormitories, and of those 25–34-year-
  olds who live with their parents, 25 percent neither work
  nor are enrolled in school—that's 2.2 million millennials
  in the United States.[8]
- In the 2016 Inc.com article "29 Surprising Facts That
  Explain Why Millennials See the World Differently,"

author Gordon Tredgold presented statistics to help us understand what drives this generation.

◊   54 percent either want to start a business or already have

◊   74 percent want flexible work schedules

◊   84 percent say that helping to make a positive difference in the world is more important than professional recognition

◊   88 percent prefer a collaborative work culture rather than a competitive one

◊   92 percent believe that business success should be measured by more than just profit[9]

In a recent survey, our company conducted its own study and asked leaders to list all the frustrations they experience in working with millennials. Over 270 responded. Of those, 60 percent said they have deep concerns with how to work with this generation. The top three response categories were:

•   character traits (45 percent)

•   confidence (34 percent)

•   collaboration (21 percent)

Their strongest complaints were:

•   a lack of determination and resiliency

•   a lack of accountability

•   a know-it-all attitude

•   a disregard for the value of work

To complete the picture, let's not forget about the stereotypes: entitled, lazy, self-interested, narcissistic, job-hopping, addicted to technology, unfocused, craving instant gratification, disloyal, impatient, difficult to manage, restless . . .

This is the millennial generation. Or is it?

You can choose to jump on the bandwagon, become frustrated, anxious, and even sad about this generation, or you can choose to focus on the positive.

When you think of the millennials in your sphere of influence, what do you see? Do you see the up-and-coming leaders from the first hump of the camel, the emerging leaders who give you great hope for the future? Or do you see young people who are from the second hump, those who are struggling to find their way in our fast-paced, sometimes chaotic world? Either way, you have a stewardship responsibility to prepare them to meet the challenges of the future.

As a mother of three millennials, I choose to celebrate and embrace this generation. I believe that to ensure vibrant, thriving compassion ministry growth we need to tap the myriad of unique skills, talents, and strengths millennials bring to our organizations.

Why and How Should We Involve Millennials in Compassion Ministries?

Why should a church or compassion ministry consider hiring millennials? And if they do, how can they develop these emerging leaders for compassion work?

Here are some things to consider:

• *The "Collaboration Generation."* Many people believe that millennials are expert collaborators. After all, they've been working in teams since first grade. They have digital technology at their fingertips, so they can collaborate on a global scale in a matter of seconds. And yes, many of them know the importance of really listening and valuing others so that synergistic collaboration happens.

It would be wise though to keep in mind that some emerging leaders haven't had enough working experience to know how to function in a true collaboration.

• **Break the collaboration stereotypes.** Are they addicted to their technology? Then use it to your advantage. Your millennial leader's affinity with the digital world is one of the defining characteristics of their generation. They have a better grasp of these key business tools than more senior workers. Who better to rally their vast networks to further your cause or to spread the word on your compassion project?

• **Strengthen their collaboration.** Based on my personal experience with young leaders, millennials welcome mentoring and coaching from people they respect. They want to be with honest, authentic leaders; favor a trusting, transparent relationship with their superiors; and work best with clear guidelines and frequent feedback. This mind-set will make your job that much easier when you mentor them on the best way to collaborate on your project.

• *Beware of the confidence crushers.* Some millennial leaders struggle to connect what they're doing today with what they want to be doing in the future. They can become disheartened and have their confidence shaken. Under these circumstances emerging leaders might think the best solution is to find another job or project.

Emerging leaders want to have meaning and purpose at work, but they may experience a misalignment with their gifts and talents. Because they're not operating in their sweet spot, they feel they're not getting anywhere.

An emerging leader I'm coaching told me, "As much as millennials are eager to give back and help others, we're all different in our own way. Getting to know each person and how they work is the strongest tool a leader can have."

I learned about an ancient Hebrew word in my transformational leadership studies at Bethel Seminary. This word is used for both work and worship: *avodah*. Having one word for such different meanings really caused me to think. Historically, our Western culture has divided life into secular and sacred: Work is secular; purpose and meaning are spiritual. Millennials want purpose and meaning in their everyday lives but don't know how to bring that about. They feel left in the dark.

Experienced business leaders can teach next-gen leaders that how they do their "ordinary" work becomes "extraordinary" when they see it as a way to honor God and serve their clients and colleagues.

The YouTube video *Work as Worship* by RightNow Media is a great summary of the struggle between what is regarded as work and what has spiritual meaning. Where is the dividing line? This resource helps millennials as they seek out the purpose of their own lives and try to understand how they can be a light in their current work environment.

By coaching and mentoring your up-and-coming leaders to build a center of courageous character strength, you provide a firm footing so they can have a positive influence in your compassion work.

• ***Break the character stereotypes.*** Self-absorbed, disloyal, and entitled? Might we consider it our privilege and, in fact, our calling, to mentor and coach our emerging leaders on the sensitive subject of character? A word of warning—you'll almost certainly be challenged by your millennial leaders. This is what one of the young reviewers of *Millennials Matter* had to say:

> Millennials often see leaders from the previous generation as the single bottom-line thinkers that justified false advertising, pollution, factory farming, and human rights

violations. We see them as having lost much of their credibility when it comes to talking about the right thing to do.

By openly sharing our own stories of success and failure, we can make it easier for our millennial leaders to look inside themselves and find the areas where they need to change.

Millennials are often described as a hopeful generation. But being hopeful doesn't guarantee they'll be able to deal with obstacles and rebound quickly. Their hopeful mind-set is often linked to their ability to dream big and to expect they can get whatever they want from life. That can be a great mind-set to have—if it goes hand in hand with the reality of what it takes to achieve those dreams. This reality calls for intense resilience, the grim, gritty, white-knuckle form of courage that is typically presented in situations where success is against the odds.

Do you think the emerging leaders in your sphere of influence are equipped to deal with the challenges they'll face in your compassion work?

During the many hours I've talked with trusted mentors, colleagues, family, and friends, one realization has stood out: millennials need us. The world is undergoing a rapid shift, and millions of young adults struggle to find their footing. Amid this cultural chaos, you get the opportunity to give millennial leaders the benefit of what you know. Your wisdom and insights can be the catalyst that equips and energizes them to become influential and valuable role players in your compassion ministries.

33

How Churches Can Provide Affordable Housing

Jonathan Reckford

This is an interview with Jonathan Reckford, the CEO of Habitat for Humanity.

Q: What is the biblical imperative for providing shelter for the homeless?

Reckford: God tells us throughout the Scriptures to care for the poor and to love our neighbor. Certainly, the Parable of the Good Samaritan in Luke 10 reminds us that we are called to respond to the needs of those who are hurting. Proverbs 19:17 and Matthew 25:40 tell us that when we minister to the poor, it is the same as serving the Lord.

I also look to Micah 6:8 (NKJV), the Scripture that I refer to as my life verse, to see how God clearly directs us in all situations: "He has shown you, O man, what is good; and what does the LORD require of you but to do justly, to love mercy, and to walk humbly with your God?"

Q: Why are you personally involved in providing shelter?

Reckford: I was drawn to Habitat for Humanity for two important reasons. First, I believe that a safe, decent, and affordable home is the foundation of a better life for every family. Second, the way Habitat engages volunteers to partner with families in need transforms everyone involved in the process. Because families put in sweat equity and pay an affordable, no-profit mortgage, they receive the chance to build a better life. I observed that transformation firsthand as a volunteer back when I worked at Disney in the early 1990s and have been a fan of Habitat ever since.

Q: What are some ways shelter affects a person's life (i.e., self-worth, family, job, etc.)? Can you give a real-life story of how Habitat provided shelter for a person/ family and the impact it made?

Reckford: Research supports strong connections between stable housing and improved health, better education outcomes, and new income opportunities.

> Seeking to put God's love into action, Habitat for Humanity brings people together to build homes, communities, and hope.

I was particularly moved by the story of Lorng, a widow in Cambodia who had once lived with her mom, son, and daughter in a tiny shack in a garbage dump. Ultimately, they couldn't even afford that. They ended up on the street with their meager possessions.

I had the privilege of being part of a team that helped build her a four-by-six-meter Habitat house. She told me about the difficult night she spent before the dedication of her new home. It rained hard and she had only a tarp to protect all their belongings from the storm. She spent that night standing up, trying to keep the rain out.

The next day, when we all gathered inside her new concrete-block home for a dedication service, the pounding rain started again. I watched as Lorng and her daughter examined the ceiling. Their concern turned to relief when not a drop of water seeped in. Big smiles broke out across their faces.

We all took jasmine and lotus blossoms and threw them over the family standing in the middle of the house. My daughter, who was part of our team, remarked, "This was so different from any other experience I've ever had. It really makes you think about everything you take for granted. I don't even think about the fact that my house is dry when it rains, and I always have a roof over my head, food to eat, and clean water to drink. It's amazing how much a Habitat house can change people's lives."

I remember thinking what a change this would be for Lorng's family. At a basic level, this family would have a door they could lock; they would be able to access water and sanitation and be afforded protection from the elements. But her story is about so much more than a house. Lorng no longer felt so burdened about giving her kids the foundation for a better future. Now they could go to school and think about more than just surviving.

Lorng has remarried, and she and her husband sell vegetables in front of a garment factory near their house. They earn about five dollars per day, which is much greater than her income just a few years ago. She's relieved that she owns her home and the land it's built on. She no longer needs to worry about eviction. The cost of water and electricity is less and, unlike before, they have enough healthy food to eat.

Until our team helped build her home, Lorng had never met an American or a Christian. Now she knows that some people who love Jesus traveled around the world to help her build her home.

Q: What is the mission of Habitat?
Reckford: Seeking to put God's love into action, Habitat for Humanity brings people together to build homes, communities, and hope.

Q: How does it work? How do you partner with the community and the family to secure the land, build the home, and then pay for it?

Reckford: Through volunteer labor and donations of money and materials, Habitat builds, repairs, and rehabilitates safe, decent houses alongside future homeowners. In the United States, those in need of decent shelter apply to local Habitat groups called affiliates. Family selection committees choose homeowners based on level of need, willingness to become partners in the program, and ability to repay the loan. Every affiliate follows a nondiscriminatory policy of family selection. Habitat is not a giveaway program. In addition to a down payment and monthly mortgage payments, homeowners invest hundreds of hours of their own labor (sweat equity) into building their Habitat house and the houses of others. Those who partner with Habitat take out no-profit, affordable loans. Their monthly mortgage payments enable affiliates to build more houses.

Q: Why is it important to build collaboration around providing shelter for the poor? What is your strategy?

Reckford: Habitat for Humanity cannot be the sole answer to the problem of affordable housing around the world. It's going to take the public, private, and social sectors working together on a large scale and in local communities to develop housing solutions. Together, we can accomplish more than each of us can do alone.

On this larger scale, Habitat is working with governments to seek land tenure for families in many locations. It makes no sense to invest in a home if you aren't sure you can remain on the land. Habitat also partners with other NGOs and organizations to help communities address needs such as accessing safe drinking water. We seek to make affordable housing markets work better for low-income people. One of our most successful funding initiatives has been the establishment of our MicroBuild Fund, which helps families make incremental improvements to their houses as they take out and repay multiple small loans. More than two million people are now living in better homes because of MicroBuild investments.

Q: What is your vision for engaging the church in providing shelter to the poor around the globe?

Reckford: The church has always been at the heart of Habitat's work, and we see church partnerships as critical to our mission. Habitat can be an effective way for churches to engage in intentional ministry—locally and globally—by raising up volunteers to build, to work with partner families, to donate, and to advocate on behalf of those in need of shelter. This partnership can further both Habitat's mission and that of the church, as a tangible demonstration of Christ's love in the world. It's my personal experience and opinion that for this emerging unchurched generation, effective evangelism will look more like an invitation to come serve in the community, which will open the door to spiritual friendships.

> Ultimately, Habitat seeks to be a vehicle through which churches can experience serving the poor.

Ultimately, Habitat seeks to be a vehicle through which churches can experience serving the poor, not as a mandate but as a joyful privilege that comes as a natural response to God's abundant love. Jesus needed shelter at the time of His birth, and since His resurrection, the church that bears His name has been given the opportunity to serve Him by serving "the least of these." Habitat is privileged to provide opportunities for the church to be in service throughout the world.

Q: What are some challenges to meeting shelter needs?
Reckford: Some of the root causes of poverty are extremely difficult to overcome. For example, some families have developed a generational cycle of dependency. The family story of being surrounded by poverty is the only thing they know. It's what they believe about themselves and something they believe can't change.

Another huge challenge is unequal access to assets—land, credit, information, technology, education, and other important resources. Leveling the playing field—seeking to spread the distribution of assets—is how partnership housing started.

Clarence Jordan, who's often called the spiritual father of Habitat for Humanity, urged those with resources to share with the poor who needed capital—not charity.

Social capital is another important issue. If a group of people has no power—no voice—they're often dismissed to fend for themselves.

Responding to natural disasters is also a tremendous challenge. We can't predict how and when the immediate need for shelter will occur, but we feel called to help those who are affected by storms, earthquakes, and other disasters.

Q: How can someone volunteer to participate in Habitat?
Reckford: Our work in the United States is done through local groups called affiliates. Using the search engine on our website you can locate the affiliate nearest you and talk with the leaders there about volunteering to build or repair a home, serve on a committee, donate funds or services, or advocate for just housing policy and more. If you prefer to work at a location in another part of the world, you may join a Global Village team. Check out the web page for teams that are forming to go to a location that interests you.

Part 5

MARKETING AND FUNDING

Some time ago the *Chronicle of Philanthropy*
published an article related to how major donors
are beginning to think about funding.
They noted a recurrent theme:
major donors are looking for models, not causes.
Because there are thousands of causes to choose from,
and many of them are duplicative,
as a nonprofit leader you must show
how your model of ministry is different.

—Bill High

34

Engaging High Net Worth People in Your Church

Bill High

He came in the door breathless. His hands shook as he took out a carefully prepared tricolor brochure. The graphics were impressive, and the statistics seemed to blur with their meaning. He leaned in, passionate to tell me about his ministry.

He described in rapid-fire succession the work with the homeless, the feeding programs, the education initiatives, and even the jobs program. The scope was broad. The detail was there. His eyes glowed with energy for the project.

Finally, he turned to the final page of his brochure: They were looking for a grant of $750,000 to continue. He'd talked for forty minutes straight and insisted that he show me his eight-minute video to cap things off. He beamed at the end of the video and with a flourish asked what I thought.

I wasn't interested.

And he was left to wonder why. He simply couldn't understand why anyone would not be moved by a compassion ministry to the city.

But he'd missed the point. There are many tremendous opportunities to grow and fund compassion ministries and engage with major donors—but the approach needs to be different if you want to convince high net worth donors to become your partner.

Look for Models, Not Causes

Some time ago the *Chronicle of Philanthropy* published an article related to how major donors are beginning to think about funding. They noted a recurrent theme: major donors are looking for models, not causes.

That idea warrants some explanation.

There are thousands of causes: global evangelism, local evangelism, church planting, youth ministry, addiction recovery, homeless ministry, and the list goes on. There are over 1.6 million nonprofits in the United States alone. And the nonprofit world continues to grow and add more each year.

Every one of those nonprofits wants to get you on their mailing list, send you their letter or video, or get you to come to their event. I remember one donor complaining that he was getting twenty pieces of mail a day from different nonprofits. It can be overwhelming.

Early in my foundation career, an acquaintance invited me to a major fund-raiser for a youth ministry—their biggest event of the year. As I walked in the door I expected to see a room full of people but was surprised to find attendance at about half of what it normally was. As I talked to one of my friends at the event, I asked why the attendance was so low. He said another ministry who shared many of the same major donors had inadvertently scheduled their major fund-raiser on the same night. People had been forced to choose between the two events.

Because there are thousands of causes to choose from, and many of them are duplicative, as a nonprofit leader you must show how your model of ministry is different from all the others. Major donors like to fund models. Models are replicable, repeatable, and sustainable. The beauty of funding a model is that a major donor can make a gift or a series of gifts and then, in theory, the ministry will be self-sustaining. The donor can go on to find the next model.

For instance, there are hundreds of rescue missions around the country. Generally, the cause is the same—ministry to the poor, the homeless, the needy. From a funding perspective, these organizations seek gifts-in-kind, regular monthly donors, the occasional major gift, and some planned gifts.

But what if someone changed the rescue mission model? Some have already varied their funding model by adding thrift stores or even used-car lots. But what if they flipped the model on its head? What if the rescue mission became, at its core, an employment agency? The employment agency could provide outreach to refugee groups and single moms, and education and placement for the homeless in real jobs. What if the employment agency became the economic engine for the rescue mission?

> Major donors look at the leader's capability and past capability to execute. I like leaders who lean in and say with the force of their personality, "I can get this done."

This is all conjecture, of course, but it's a unique model that could very well attract capital, sustain itself, and allow for the creation of other models.

Cast a Compelling Vision

Another key to engaging major donors in compassion ministry is casting a *compelling* vision.

What makes a vision compelling? A compelling vision is more than just a big vision—it's vision combined with effective leadership. A vision without proper execution is just a dream. Major donors have an acute sense of the difference between leaders and dreamers.

What do major donors look for in leaders? Humility. Are they self-effacing, or self-promoting? Are they people of prayer? Do their lives reflect a life in the prayer closet and reflection on God's Word? As part of their humility, do they similarly express an interest in the life and work of the donor? Are they interested in the business of the major donor? Are they willing to pray for the business endeavor of the donor? All too often I've seen ministries eager to talk about the vision of their ministry, but they have no interest in the person in front of them.

Here's another intangible of leadership: Major donors look at the leader's capability and past capability to execute. I like leaders who lean in and say with the force of their personality, "I can get this done." Part of the communication in "getting this done" is to recount past accomplishments and endeavors along with real metrics—the number of people served, the people who prayed to receive Christ, and so on. It's essential that you move beyond the stories of touched lives to the underlying metrics of the activity.

It also takes a big vision. In *Giving It All Away and Getting It All Back Again: The Way of Living Generously*, David Green describes a meeting with a ministry leader who described a big vision. The vision in simple terms was to reach the nation of the Philippines with the gospel by way of a children's book of the gospel. It was a simple plan. The team was in place. They had a good history of execution. And they talked about reaching a nation—something big!

That's the key to a big vision: a big problem with a bold plan to alleviate it. Big vision captivates big thinkers and big givers.

Value and Support the Businesspeople among You

The high net worth guys I know say the loneliest place in the world is church on Sunday morning. Most people in attendance share prayer concerns about getting a raise at their job, or how they hope they can pay the bills that month. But if you're the guy restructuring a one hundred million dollar financing deal and you'd like prayer and wisdom about some aspect of that, who are you going to talk to? Most likely, you'll clam up and simply get through the church experience.

Even the pace of a church can cause a high net worth person to feel they don't belong. They are often visionaries and architects of vision, fast-paced multitaskers. They see problems and want to fix them. But churches don't generally move at that speed, and this creates a disconnect. These people end up sitting on the sidelines or going someplace more interesting.

Let me say this gently: pastors themselves are often the problem. Too many pastors see themselves as being in the ministry and the high net worth people as those who fund it. I've heard that sentiment come out of the mouths of church and parachurch leaders.

Other pastors feel intimidated and deficient. They don't know how to make money and sometimes don't even know what questions to ask someone who does. They have great curiosity about God's Word, but they aren't as inquisitive about the life and perspective of someone running a business, which is really just as fascinating and illuminating. Some pastors simply think their work is more interesting than the work of some guy making widgets.

I offer three solutions that I've seen work effectively in developing good pastor-businessperson relationships and partnerships:

• ***Value the person.*** Care for them. Cultivate a genuine interest in and concern for their lives, families, businesses, and goals. Seek to understand their business and how it works. Pray for them and tell them you're praying for them. This makes a huge difference in their lives, spiritually and practically, and lays a foundation of trust on which to build a powerful partnership.

• *Be their distributor, not their answer.* There's no need for pastors to develop expertise in financial planning, wealth management, or business entrepreneurship when there are Christians gifted in these areas who can help. I compare the pastor's role to that of a point guard on a basketball team. He dribbles down, assesses the situation, then passes it off to a teammate who's likely to score. Perhaps he puts one businessperson in touch with another. Maybe he feels the nudge of the Holy Spirit to connect a high net worth person in his church with a foundation that will help their family get on the same page about multigenerational stewarding of resources to effectively accomplish kingdom work.

One of the best phrases a pastor can use is, "I don't know how to answer that, but I think I know someone who does." In this way, churches can become go-to places for people seeking advice on how to be good stewards—by connecting the right people in the right way under the guidance of the Holy Spirit.

• *Sometimes the vision of the pastor and the businessperson will align in a common task.* Discovering this requires patience, a listening ear, humility, freedom from intimidation or feelings of deficiency, and shedding an "I'm the minister, you're the funder" approach. When speaking with high net worth people, pastors should look for skills, gifts, talents, and abilities that call for engagement with the church beyond teaching Sunday School or serving as a greeter, as valuable and honorable as those things are. Some businesspeople should be brought in at a strategic level to help with the vision. That's where organizations like CityServe are so valuable. They encourage and facilitate meetings of powerful, anointed businesspeople who can sit around a table and say, "How do we win the city to the Lord? What's possible?"

Some high net worth people's needs are deeply personal and financial at the same time. I've seen this up close at The Signatry, the foundation I run that helps high net worth families come to a biblical notion of family and legacy. The Western world has created the idea of a one-generation family with little connection to the generations that came before or will come after. We raise our kids to independence, then boot them out and expect them to go their own way. Many families, not just those with large financial blessings, need to think in terms of what's good for the family legacy across multiple generations, versus what's good for me.

Many high net worth families struggle to get in the same room, let alone on the same page about their finances and legacy, their family vision, mission, and values. But when they do, the results are powerful. We facilitate these conversations and help families put together a "family constitution," just as a country makes a constitution by which it is governed. Technically, this is a trust document, but it's about much more than transferring wealth. It's about family unity and strength around a common vision for its legacy and the good it wants to do with the financial blessings God has given. It's healthy when a family asks questions such as, "Is there something we should own in this city? Are we about eradicating poverty or opioid abuse, or helping kids in foster care? What's our big idea? Where is our Jerusalem, Judea, and Samaria?"

Churches don't need to be experts in those discussions. They just need to know how to point people to those who do it well.

Everyone—pastors and businesspeople and all other believers—want to be meaningfully engaged in the work of God, with and for the people of God. When we humble ourselves and honor each other in our distinct areas of talent and ability, the Kingdom moves forward much more effectively—and the journey is more fulfilling.

35

Becoming Attractive to Major Donors

Barry Meguiar

This is a candid interview with Meguiar's CEO, Barry Meguiar, about how nonprofit leaders can better relate to businesspeople and major donors.

Q: What has been your experience, generally, with development people and fund-raisers for ministry and nonprofit organizations?

Meguiar: If someone approaches me as a development person, I want to run. After a lot of years and encounters with many development people, I've met very few who were interested in me more than my money. Usually, their questions are focused on sizing me up for my giving potential and preclude any interest in me as a person or my needs.

There are, of course, wonderful exceptions. This afternoon I'll meet with a development person for a major ministry. I already know I'm going to be generous with him. Why? Because he cares about me and my needs, and knows the names and has prayed for my family members and my business. In addition, the ministry he represents is doing great work for the Kingdom. He's worked hard at becoming my friend. And by being my friend, he obligates me to ask him about the needs of his ministry and how I can help.

Q: What are keys to dealing with businesspeople who have the capacity to give?

Meguiar: It boils down to relationship. Development people must build a relationship with donors before effortless, generous, and continuous giving can commence. I recently received a call from a development representative on my way to a ministry conference that he was attending. He had been hounding me for the previous month, and I had been too busy to respond. After I told him I couldn't give him any money at that moment, he quickly hung up and never spoke to me at the conference.

> Every ministry supporter wants the confidence of knowing they've made a good investment.

Here's where he made his mistake. He failed to realize that the moment would pass and my ability to support him could be cultivated. He was more interested in my ability to write a check at that very moment than in establishing a relationship with me.

Relationships matter! We give our business and our ministry dollars to people we like and trust and who share like-minded passions—those who can make us feel like their ministry is our ministry. This leads to the long-term goal of every ministry and supporter, which is consistent, long-term giving.

Having said that, the establishment of trust is even more important. Every ministry supporter wants the confidence of knowing they've made a good investment. Business people are focused on ROI—return on investment. Why should they give to one ministry over another? That decision hangs on a documented point of differentiation that separates one ministry from all other ministries: trust.

Critical to the development of trust in a ministry is communication, accountability, and transparency. While relationships open the door to generous giving, trust plays the critical role in the development of generous, long-term supporters. And that trust must be verified with regular, transparent communication that emotionally places the donor inside the ministry . . . letting them feel like it's their ministry!

Q: What's another key?

Meguiar: Ministries need to stay focused on God as their source rather than on their donors. God provides the resources for individuals and organizations that exist for His purpose: to seek and save the lost. A God-orchestrated appointment with a high-potential giver may have nothing to do with raising money. It may have everything to do with moving that person closer to Jesus, which is of far greater value. And God keeps the books!

Q: What are some make-or-break principles for you when relating to a nonprofit or ministry?

Meguiar: Integrity. Integrity is nonnegotiable. The individual and the organization they represent must have absolute integrity. Why else would anyone trust them with their resources?

A ministry asked my wife and me to make a gift that would require us to go into the principle that generates our funding for ministries. Nevertheless, the opportunity to give this lifetime gift to fund an amazing project caught our attention. The drawings of the completed structure sold the deal. While we didn't want our name on the structure, the fact we would always know that our faithful use of God's money made it all happen is what appealed to us.

Six months later, we saw a mailer soliciting funds for the same structure. They had used the idea of meeting the entire need to convince us to give more than we normally would have given . . . and far more than we would have given if we had known we were one of many givers funding the project. To make matters worse, they never had a second thought about this type of fund-raising. That's lack of integrity!

Q: In a general way, how do you decide to give?
Meguiar: We rely on the Holy Spirit to prompt us. We don't move unless we feel the leading of the Holy Spirit. And Karen and I are almost always on the same page and getting the same message about a ministry. She'll look at me or I'll look at her and say, "We need to support this." Knowing we can easily express concern or pushback to each other and immediately stop the process, we rarely ever do that even when we don't have funds available.

When the Holy Spirit prompts us to give, we give. While we're not major donors with endless resources, we do as we're told. It's God's money and not ours. In a sea of requests from wonderful ministries, we can only do so much, so we leave that up to God to decide. I don't want to sound overly spiritual, but no amount of pressure and tenacity can prompt us to support ministries we're not led to support.

The key factor for us is how many people have been saved over the last twelve months as a result of the ministry. If the people promoting the ministry can't answer that question, we have no further need to talk. There are multitudes of ministries doing good things that non-Christian organizations can do just as well. But being good and doing good things doesn't get anyone into heaven. The entirety of life is about redemption! A hundred years from now, nothing else will matter.

Q: What have you learned about ministry from being in business?
Meguiar: When I entered the family business out of college, Meguiar's was a cottage business doing six hundred thousand

dollars a year selling to body shops and car dealers. As the third-generation leader, I took Meguiar's into retail, focused on selling to car guys. Without any resources for launching a mass market campaign, I went to where the car guys were—at car shows—and won them over one guy at a time by loving on them and showing them the best product in the world for making their cars shine. And every one of them told their friends who told their friends, which generated exponential growth and made us the top-selling car wax in the United States.

My point is this: the gift of eternal life, being the gospel, is the best "product" in the world. And no matter how much noise we make, mass marketing is way too expensive and has never worked. The best and easiest way to market the gospel is to ignite one person at a time, who will ignite their friends . . . who will ignite their communities . . . who will ignite the United States with revival. It's called the Great Commission, and it's God's formula for making our lives and our country shine again. The Christians of the Early Church added to their numbers daily and turned their godless world upside-down without resources, churches, Bibles, or even literacy. Whether or not we're in formal ministry, everything we do and say on a personal basis is moving everyone watching us either closer to God or further away from God. Indeed, we're all in full-time ministry!

As Christians we have a product that people want and need. Once it's sold, it'll stick. Those people affect ten or a hundred more and it grows exponentially. That's what the early Christian church did—moved people closer to Jesus every day.

36

Writing Winning Grants

John Hughes

Sunday after Sunday pastors are successfully presenting the basic components of a winning grant: describe the need in the community, the program to meet that need, and the goals to be achieved with the raised funds. Writing winning grants begins with a basic understanding of the request-writing process.

Where Do You Find Grants?

There are several places to find grants for your projects. They can be as local as a family foundation or as far away as the state and federal government. Before you begin seeking grants, consider these three important points.

First, foundations, government, and major donors are dispersing money for areas of focus they want to fund. Secondly, whenever possible, it will be beneficial to try and meet with the funders in advance of submitting a proposal. Cultivating a relationship with the funders can be difficult, but it's key to moving your request to the top of the pile. Third, the funders need people to ask for funding. Think about that for a minute. Government offices and foundations are required to grant a certain amount of money each year, so they want to find and fund capable people doing good work.

Local Grants: A Good Start!

The business section of the paper is a great place to identify local business leaders and companies who are interested in engaging the community. You can also do a Google search or look in the society section of the paper when there's been a black-tie event to see who sponsored or attended the event. It doesn't take long to develop a target list of names to search on the Internet and determine if they have a family or corporate foundation.

Community foundation websites regularly provide information about how to access local and national grants. Whether you're new at looking for grants or a professional fund-raiser, local community foundations are a valuable resource. I also recommend Foundation Center (http://foundationcenter.org) as a source for foundation funding opportunities. One of the best sources to understand what foundations fund is the trade publication *Chronicle of Philanthropy* (https://www.philanthropy.com). The *Chronicle* provides a wealth of understanding on trends, current activities, and contact information for foundations.

Federal Grants: The Big Leagues

No search for funding would be complete without registering for notifications on www.grants.gov. This site provides information concerning all the grants being funded by the US government. A word of caution: When you start applying for grants at the federal level, you're competing nationally against hundreds of other organizations for the funding. This is the big leagues. A critical step is to register with Dun and Bradstreet (call 1-866-705-5711) and obtain a data universal number system (DUNS), or you can go to: http://fedgov.dnb.com.

You must also register with the office of System Award Management (SAM) at: https://www.sam.gov. The completion of the DUNS and the SAM can take weeks. It's critically important to complete both before you begin to apply for a federal grant.

Pick the Right Grant

Once you've located funders and have identified a wealth of grant options, you need to pick the grants that are right for you. Carefully read the Request for Proposal (RFP). Generally, the RFP for smaller communities and programs will be under five pages, but with many federal, state, or local grants the RFP can be fifty to seventy-five pages or more. As you read the RFP, you'll need to consider some key questions: (1) What do they want to fund? (2) When is it due? (3) How much money is available? (4) Do we have the capability to do this? (5) Is this in your mission or are you chasing the money? (6) Who else in the community might be applying for the grant?

> To convey the message of your compassion program, you need to enlist the help of the best writer on your team. Hopefully this is someone from your church and community who's acquainted with your compassion program and can communicate your vision and desired outcomes.

Researching and Writing the Grant

I'm reminded of a quote by Mark Batterson, "Writing is praying with a keyboard." To convey the message of your compassion program, you need to enlist the help of the best writer on your team. Hopefully this is someone from your church and community who's acquainted with your compassion program and can communicate your vision and desired outcomes. During the writing process, you need to gather information to fulfill the grant's request for demographics, statistics on crime or poverty, the best approach to finding a solution, and so forth.

Forms, Letters of Support, and Checklists

Many grants require multiple forms. I encourage you to read the RFP three times—so you know *exactly* what forms and letters the fund requires. Many grants ask for a letter of support from a local partner, politician, or government official. These letters are essential. I would also encourage you to build a checklist of all the requirements of the grant and the corresponding evaluation points. This gives you a chance to evaluate your work before the grant reviewer does. As one of my professors in graduate school said, "Do it to yourself, before they do it to you."

Budget

Many grants require a written budget along with a narrative explaining in detail the justification for the proposed expenses. For example, if you tell them you need a full-time staff person for the project, you need to make the case for the salary, taxes, and benefits involved.

Components of a Winning Grant

Abstract. This is a one- to two-page summary of your entire grant. If the fund requires an abstract, I recommend you write this last. You'll already be finished with all the heavy lifting of the grant proposal so it'll be much easier to write a concise summary of the grant.

Need of the target population and geographic area. This is where you make a case for the need the grant will address. This component can include poverty levels, educational levels, income, crime statistics, etc. Much of this type of information is available through the US Census American Community Survey (https://www.census.gov/programs-surveys/acs).

Program design. In your program design you outline your ideas to fix the problem you are presenting. For example, if you want to develop a mentoring program, you would need to address questions such as: How will you recruit mentors? How will you orient them to the expectations? How will you screen people to ensure those being mentored are safe from predators? How would you match mentors and those mentored? What is the first step after they are matched? Do they meet in a group or one-on-one? How long will the intervention take from start to finish?

Goals and objectives. The funders want you to outline clearly the goals and objectives for your project. Goals state a desired long-term achievement. Objectives outline the steps necessary to achieve that goal. Goal has the word *go* in it. Goals describe a movement forward. For example, my goal could be, "I want to run a triathlon." My objectives will describe the steps I need to take to achieve that goal. Objectives follow a SMART format. They are *specific, measurable, attainable, realistic,* and *time sensitive.* My SMART objective to achieve my goal of running a triathlon would be: to complete the San Diego International Sprint Triathlon by June 2018 with a time under two hours as evidenced by my registration and written documentation of the finish time. Do you see how my goal, along with the SMART objectives, provides a clear picture of what I want to accomplish?

Implementation time line. Outline the key steps to be accomplished during the grant's life span. Time lines are usually shown in a table with some narrative.

Key personnel. Potential funders will scrutinize the experience and education of the key personnel working on your project. In this section, you want to outline your personnel's previous experience with externally funded projects, unique qualifications, and certifications or licenses.

Evaluation. This describes the process you'll use to evaluate the goals and objectives. Funders want to know that you have a management information system (MIS) that captures various data points and can produce reports to the funders on a monthly, quarterly, or annual basis. You can purchase various MIS systems with an annual subscription. Salesforce or Efforts to Outcomes are industry standard in nonprofits. If this is one of your first projects, you may not need an off-the-shelf MIS system.

Budget and narrative. In the budget, you detail how you plan to use the funds in two primary areas: personnel and operations. The personnel section will outline key staff positions, salaries, benefits, taxes, and percentage of time on this project. Operational costs will include the essential elements of rent, technology, supplies, etc. The budget should include a written narrative providing a detailed explanation of the use of funds. The budget and narrative together should provide the funder a clear picture of how you will use the funds.

> Objectives follow a SMART format. They are *specific, measurable, attainable, realistic,* and *time sensitive.*

Conclusion

Remember, each funder will have unique requirements that are important to their work. These could range from logic models to letters of commitment from community partners. Always refer to the RFP when starting a new grant. Your ability to articulate your ideas clearly helps to ensure the success of your grant. It can seem like a daunting task, but each grant proposal you write will provide new lessons and bring you closer to success.

37

Messaging Your Ministry with Dignity

Dr. Julie Horner

Social media and the interconnectedness of today's society have changed how compassion ministries market their services. One major challenge of marketing a compassion ministry is how to communicate respectfully about your target audience, the people who will benefit from your ministry.

In the past, nonprofits could communicate discreetly with board members, donors, and supporters. These days, communication happens on social media or other parts of the Internet, or by e-mail, so all communication is essentially public. While a photo of a starving child or a blighted neighborhood might communicate the need quickly to your supporters as you seek volunteers or funding, how will the people feel who live in that neighborhood (or their relatives and friends) when they see your post on social media? Or on a PowerPoint presentation at church? Or on your web page? Or on your YouTube channel?

It's almost impossible to control your message based on an intended audience anymore. The only safe assumption is that everything you communicate will be read and heard not only by potential donors, but also by potential recipients of your compassion ministry. This can create awkwardness or even hard feelings.

Here are some forward-thinking questions to help you plan for dignified communication:

- How will we refer to the recipients of our ministry efforts? As guests, clients, friends, or recipients?
- Who will be responsible for reviewing information and images before we make them available to the public to ensure they meet our standards of honor?

While creating your marketing materials, you should also ask:

- Have we reported our involvement accurately, without embellishment or self-gratification for what we've done?
- Have we communicated the facts accurately and in a way the recipient of our services would condone?
- Have we used people-first descriptors by identifying the person first and then their need (children who don't have enough to eat instead of starving children or the hungry)? Even though this often takes a few more words, it honors the individuals instead of labeling them.
- Have we received permission to share recipients' quotes and images, especially if they're identified or singled out in photos?
- If we read this aloud to the person we're serving, would we be embarrassed by how we refer to them?

The importance of these items hit home for me at church one Sunday when the grandmother of a boy with a brain injury approached me. Her grandson and our son, who has cerebral palsy, are friends. The grandmother said to me, "We're so glad your son is a friend to our grandson. He treats our grandson like a person, not a project." Those words struck my heart and began to inform my marketing strategies as well.

When helping people with needs, it's easy to see them as

projects rather than people. Instead of focusing on who they are— their personalities, likes and dislikes, hopes and dreams—we may focus on the good things we're doing for them. If our primary attention is on us and how we grow and gain from serving, that's not the best strategy.

We need to wrap marketing around relationships instead of just needs. Marketing compassion ministries today ideally requires forging genuine relationships, or being open to genuine relationships, with the people we serve. This might mean finding someone who already has a friendship with someone in your target audience before you form your own. That connection is vital. Every part of compassion ministry marketing should keep people as the focus. Discuss with everyone involved how all of you will refer to those you serve. *Guest* might be a great term of honor until you have a deeper relationship with someone; then *friend* might be a more accurate option.

> **Every part of compassion ministry marketing should keep people as the focus.**

When serving others, I ask questions to hold myself accountable: Am I treating them as people or as a project? Do I talk *with* the people I serve, or do I talk *down* to them? Am I willing to be seen with them in public without thinking I need to give someone an explanation? I continually check how I speak with and about the people I serve, how I posture myself toward them, and what expectations I have for a relationship with them going forward.

Forming relationships has the added benefit of illuminating your target audience accurately. The more you know about the people you want to serve, the better you can help them in ways that matter, and the better you can define your goals. Are you helping kids in a local school? Or the neighbors around your church? Or local seniors? Write down specific information about the people you want to reach. The more detailed a description you can provide, the better. This will also help you determine with sharper focus how you can best assist them.

The Four Ps of Marketing

Once you've clearly defined your specific efforts and begun to form relationships with the people you'll serve, you can use basic marketing principles to guide your efforts. The four classic Ps are (1) product, (2) placement, (3) price, and (4) promotion, and they still apply.

Product

The "product" of your compassion ministry is what you want to give or how you want to serve. Marketing is a lot easier if you narrow your focus to a specific event or effort. For example, my church recently chose to help kids who qualify for free lunch at the local school, and we needed to identify how to do that. What was our "product"? We decided to throw a back-to-school party for them. That was a lot easier to market and plan and was essential in helping us identify the children who needed our help.

Placement

Where and when will you offer the event? A relationship with someone in your target audience can help you choose a time and location where guests are available and comfortable. If you're going into their community, go with a great deal of respect and advance understanding of how they'll feel when a group of volunteers arrive. Again, openness to ongoing relationships makes a big difference in the tone of the event, and their receptivity to your help.

Price

Price introduces a marketing challenge because compassion efforts are usually offered for free, which means someone other than the guests must pay for the product. Reach out to donors, volunteers, and nonprofits—anyone with an interest in what you're doing. Just remember to honor the people you want to serve when you communicate the need.

Promotion

Promote your compassion ministry and do it personally if possible. Traditional advertising through newspapers, television, and radio may not be as effective as in the past. Personal invitations are always meaningful and effective.

When our church did the back-to-school outreach, the elementary school staff helped us invite the families. This was possible because we had laid relational groundwork in advance. Our pastor had met with the superintendent and principal previously. Also, we'd taken Christmas cookies to the teachers and interacted with them in other ways to get to know them.

If you want to give food to kids lacking good nutrition, a local food bank, day care center, or public school might connect you with people who would appreciate your help. Another option is to begin by serving alongside ministries who already have established relationships in that area.

Personal invitations should be written down, reinforced verbally, and include all the details of your outreach along with a phone number and website. We found it helpful to ask people to register so we knew how many to expect. This also provided some basic information about the guests.

Simple posters on brightly colored paper work well to get the word out. Hang them at grocery stores, gas stations, laundromats, and businesses where potential guests gather. These take a little more time to create, but they strike a personal note, and if you put small tear sheets across the bottom, people can take home a reminder of the details.

Social media is a must, but keep in mind what was discussed earlier. Don't write something clunky and insensitive that might be understood as, "We're going to help some poor people in a rundown neighborhood this weekend. Come join us." Instead say, "This Saturday we're going to such-and-such neighborhood to pull weeds and help clean up yards." The difference is subtle but important.

Promote your compassion ministry and do it personally if possible.... Personal invitations are always meaningful and effective.

At the event itself, you aren't just performing a service but marketing for future events. People will sense if you're swooping in to do a good deed and then leaving. Talk to your team about letting relationships develop naturally. Maybe someone you meet will come to church with you one day . . . or maybe you will go with them. If you live locally, chances are you'll bump into them at the store or the post office. The more comfortable you are in their space, the less the event will feel like a do-good charity moment.

After the event, as much as possible, let the people you served tell the story on social media. Adopt their perspective. Don't make it about how you helped and how that affected you. Let *them* say it. Think about how you would celebrate something with a friend.

Marketing compassion ministries can be effective, affirming, and even relational when we treat everyone involved as people . . . not projects.

38

Kingdom Investors—Involving Business Leaders in Solutions

Mark Lehmann

An interview with Mark Lehmann, the lead pastor of Cornerstone Church in Bowie, Maryland, about Kingdom Investors.

Q: Tell us about Kingdom Investors, and why you started it.

Lehmann: We saw a niche for business leaders who wanted to support humanitarian works and do something that matters, because everyone longs for that. We considered, *What if we connected them to projects around the world? They may not want to go to our church, but they believe in what we do and want to be part of it.*

So, we started Kingdom Investors in 2002 in a room at a Chinese restaurant with George, a businessman in our congregation, seven other businesspeople, and me. I invited John Bueno, founder of Latin America ChildCare (now ChildHope), to speak and challenge us, not knowing what would happen. From small beginnings came this incredible thing. After that meeting I knew it had potential, big time. There was such a great need for it. People were looking for an answer.

Since then, Kingdom Investors has raised $2.5 million for projects. I didn't know it would grow as big as it has grown. It's run on a shoestring budget but is having a major impact.

Q: Many supporters aren't from your church, correct?

Lehmann: Most of them have never been involved in our church, and a large percentage are not followers of Jesus, but they want to make a difference. They don't care who does it; they just want it to get done, whether it targets human trafficking, feeding programs, child care, digging wells, Teen Challenge, inner city projects, compassion outreaches, orphanages, or adoption. Whichever project grabs them, we'll put the money right toward that. They don't feel pressured to participate in a specific project. We give them options. They see it as, "What's my return on investment? I helped to change that life. I gave that person hope and a future."

We make no bones that we're a Christ-centered entity, and many of them have come to faith in Jesus through this program. They get involved, see the good that's happening, and God uses it in great ways.

Q: What questions do businesspeople ask before getting involved?

Lehmann: Most businesspeople are skeptical of compassion programs, and rightly so. Our people near DC are leery of anything. They've seen government and business at its best and worst, so they want to know, "Why are you doing this? What's the reason?" We make it clear that though our church gives one-third of our money to missions every year, we believe strongly that God wants us to engage people who aren't engaged yet. We have a separate website, so people can give directly to Kingdom Investors, not to the church. Checks are made out to Kingdom Investors. It goes through our 501(c)(3), and we do business as Kingdom Investors.

When they say, "This is funneled through a church, so how is that not proselytizing?" we answer that every penny goes to their designated project. And they can look in the financial books at any time. We don't take a dime for administrative costs. We underwrite it all. How many organizations can say that? Every penny goes to the project, which is almost unheard of. It gives credence and credibility that this isn't just a fund-raising tool or a nonprofit making 30 percent off it. We say anytime you want to see where the money goes, we can show you.

I've learned that businesspeople want to say, "I trust you." Because the director of Kingdom Investors isn't on staff at the church, that little bit of distance helps businesspeople to buy in.

> We give report after report on what's done with it. We're going to India this year to verify where the money is going for a project there. We come back to businessmen and say, "We've been there and seen it ourselves."

Q: What other ways do you build trust with supporters?
Lehmann: We make sure we personally vet every project. George and I travel a lot and do reconnaissance at sites so we can say, "We know where this money is going." We give report after report on what's done with it. We're going to India this year to verify where the money is going for a project there. We come back to businesspeople and say, "We've been there and seen it ourselves." We can't go on-site to each one, but we do due diligence as much as possible. Credibility and accountability are huge for us.

Q: This is separate from your church's missions giving, correct?
Lehmann: Yes. Cornerstone gives one million dollars to missions besides Kingdom Investors, but this adds influence. People in our church love it because we have a passion to touch more people.

Q: A big part of Kingdom Investors' success is your unique and powerful partnership with the businessman you mentioned, George. Tell us about that.
Lehmann: George was in the HVAC business in Washington, DC. God has given him a huge heart for evangelism, so I asked him to help reach this niche of people with potential to do great things. He prayed about it and said, "I can try that." He began making connections. George has an incredible way with people. He's six feet five inches tall, drives a Smart Car, and has a great joy for the Lord. He's a fun guy. When you're around him, he exudes the love of Jesus like a big kid. Anyone who meets him knows he's genuine. That's a key with businesspeople: they want to know you're genuine.

George works from his home. The church pays most of his expenses. That's why there's no overhead for him. He hustles and makes contacts with people who have needs and those who can meet those needs. He goes to lunch and is bold with people: "Here's a project. I know you want to do something. Why don't you help me with this one?" These donors aren't believers, but soon they're giving sixty thousand dollars. George activates that.

These guys go on trips, too. Some have gone with George to Haiti several times. We have bankers come for food distributions. If a hurricane or project comes up, groups go to help build houses and churches. Kingdom Investors spearheads that for us. Because George was one of them—a businessman first—it gives great credibility to the fact that we're not trying to take their money. We want their partnership.

George now runs two Kingdom Investors golf tournaments a year, drawing more than two hundred people. It's a great way for businesspeople to tie in. They give away awards and people sponsor holes. One businessman knows someone else, invites him to a golf tournament, and they get connected to what Kingdom Investors is all about.

Q: What makes the relationship between you, a pastor, and George, a businessman, work so well?

Lehmann: George and I talked about this recently. The reason the relationship he and I have works is because it has a huge amount of trust. I've been here twenty-five years. He was in the church before I got here, and this is a big part of his life now. If he wants to do a project he'll ask, "Pastor, what do you think about this?" I've never said no. If people are being changed and lives are being touched, I'm with it.

Sometimes I'll go to him and say, "We're building this children's home in Moldova. Would Kingdom Investors be willing to help out?" He'll say, "Absolutely." Or he'll propose something to me, and I'll say, "Absolutely." It's a partnership, and our mutual heart isn't about my ministry or his ministry but what we do together. It's always been "our" thing.

> What if you let businesspeople run with it and go? Think of the thousands of people you can help.

George can do this without me, but he wants me to be part of his covering. I want to empower him to reach people I could never touch. Ultimately, if we do it together, we can reach far more people than either of us could by ourselves. Hopefully, other churches and businesspeople can model this. It's a beautiful thing when both parties trust each other.

Q: Can other churches replicate what you're doing with Kingdom Investors?

Lehmann: Without question. I think there's a businessperson in every church who can take ownership and have kingdom impact on whatever scale. Maybe it's at one thousand dollars or two million dollars. How do you know unless you try? We were small when we started.

Pastors are often afraid to ask businesspeople to do something like this, but that's an untapped resource. People sitting in your congregation want to be activated and become part of the answer. Guess what? They're giving money to someone else. What if you let businesspeople run with it and go? Think of the thousands of people you can help. If there's a guy sitting in your church who wants to run with it, let him run. You need to trust him. If I hadn't done that, and if George and I hadn't trusted each other, none of this would have taken place.

Church leaders must realize how dynamic it can be to interact with the businesspeople in their communities. You can do it no matter the size of your church. To learn more about Kingdom Investors, visit www.kingdominvestors.info.

39

Workplace Compassion

Doug Heisel

This is an interview with Doug Heisel, a leader and communicator who's passionate about sharing timeless truth in relevant and interesting ways. He's the founder and lead pastor of New Life Church in Alamo, California, one of the fastest-growing churches in the San Francisco East Bay.

Q: You thought you would be a marketplace leader, but God made you a pastor to marketplace leaders. Tell us about that journey.

Heisel: My dad was a small business owner, but I called him the evangelist of tithing. He would tell people how good it is to tithe, so I heard it from him, not just our pastor. I thought, *I want to do what my dad did, but in the corporate world rather than a small business context . . . and with larger numbers.*

When I was in college, God called me to full-time ministry. I felt like I was giving up a first love, which was to be a marketplace leader. When we came to the Bay Area I kept thinking, *This is a weird demographic. I'm a kid from northern Minnesota. God, why in the world did you stick me in the Bay Area of California?* I can't fully answer that. I just know He has placed me here, perhaps because I come from a grounded place. I'm neither enamored by stuff, nor do I think stuff is evil. I think God needs Christians in every zip code in the country. So, I feel He's called me to the Bay Area, and I can't redefine the missions field, I can only react to it and attempt to influence it.

Six or seven years ago God said to me, "You had a desire to be a marketplace leader, but I want to use you in the Bay Area to raise up marketplace leaders. Set a goal to raise up a thousand marketplace leaders to take your place." That fuels me and does two things specifically: First, I get to feel I'm in a position as a marketplace leader because part of my ministry is uniquely aimed at them. Second, I started learning their language, how to speak to them, what questions to ask, what doesn't work. Today, we spend a lot of time equipping marketplace leaders and raising them to thrive in their missions fields here in the Bay Area. I have a genuine interest in their world, in them as people, and in what they do. I tell them, "I love what you do because there was a time I thought God would put me in a similar field."

Q: How do you talk about stewarding wealth in your context where many people have so much?
Heisel: I find I need to salt stewardship into many of my messages. A little comment or paragraph or five minutes on something related will begin to tilt their mind-set. But on the spectrum of discipleship, my bigger thoughts about stewardship won't all happen on Sunday morning. I've carved out a different, new lane for that, and for us that has been our Kingdom Builders nights, three or four times a year. It's about investing in them to become better leaders and helping them leverage their resources as God blesses them. I know I have no skeptics there. If they come, I'm going to hit it hard. It's not about "ask, ask, ask." It's about me as a leader asking, "What can I give them so they feel enriched? And where else can we stretch them?"

I often have marketplace leaders tell their stories. When I bring someone in who's committed to being generous and is a marketplace leader and is leveraging resources for the Kingdom, that's a megaphone to people. They think, *"I've been hearing my pastor say it, but this validates it."*

The skill of working with marketplace leaders is more developed than downloaded. It can and should be learned, especially if you live in a community of marketplace leaders like I do. If they come to a night like Kingdom Builders, I can ask them to do more, but it's not just a request. It's an investment first.

Q: How do you encourage generosity without coming across as being after people's money?

Heisel: An interesting spectrum of people sit in front of you on a Sunday. Some are skeptical about your motivation for talking about money. Others are uncomfortable and feel guilty with what they have. Then a whole bunch are just comfortable enough that they don't want to stretch themselves to do more. But, there are also others wanting or ready to increase their giving.

> As Christ-followers we have a new identity, and part of that is to become givers because God is a giver.

I think of a CEO of a software company in Palo Alto. He's a committed Christ-follower and would refer to himself as the pastor of his company, which has twenty thousand employees. He said something one time to the effect of, "The Bay Area is the most unchurched city in America. The net income is one of the highest, and per capita giving one of the lowest. I live around rich pagan misers."

I don't know that most are miserly, but I do think many are fearful, or just driven and competitive. They're making more money for the sake of it, and they haven't thought about living a different story.

Part of my theology is that we're created to be generous, and it's the best way to live. If I don't have that as a core conviction then I'm prying people's fingers open rather than leading them to their best life. It's trying to change the operating system from self-centered, which is how we're all born, to the people God made us to be. As Christ-followers we have a new identity, and part of that is to become givers because God is a giver. As a pastor, I believe that to my core. People who tend to make money are shrewd with money; they smell good deals and bad deals and are intuitive about people. They'll know if you believe what you say or it's a line and they're being worked.

Q: How does compassion ministry happen in your high-earning cultural context?

Heisel: "To whom much is given, from him much will be required"[10]—that app runs in the background of my head all the time. We must communicate the message of compassion differently in our context because, in many regards, compassion ministry can't happen in our backyard. People aren't asking for it. It's like giving bread to people who are full. They'll buy their own designer bread, but they don't want or need your bread.

We try to put people who are somewhat isolated and insulated from world problems in proximity to those problems so they grow to care about them. We want to show them there's a moral cause and impress on them that God didn't put them where He did just to enjoy the lifestyle but to leverage it. That's one of the most common words we use: *leverage*. We leverage the resources of the East Bay for the benefit of the world. We should do a disproportionate amount of the heavy lifting.

Recently, I've been saying to some of our people that if you get to a place where you've earned enough money while you still have good working years in front of you, why retire? Why not work the rest of your working years and give away what you earn? Lowering your golf score can only be so fulfilling. Go on a mission trip and feed some hungry kids.

Q: How do you teach about money in a persuasive, biblical way?

Heisel: I believe in the innate power of Bible stories. One story convicted a guy I know, and I didn't even tell it! He just read it for himself. It was the story of the foolish man who built bigger barns and said, "Eat, drink, and be merry." God told him, "You fool! Tonight, you're going to die."[11] That had a catalytic effect on this man and arrested his notion that putting more money in the bank would give him more security. That lie is the reason many people are so driven. But it's a mirage.

One man in our church believed he needed a certain amount of money in the bank to feel secure, and after accumulating that amount he would give more. Seven or so years ago when the economy went down, he was at church one day feeling frustrated and saying, "God, give me back my money." In the service that day someone from Mexico spoke about her ministry. This man sat there thinking, *Too bad she came today because I'm here to get, not to give. I'm here to say, "God, give my money back!"* Then the Holy Spirit convicted him with an extreme challenge: "You're responsible to talk to her and say yes to whatever she asks you to do." Suddenly, he was in a spiritual wrestling match.

Finally, he said yes to what the Holy Spirit had told him to do . . . to the tune of tens of thousands of dollars. That yes changed his life. Salvation was first, giving was second. He would tell me that his life is better because he's learned to be generous.

When I heard that, I thought, *Thank God I'm not alone in this! I just need to set the appointment with the Bible and the Holy Spirit, and get out of the way.* The Holy Spirit will work on them more than I ever could.

Q: What can pastors do to help high-capacity financial people steward their wealth?

Heisel: Often the church doesn't recognize the unique opportunity high-capacity people have as givers. That's their ministry, and they need the freedom not to do it all through your church and solve all your problems for you.

I run into people in the Bay Area who, when they get generous, control instead of release. They set up foundations and want to control 100 percent of everything. Yet pastors do a similar thing: they want to control 100 percent of everything. Both equations are wrong. God essentially says to give 10 percent to the storehouse (your local church) and do what you want with the other 90 percent. Pastors need to bless marketplace leaders to give their money directly through the church and indirectly through other organizations.

> **Pastors need to bless marketplace leaders to give their money directly through the church and indirectly through other organizations.**

I learned this from a man who was touched to give to a work in another country and wanted to give the money directly to them. I said, "Great! I don't need to have my hands on that money or know what you're doing with it. I just want to know that you're giving it." In my denomination, the Assemblies of God, our church doesn't get giving credit for that, but if you care too much about getting credit, you won't do it right. It's amazing what you can do if you don't want the credit. You can't go into meetings with marketplace leaders with the wrong mind-set. If you don't readjust your thinking, you'll have a mental scorecard somewhere. Maybe getting credit won't be your scorecard, but it'll be something else and you'll unintentionally be after something that's not helpful.

On the other hand, another high-capacity person told me something that changed how I think. He's a more mature and spiritually gifted giver. He told me, "Doug, I feel like at church you're more concerned about not offending the bottom 10 percent who are skeptical than challenging the top 10 percent who want to learn more and do more! I want you to challenge me and speak into my life so I can become the best marketplace leader I can be. Stop worrying about offending the person who won't be motivated anyway." In other words, I was focusing on the ultraskeptical person and spending too much attention in that direction. I realized that on any given Sunday, there's someone sitting there who wants to be more generous and they're saying, "Convince me." That day I changed how I talk about these things.

Q: Can you share any other stories about God moving people to radical generosity?

Heisel: I was recently with one marketplace leader who told me that he was in a church on a Sunday where a guest speaker said: "Some of you are giving the same amount you did ten years ago. You've learned to tithe, but that's all you'll do unless you change." This man and his wife, who were in their thirties, decided to increase their giving by 1 percent every year. That was thirty years ago. They now give away 50 percent of their personal net worth. Because of their generosity, a certain Christian university exists, and their foundation is the primary funder of a ministry that reaches hundreds of kids in Kenya.

That came from one person saying one thing to the top 1 percent on a Sunday morning. That's fanning the flame of generosity.

40

Labor of Love—The Church Honoring Job Providers

Dave Donaldson and Ryan Odle

Charlie, I have an idea I want to run by you because your company (O'Reilly Auto Parts) is one of the top job creators in America. What do you think about the idea of churches honoring employers in their communities for providing jobs? We could do it over Labor Day weekend at a host church and call it Labor of Love."

Charlie thought for a moment and clearing his throat said, "That's a great idea! How can I help?" Over the years I've come to value Charlie's counsel, and this was the confirmation I needed.

O'Reilly Auto Parts was founded in 1957 as a single store in Missouri and has grown into a corporation of 5,097 stores in 47 states and more than 77,000 team members. In communities across the United States, O'Reilly's Auto Parts, along with other quality companies, is spearheading the best antipoverty strategy ever—jobs!

I then took the vision to my pastor, Jeff Peterson, formerly at Central Assembly in Springfield, Missouri. Jeff was always looking for ways to encourage people and affirm good works, so I thought the idea would resonate with him, and it did.

"Jeff," I asked, "where would churches be without the four-letter word, *work*? If not for jobs, where would tithes and offerings for the church come from?"

Jeff replied, "Too many of us well-meaning pastors see businesspeople as dollar signs instead of valuable partners in bringing meaningful work to families in our churches."

"Amen!" I replied, "And I think a good mission statement for our churches would be: 'Jesus and a job.'"

Jesus and a Job

That tagline was a phrase born out of an experience I had years ago at a Convoy of Hope outreach in Baltimore, Maryland. From a distance I spotted a man standing beside his son, gazing dejectedly at the ground. His beaten-down demeanor caught my eye as I mingled with other "guests of honor" at the event.

"Will there be clowns and balloons?" the boy asked as I drew near.

"Yes, and hot dogs, games, bouncing gyms, and even prizes."

I offered my hand to the father. "My name is Dave. I want to thank you for coming today." He shook my hand and replied with little emotion, "I'm Jim."

> With tools like Labor of Love, the church can cultivate relationships with business owners and join them in incubating programs for job training and placement.

"Jim, how long have you lived in the area?"

"A few years." Then he sheepishly looked me in the eye and said, "I've tried to find work, but it seems nobody wants me." Jim's son had walked away a pace or two. "I don't want my boy to think his dad's a bum," he said urgently. "I don't want him to grow up to be like me either."

The pain in his face and voice troubled me deeply. "We have people here today who will help you put together a good résumé, and there are also employers here who are looking for someone just like you who is eager to work."

A few days later I visited Jim and his son at their home. They lived in government housing that was cold, dark, and cramped. The door was cracked open, so I knocked while saying, "It's Dave from the outreach," hoping he would remember me.

From a back room, Jim summoned, "C'mon in, Dave."

As I walked past the open door, I noticed his little boy. Holding up my hand he jumped high to "slap me five." Jim was sitting at the kitchen table completing some forms, and there was a new energy about him.

"Do you know what this is?" he asked with a smile. "These are employment forms I need to finish for my new job." I reached out my hand to congratulate him, and he grasped it with confidence. "Dave, thank you! At that event you guys put on last Saturday, well, I found Jesus and a job!"

Jim represents the best opportunity for the church to bridge the gap between the unemployed/underemployed and job providers. According to Hudson Institute, by 2020 there will be over forty-one million jobs vacated by retiring baby-boomers in the United States.[12] Most of these jobs require medium- to high-level training. With tools like Labor of Love, the church can cultivate relationships with business owners and join them in incubating programs for job training and placement.

Labor of Love Program

After my talk with Pastor Jeff, he, David Mayne, who designs for Bass Pro Shops, Chris Huff from Convoy of Hope, and I began working on a plan to host a Labor of Love in a Sunday morning service at Central Assembly. This service would be completely dedicated to honoring job providers in our Springfield community.

The event, held on September 4, 2016, was a huge success. The program included the mayor making a proclamation for Labor of Love, the city manager, the president of the Chamber of

Commerce, the superintendent of public schools, executives for two major hospitals, a panel of entrepreneurs, and Anne Beiler, founder of Auntie Anne's Pretzels, as the keynote speaker. There was even a touching moment when a city official presented the Labor of Love Community Award to a security guard who had been serving the public schools for over twenty-five years. The instant standing ovation for this unsung hero left many of us in tears.

Another highlight was a Charlie O'Reilly video interview hosted by Robert Spence, former president of Evangel University. The interview between two longtime friends and seasoned professionals underscores O'Reilly's religious background as the foundation to job creation and "giving back to our community."

My brother, Steve, founder of Rural Compassion, put it best, "Labor of Love can be hosted by any size church and community." In fact, in smaller communities Labor of Love could be one of the seminal events of the year and become a tool to attract business entrepreneurs to their area.

Community Balance

Since the first Labor of Love weekend, the feedback has exposed how removed the church often is from the business community. It also demonstrated how the church can bring the community a balance of good news and bad news. For example, a city manager's job is to bring problems to the surface and resolve them. However, if city officials place too much focus on the community's negative issues, they'll get pushback from the marketplace, real estate companies, homebuilders, and others who are trying to attract people to the city to buy homes and patronize their businesses. One business owner told me privately, "All this talk about homelessness is sullying our community's image." Labor of Love is one way for the church to lead in celebrating the livelihood and strengths of the community.

I followed up with Pastor Jeff to get his comments on the inaugural event, and he replied eagerly, "It was a great day for our church! Our congregation left with a heightened awareness of our city's needs and were encouraged with our own community engagement ministries. Our people were challenged to support and celebrate what others are doing to positively affect our culture. I would highly recommend Labor of Love for any church to bridge the gap between civic and commerce leadership and the local church's efforts to impact their community."

For more information about Labor of Love, go to the cityserve.us website and click on the link for "Hosting a Labor of Love in Your Community." The site includes resources, sample program run sheet, and the Charlie O'Reilly interview. Many ideas are emerging from that event including a job fair and symposium on "Workplace Strategies for Economic Development" that can be hosted on the Saturday before the Labor of Love Sunday or on Labor Day itself.

Part 6

CHURCH AND GOVERNMENT

Go after government funding for the sake of
those who need your good service.
The point is not to simply find
another source of funds but rather to
extend the good you do in your community.
If your services honor God by being excellent
and effective, then it is good for everyone that
more people can access them because of
government financial assistance.

—Stanley Carlson-Thies

41

How the Church Relinquished Social Services to Government

Marvin Olasky

In Marvin Olasky's landmark book, *The Tragedy of American Compassion*, he makes a compelling case for how we've allowed a culture of dependency to emerge to the point that it's socially acceptable for a person not to work and contribute to society. In his more recent book, *Renewing American Compassion*, he writes, "In the 1920s and 1930s we were productive, but now we are consumer-oriented. People don't want to produce, don't want to get a job. It used to be that a person's not working had a direct impact on his ability to eat. Now, folks that don't work are idolized—they're cruising around in a nice car, not having to work. We should be saying, 'We will help you if you help yourself.' "[13]

In the following interview, Marvin Olasky discusses how we got here and what lessons from history we can apply to a godly vision for social renewal in the United States.

Q: Why did you write *The Tragedy of American Compassion?*

Olasky: The key to the future, as always, is understanding the past. Americans a century ago faced many of the problems we face today, and they came up with truly compassionate solutions. This book, by laying out this history of charity in our country, attempts to recapture the vision that changed lives up to a century ago.

Q: What was charity like a century ago?

Olasky: At the turn of the twentieth century, the natural course for Americans was personal responsibility to care for yourself and your family. When an able-bodied man in almost any city asked an agency for relief, they asked him to chop wood for two hours or to whitewash a building. They gave a needy woman a seat in the sewing room. Charities didn't treat everyone equally, and since they were private they didn't have to. Instead, charitable societies considered people "worthy of relief" who were poor through no fault of their own and unable to change their situation quickly. This included widows unable to work, orphans, the elderly, and a person suffering from a temporary illness or accident. When a person needed material support, charities tried to raise the funds from relatives and others with personal ties to the individual instead of appropriating funds from general income. This approach enforced family responsibility and set a pattern for the next generation.

Q: How did we move from charities providing temporary aid until a person could get back on their feet, to a culture of entitlement where relief becomes a way of life?

Olasky: The change began with the advent of the Great Depression in 1929 and an unemployment rate of 27 percent. The Depression increased demand for assistance, but from 1929 to 1932 at least four hundred of the nation's private welfare agencies went under. When the major economic crisis emerged in the early 1930s, many believed it was not only natural but inevitable to rely on governmental programs run by professionals and emphasizing material transfer rather than individual challenge and spiritual concern. Franklin Roosevelt nationalized the idea called the Federal Emergency Relief Administration, or better known as the

"New Deal." Even Roosevelt himself acknowledged the danger of welfare programs becoming "a habit with our country" and pledged to avoid it.

This set the stage for what I call a new charity order. Although this new charity order afforded greater dependence on government support, many chose to avoid what they esteemed a handout subject to personal shame. As late as the mid-1960s, only about half of those eligible for welfare payments received them, and many of those enrolled took only part of the maximum allowance. The decades to follow became a slippery slope that led to a federal monopoly on "caring."

Q: In the 1960s my family went on welfare following the accident that killed my father and debilitated my mother. I recall that although my mother was severely injured and had been out of the marketplace for many years, she saw government support only as a temporary safety net. To her, living off the public dole was embarrassing, and she couldn't wait to get a job so she could take care of her family as the breadwinner.

Olasky: In the case of your family, society would say you were "worthy of relief" because your dependence was no fault of your own and you were unable to change the situation quickly. This was the case for Americans in the category of orphans, the aged, the incurably ill, children with one parent unable to support them, and adults suffering from temporary illness or accident. Still, through the 1960s most viewed welfare like your mother did—temporary and used only as a last alternative.

Since then, we've fought a war on poverty that has also struck down three of the best allies against poverty: shame, family, and God. When we take away shame, we take away deterrence. When we take away family, we take away the soil in which compassion grows best. When we kick out religion, we also remove the greatest incentive to help and be helped.

Q: Then, in the 1960s, was President Lyndon Johnson's "Great Society" a catalyst for this shift toward permanent welfare?

Olasky: Yes. Johnson declared "a Great Society: a society of success without squalor, beauty without barrenness, works of genius without wretchedness of poverty." Johnson's legislative triumphs—the Economic Opportunity Act, food stamps, Medicare, Medicaid, public works programs, and so on—were immense. The Great Society was truly a triumph of faith, the social gospel walking on earth. The speed of passage, unrivaled since the New Deal, showed disregard for real-life effects. In the words of biographer Doris Goodwin: "Pass the bill now, worry about its effects and implementation later."[14] This paved the way for the modern welfare state.

Q: Where did religious denominations stand on the Great Society?

Olasky: The National Council of Churches went on the record in 1968 with a proposal for "a guaranteed income" for everyone regardless of conduct. On the other hand, the US Catholic Conference stayed aloof, and largely white evangelical, fundamentalist, and Reformed churches responded negatively, as did their brethren among the black churches.

Q: Can you give an idea of the welfare explosion that occurred in the middle and late 1960s?

Olasky: During the 1950s, Aid for Dependent Children (AFDC) rolls rose by 17 percent—but during the 1960s the increase was 107 percent. About three-fourths of that increase occurred from

1965 to 1968 alone during a time of general prosperity and diminishing unemployment.

Q: What part did the retreat from the "social gospel" play in all of this?

Olasky: The answer to that question is lengthy but the short answer is, the "social gospel" emphasized God's love but not His holiness. It purported that basic human nature wasn't corrupt but was good; there were sins but not sin, evil acts but not evil. Problems arose from social conditions rather than inherent moral corruption. The social gospel declared that pressuring someone to work was cruel because a person who has faced "crushing misfortunes" wasn't at fault. The government was the best institution to transfer materials to the poor and change their environment. This led to crowding out private charities and mushrooming welfare programs.

Q: Shouldn't faith-based organizations share the blame for this "crowding out," for abdicating their responsibility to care for the poor?
Olasky: Most of us have grown up with personal peace and affluence. We like the way a welfare system—corrupt and inefficient though it is—removes the burden of basic care from our consciences. Church leaders forgot that compassion means "suffering with." They looked more and more to government to fulfill the biblical mandate to "care for the least of these."

Q: In your book, *Renewing American Compassion,* you use Ezekiel's vision of God connecting knee bones to thigh bones, bones with muscles, tendons and skin. Then God breathes new life into the creation so that it comes to life and stands on its feet.[15] **How does this relate to a new vision for American compassion?**

Olasky: We must envision a revitalized community where the parts of the community body are knit together to become a vast army. In *Renewing American Compassion,* I present seven principles to practicing responsible compassion that can restore the moral authority of our country as a beacon of freedom for the world:

• *Principle 1 Affiliation (connect with families and community).* Responsible compassion begins with first trying to restore family ties.

• *Principle 2 Bonding (help one-by-one).* Effective compassion recognizes that one size does not fit all—only a personalized, face-to-face approach offers any hope for turning lives around.

• *Principle 3 Categorization (treat different problems differently).* For example, those who are orphaned, elderly, or disabled receive aid. Jobless adults who are able and willing to work receive help in job finding.

• *Principle 4 Discernment (give responsibly).* Today, lack of discernment in helping the poor is rapidly producing an anti-compassion backlash as the better-off people, unable to distinguish between the truly needy and freeloaders, have an excuse to give to neither. We must help wisely, giving with our heads as well as our hearts.

• *Principle 5 Employment (demand work).* If individuals are paid not to work, unemployment multiplies, chronic poverty sets in, and generations of young people grow up not seeing work as a natural and essential part of life. Programs that stress employment, sometimes in creative new ways, need greater emphasis and deserve our support. Why shouldn't able-bodied homeless persons remove graffiti, clean up streets, and pull weeds at parks?

• *Principle 6 Freedom (reduce barriers to compassion and enterprise).* Perhaps this was the wisdom behind charity workers' past reluctance to ask government to come in and take charge of the poor—they chose instead to show perpetual dependency.

• *Principle 7 God (reliance on the Creator and His providence).* Successful antipoverty work, past and present, has allowed the poor to earn authentic self-esteem, not by offering easy, feel-good praise, but by pointing them to God.

42

How City Government Can Collaborate with Churches

Greg Burris

For almost a decade I had the opportunity to see things from a chair in which few get to sit. As city manager of Springfield, Missouri, I got to see things most citizens either never see or only see in snapshots on the evening news. I call it "Breaking the Bubble, Boiling a Frog, and Moving the Needle."

From that chair, I got to see the thousands of moving parts that create a community and how they influence each other. I got to see the unintended consequences. I got to see the victories, and the years of work accomplished behind the curtain by people who will never see the spotlight.

I got to see the complexities and the struggles. I saw things that occurred in my community that made me grimace . . . and I saw things that made me swell with pride.

Before taking the job as city manager, I lived in a bubble.

Breaking the Bubble

In fact, I've lived in a bubble for most of my life.

Growing up, I witnessed poverty and other social issues mostly through the media. We didn't have cable TV so I saw poverty and other issues portrayed on crime dramas, a few documentaries (but not many; they were too depressing), and even some sitcoms (typically as quirky, but funny, homeless characters). As you can see from these experiences, I must have known a lot about poverty and other related social issues. Well, maybe not.

After becoming city manager, I quickly discovered I didn't know squat about poverty, the people living in poverty, or what they needed to climb out of poverty. I also didn't understand the hundreds of factors that impact poverty, how poverty impacts a community, or how a community can impact poverty.

I also didn't realize how hard it would be to turn away from these issues and pretend they didn't exist in my city. After all, as city manager, I considered Springfield to be *my* city.

Seeing Is Believing

When speaking to groups about this issue, I often state that if someone has a car, a garage door opener, and Netflix, they really don't have to deal with many community problems. They can just drive home, pull their car into the garage, and escape inside their home. Modern conveniences have removed much of our need (and perhaps some of our desire) to build a community. It's easy for us to stay inside with our technologies and just nest.

What we need is a way for people to see behind the curtains of their communities. Once they see their own community's challenges (and all communities have challenges) and the good work being done to address those challenges, they're "infected" with knowledge. Once you see your community's challenges, you can't unsee them. A word of warning: if you decide to take your community's challenges head-on, you won't receive unanimous support.

Infecting a Community

How does a community address any large-scale, complex challenge? For example, how does a community try to reduce poverty? Will one more governmental program do it? Can a ten-member task force get it done? What if I issue a memo or elected officials pass a bill? I suppose a leader has three choices.

First, a community can ignore the problem and hope it goes away (or at least can be avoided until it's the next generation's problem). Passive resistance may come in the form of just ignoring the data, claiming the problem isn't as big as it's being made out to be, stating that "those people" are getting what they deserve, or just sitting on their hands. Active resistance may appear in the form of direct requests to halt the public dialogue about the community's challenges for fear awareness about the issue will somehow make things worse or will make the community look bad.

Or a community can add a program here and a policy there, talk about the problem a bit, and sort of poke the problem with a finger.

But I propose that the only way a community can really address issues as big and gnarly as poverty is by educating the populace about the issue ("infecting" them with knowledge), mobilizing and motivating an army of organizations and volunteers, then aligning its resources: nonprofits, government agencies, churches and other faith-based groups, businesses, and community leaders. I believe nothing less will work. The government can't do it alone. Nonprofits can't do it alone. The faith community can't do it alone. It requires a partnership of all sectors working together.

During our experience, Springfield's faith community stepped up. It was almost as if they were just waiting to be asked. And when we asked, they responded in a big way.

However, I must admit, there's a need for some balance. While we don't necessarily need a front-page story in the newspaper every day proclaiming "Our City Has Poverty," there's a need for a counterweight of positive messaging, which we provided. Dave alluded to this in chapter 40 about the Labor of Love event to honor job creators.

Every community has its challenges. Some treat those challenges as dirty little secrets that no one should discuss publicly. Others take those challenges head-on. Personally, I believe community leaders gain political capital when they acknowledge their community's problems and firmly state, "We aren't looking the other way. We're taking this head-on!"

I believe that during the next few decades globally conscious companies will want to locate in communities that acknowledge their challenges and show the guts to take on those challenges. We can't nibble around the edges of our community problems and provide nothing more than window dressing. The issues are too complex and too deeply ingrained to move the needle in that way. We must dive in!

Boiling a Frog

Do you know how to boil a frog? I've never actually tried it, but I've always heard that if you try to place a frog in boiling water, it will immediately jump out of the pot. But if you place a frog in tepid water and slowly raise the temperature, the frog will gradually adjust to the changing temperature and will remain in the pot, even until the water reaches the boiling point.

We do the same thing. Most of us react similarly to slow-changing macrotrends. For example, if the free and reduced lunch rate in your local public school system suddenly increased from 20 percent to 50 percent in one year, your community would react strongly and quickly (and correctly so). They would move to action!

But if the free and reduced lunch rate in that same school increased gradually by 1 or 2 percent each year over a span of twenty-five years, your community likely wouldn't react as strongly or quickly. Instead, they would adjust their expectations and their view of the world each year. So, when the rate increased from

20 percent to 21 percent in the first year, their reaction might be, "Gosh, that's a shame. I hope it doesn't continue. What did we need from the grocery store?" And each year, that same type of reaction might be expected. Then, all a sudden, after twenty-five years the community wakes up to a 50 percent level and wonders how this happened "overnight."

Obviously, it didn't happen overnight, it happened slowly over time. But our community adjusted their view of the world each year, and life went on.

Empathy Changes Everything

It seems to me there's been a loss of empathy in our modern world. We retreat too easily to an "us vs. them" narrative.

I attribute some of this decreasing empathy to the source of our news (if we look for news at all). As social media and cable news options allow us each to seek our own "echo chamber" of news, our society is quickly moving from a one-size-fits-all to one-size-fits-Al model. At one time, most of us got our news from Uncle Walter—Walter Cronkite—considered the most trusted man in the country at that time. Now we have hundreds of "news sources" to choose from. These "news sources" are available in any flavor, from far right to far left and every shade in between. This allows each of us (including Al) to find a "news source" that reinforces our preconceived notions of how we believe the world works. Right or wrong, our preconceived notions are reinforced and validated, and we become even more deeply entrenched in our views.

Getting our news within these echo chambers results in a breakdown in the "bridging" social capital of our communities. As a result, we find it increasingly difficult to relate to people who don't look like us, don't live in our part of town, don't go to our church, or don't have our same social or economic status. We find it increasingly difficult to relate to their challenges. And soon, they become "them." A senior pastor told me he attributes some of this reduction of empathy to the faith community. He said that in previous generations the rich and poor attended church services together, possibly sitting in the same pew. Now, he explained, there are "rich churches" and "poor churches," and many people with resources don't personally know even one person who is struggling to make ends meet. He feels this has reduced our ability to empathize with others. How would the world be different if people could empathize with those who are different from themselves?

Moving the Needle: The Give 5 Program

Well, if all this wasn't complicated enough, let me pile on a couple more layers of complexity, then offer a possible strategy.

- Approximately ten thousand baby boomers will turn sixty-five every day for the next seventeen years. That's an amazing tidal wave of talent and resources, many of whom will be seeking new purpose and meaning in their lives after having just retired from the thing that supplied much of their purpose and meaning previously—their jobs.
- According to the US surgeon general, the largest health risk for this population is not cancer or heart disease—it's isolation.
- As mentioned above, the levels of empathy in our communities are dropping. Similarly, our communities need to build their "bridging" social capital by getting people out of their houses and from behind their keyboards and phones to interact with other people, especially people who are different from themselves.

- Federal and state funding is dropping for the nonprofits in our communities that do much of the frontline work to address these community challenges. Can nonprofits survive, especially as we approach zero unemployment (more jobs than workers) and they find it even more difficult to compete for talent in a hypercompetitive labor market?

- The largest transfer of wealth in the history of the world has begun—from the boomers to their heirs. This transfer will see a handover of about thirty trillion dollars.[16]

So, what if we could address all these trends with one strategy? The good news is, we can. We created a new community-strengthening program called Give 5 (SGFGive5.org) that we've implemented in Springfield, Missouri. And it's working.

It's a "civic matchmaking" program that lets our citizens see behind the curtains by learning more about their community, including touring twenty-three nonprofits doing key work in our city. This is all accomplished in five program days, typically one day per week over five weeks. After the fifth program day, participants can sign a "letter of intent" identifying the nonprofits they commit to help. At the graduation ceremony, participants reveal where they'll volunteer, and we host a "media event" when we take their picture with the executive director, staff, and/or board members of the selected nonprofit. We then blitz social media with these photos to pique additional interest in the program. We want people saying, "Hey! What's Mary doing? What's this Give 5 thing?"

The program is called Give 5 because we ask each graduate to volunteer for at least five hours per month for five months. We set the bar low so it wouldn't intimidate potential applicants, but we also knew that these program graduates would volunteer a lot more than five hours per month once they saw behind the curtain and connected to their community through a cause that touched their heart.

Give 5 offers an opportunity for this wave of retiring baby boomers—with their many skills, talents, and strong work ethic—to find renewed purpose and meaning in their lives in a fun and social way that gets people off the couch, promotes "bridging" social capital, builds empathy, and assists nonprofits who are increasingly reliant on volunteers and philanthropy to operate.

One of the best things about the Give 5 program is that it can be replicated and implemented in small, medium, and large communities.. What if every community operated a Give 5 program? What if this wave of retiring baby boomers turned out to be the most powerful force mobilized to renew lives and communities in the world? What if we started today?

43

Peacemakers' Approach to Church-State Partnerships

Rich and Robyn Wilkerson

I arrived one morning at our church facility in Miami where we shared a building with Dade County Foster Care. They oversaw five thousand foster children from their office, so we had a continual stream of foster kids and foster parents on our elevators and staircases.

Pandemonium had overtaken the lobby that morning. People were running around, some crying. "There's an Amber Alert," one person told me. "One of the little girls from upstairs went missing this morning. We can't find her. She's four years old." It was 10 a.m.

The police arrived, and teams went out searching, but the little girl wasn't found until 10 p.m. She was safe and had been sitting all day at a public bus stop two blocks from her grandparents' house where she lived. Her brother had found her. They asked, "What are you doing here?" She replied, "I'm gonna go see my mama." Her mom was in prison five hours away.

Our ministry leader, Linda Freeman, couldn't get the incident out of her head. Three days later she came into my office. "Pastor Rich, I found out there are 7,500 kids in Dade County who have parents in prison somewhere in this state," she said. "I'm going up to the Lowell Correctional Institute in Ocala to ask that warden if I can pull together fifty kids and bring them to see their mothers."

We encourage an entrepreneurial culture with our staff, and I loved the idea. A month later, Linda had received approval and started taking busloads of kids to that prison. You've never seen emotion until you sit at those prison gates and watch those children see their mothers for the first time in years. They run screaming, hollering, and weeping into their mothers' arms. While there, the reunited moms and kids play games together, and we bring utensils and food so the moms can make sandwiches to serve their kids. The emotions upon leaving are even harder to watch. Through the years, our church has taken 2,800 children to that prison to visit their mothers. Five years ago, the state of Florida took our idea and made it a state-funded program for any 501(c)(3) that bids on it. The irony is that now we must bid to conduct the program we started!

The story of how we do things like that at Peacemakers began two years after we planted the church. We were broke. My wife, Robyn, and I had emptied our pocketbooks personally into this church plant, and we didn't know what to do. We weren't upset that we had no money. We didn't feel it was our money anyway, but how were we going to minister without money?

One day Robyn, who never, ever reads the newspaper, came to the breakfast table where I was doing my devotions. In her hands was a local newspaper.

"I came across this little ad in the want ads," she said. "It says, 'Request for proposal is being granted for day camps.' I'm going to check it out."

She went down to the county office, got the application and thought, *People fill out these documents every day. How hard can it be?* Six weeks later, the proposal she had created looked like a doctoral dissertation. It was an inch thick, and very detailed. She won the two hundred thousand dollars contract, beating out dozens of other entities and overcoming the county's skepticism about giving money to a church. Peacemakers held an eight-week day camp for kids ages four to fourteen. We've done that day camp now for eighteen years.

A revolution had begun in our approach to inner-city ministry. Robyn continued applying for grants for various projects, and we continued receiving grants from government entities—city, county, state, and federal. Today, more than half of our budget is funded by community agencies, and many of our 130 employees, except for me as the pastor, are subsidized by different pieces of contracts we bid on in the public arena. We are a church first, and a social services agency second. The two entities are not separate nonprofits but one, operating as Peacemakers Family Center. Our board of directors is from our community and are all of African descent. Our community leaders love us.

In nearly two decades, Peacemakers has started many creative programs for public schools, after-school programs, camps, and much more. For example, our employees go into the Miami-Dade school system and teach health and teen-pregnancy prevention. At the federal level, we had the number one teen-pregnancy prevention program in the United States. We're proud to report that in our county there's been a steady decrease in teen pregnancies. We also run the number one AmeriCorps site in Florida, and Robyn and I have been to the White House twice.

Because we are a social services agency, people can walk into our building seven days a week and apply for food stamps or unemployment. We have offices in the lobby of our church where people can receive emergency services and talk with a licensed social worker about applying for services. To provide these services and fulfill our many contracts across many government agencies is a highly complex endeavor. We staff each contract separately and hire people who can do multiple things and have a can-do attitude.

We get criticism all the time from both sides. On one side are governmental leaders who don't want us to get any money. But when we deliver with excellence and establish an impeccable track record through the years, they can hardly deny us. Everybody knows we deliver on what we promise, so our excellence overcomes their antagonism.

On the other side, we get criticism from Christians who don't think we should take government money. To be honest, that was probably our default position before we began this type of work, but it doesn't stand up to scrutiny. In fact, it's anticonstitutional thinking. Two recent presidents wrote executive orders stating emphatically that it is not constitutional to deny religious organizations the opportunity to receive government contracts. Nonprofits like Catholic charities and the Salvation Army have been doing effective ministry this way for decades. Why shouldn't we as churches access those dollars for people?

Peacemakers doesn't exist because of our bright idea. We were never trying to come up with a different paradigm for doing ministry. We didn't expect to become experts on poverty in the United States, but because of our church location, we discovered resources and people already in place that we can use for ministry purposes. This ministry also pushes us continually into the marketplace and the public sphere. We have influence in arenas where a lot of people choose to live in darkness. Whether they are poor families or multimillionaires, friendly politicians or antagonistic agency workers, our ministry approach forces us to interact with them in their world. If that's not being salt and light, I don't know what is.

Peacemakers' approach is complicated, difficult, and different from the way churches typically operate, so I know it's not for everyone. But any of us can be alert to the small opportunities around us, which sometimes open whole new pathways to compassionate ministry.

You can learn more about Peacemakers and its programs at www.peacemakers.com.

44

Pursuing Government Grants and Keeping Both Eyes Wide Open

Stanley Carlson-Thies

W e first met Stanley Carlson-Thies in 2001 when he worked at the White House Office of Faith-Based and Community Initiatives (FBCI). Stanley's reputation preceded him as one of Governor George W. Bush's architects for faith-based engagement and as a go-to person for helping churches and nonprofit organizations build a firewall of protection when pursuing government funding. Stanley's value to the faith community and government was evidenced by his rising above the political divide to work with President Barack Obama's Advisory Council on Faith-Based and Neighborhood Partnerships concerning religious hiring practices and other church-state issues. Ronald Reagan was credited as saying, "If you get in bed with government, you may not get a good night's sleep." Stanley and I co-authored *Revolution of Compassion* to show faith-based organizations how to keep both eyes wide open if they plan to accept government resources to deliver social services. Here are a few key questions we posed to Stanley recently for *CityServe* about the same subject.

Q: What's the first thing you would say to a faith-based organization considering government funding?
Carlson-Thies: The overarching question that every faith-based organizations should ask is: Is government funding—city, state, or federal—a snare that will undermine the Christian message of

your church or nonprofit, or a support that will allow the ministry to extend the help it gives?

Government money isn't free—it comes with restrictions and requirements. However, many of the conditions on government funding have been modified over the past two decades specifically so that faith-based organizations—churches and self-standing religious nonprofits—can participate in government funding programs. Still, the requirements and restrictions need to be evaluated prayerfully and carefully. Then, if what the government is looking for is aligned with the goals and methods of your church's service outreach, the government funds can help your church expand its contribution to the good of the community.

Q: What is the context behind government outsourcing social services to faith-based groups?

Carlson-Thies: Most of the social services the government provides, such as substance-abuse treatment, low-income housing, help for the survivors of trafficking, reentry for former prisoners, and after-school programs, are provided by private organizations, although paid for by the government. Typically, religious or secular groups were providing those same services before the government even decided to become active, so it's natural to think of partnerships that combine the government's money with a private group's expertise and passion to serve.

That idea of partnerships was championed by President George W. Bush, who, shortly after taking office in early 2001, created the White House Office of Faith-Based and Community Initiatives. A major job of that office was to ensure that religious organizations were able to compete equally with secular groups for federal funds to provide services, whether those federal funds are given out as federal grants or are passed on to state or local government agencies, which then award the money to private organizations. He also created similar Centers for Faith-Based and Community Initiatives in major federal departments such as HUD, HHS, Justice, Labor, FEMA, and the VA. All these specialized offices monitor federal rules, encourage officials to regard faith-based and smaller community organizations as valuable channels to people and communities in need, help to answer questions about federal funds, and resolve conflicts with federal, state, and local officials.

Q: Didn't this concept of government and faith-based partnerships begin under President Bill Clinton?

Carlson-Thies: Yes, President Bush's action was preceded by Congress passing Charitable Choice rules during the 1990s to ensure a level playing field in welfare and substance-abuse treatment funding—rules signed into law by President Bill Clinton. And after President Bush, President Obama maintained the federal faith-based initiative, although he put more stress on seeking the support of community and faith groups for his administration's political priorities. Now, under President Donald Trump, all the level-playing-field rules remain in place, and the Centers for Faith-Based and Community Initiatives in the major federal departments are ready to help you understand and navigate federal funding programs.

Q: How does a church create a firewall to protect its mission and methodologies?

Carlson-Thies: Keep in mind that government and church remain distinct institutions, even though there's overlap in aims and methods. Therefore, churches and other religious organizations need to proceed wisely when evaluating whether to apply for a government grant or contract to support the services they offer. Note that grant or contract funds cannot be used to pay for Bible studies, prayer, discipleship training, or other specifically religious activities or materials, and all explicitly religious activities must be kept separate and distinct from the government-funded services. However, your church or nonprofit can pay for those biblical activities and materials with private funds and then offer them, on a voluntary basis, to participants in the government-funded activities. And sometimes, as with federal funding for child care, the government money goes to the family or a student or patient in the form of a voucher, certificate, or scholarship. In this situation, when the funding attaches to a person or family, then the family or person can pick any provider they choose, and the provider can weave religion into every aspect of the government-funded services. Why? Because in this arrangement the student or family chooses the faith-filled service rather than a government official who dictates that the student or family must be subject to a religious experience.

Q: What are some key questions a church should ask itself when evaluating a partnership with government?

Carlson-Thies: How good is the fit between the services the government wants to pay for and the ministries your church desires to carry out? Your ministries often serve a broad range of people in an expansive way. For example, you may have an after-school program that integrates physical recreation, mentorship in life skills, and spiritual guidance in a single program that is open to all the young people in the neighborhood. In contrast, government programs are typically targeted: sports plus messaging about the dangers of substance abuse only directed to at-risk preteens and without any specific religious message. Will it harm your outreach to reconfigure your program to the government's pattern? Don't let the search for money undermine the mission God has placed on your heart.

If Christian teachings and activities are an essential part of how you serve youth or families, be wary of tearing that faith-heart out of the service just to get government money. If you do, you'll undermine your mission and may ineffectively help those who receive the changed services. If your church does decide that dividing the explicitly religious elements of a program from the secular service elements would harm the integrity of the program, then see if voucher or scholarship funding is available, rather than a grant or contract, or stick to private funds.

Q: What should a church or faith-based organization be aware of if it is awarded a grant or contract?

Carlson-Thies: If there is a good fit of aims, methods, and beneficiaries, then take a close look at the fine print of the grant or contract, and don't neglect the other regulations or laws the fine print refers to. If your church accepts the funds, it is also accepting all those rules. Unsure of what a requirement means? Ask for help from a lawyer, CityServe staff, or other faith organizations that have applied for the same funding.

Government programs do (and should) require financial accountability and reports on who was served and what difference it made. Be sure you know how to track funds, hours, and outcomes, and have reliable systems and routines in place. An essential practice for a church that accepts government funds is establishing a separate bank account into which those dollars go and out of which the legitimate expenses are paid. That keeps church and state in their distinct orbits and prevents auditors from having to rummage through the church accounts to find out where the government dollars went. And keep accurate time sheets that preserve the distinctions: the youth minister can direct the government-funded program, but the time sheet must show which hours were spent on the government-supported service and which hours were in gospel ministry. Clear distinctions ensure that the government funds aren't mistakenly spent for disallowed purposes.

Another practice that can be beneficial is to create a separate faith-based nonprofit to operate the government-funded services. This is a best practice if your church is planning on more than minimal engagement with government programs. A separate nonprofit with its own board of directors, bank account, and policies establishes a strong firewall between the church and the government-funded services—and aids in running the community-serving programs appropriately. Of course, this nonprofit will be faith-based, but it will be dedicated to loving your neighbors as Jesus calls you to do, a high calling but a different one than the church's vital tasks of worship, training disciples, and evangelism.

Q: Can you speak to the concern that churches have regarding hiring rights?

Carlson-Thies: Are you worried that your practice of hiring only believers is illegal? Don't be. The Civil Rights Act of 1964 has always protected religious hiring by religious organizations—not just churches but also religious nonprofits—and it protects you not only when you are hiring pastors, religion teachers, and chaplains but when you hire janitors, caseworkers, and "secular" teachers. Government funding doesn't cancel out the protection for religious hiring (in limited cases a lawyer may need to help you challenge on constitutional grounds a hiring restriction attached to government funds). But be watchful: religious organizations can get into trouble if it seems that they care seriously about religious qualifications only when a gay applicant or someone of a different ethnicity or race shows up. Be consistently religious in your policies and practices and from one applicant and decision to another. Churches, when they hire or fire "ministerial" staff, have even greater protection than do religious charities because of the First Amendment.

Q: Do you have a final message for churches and faith-based organizations?

Carlson-Thies: Don't let the requirements attached to government funds overwhelm you. Being more systematic with records, outcome measurements, time records, and financial details can help your ministry become more effective and more accountable. CityServe and experienced faith-based organizations can help you get started and assist you with questions and challenges.

Utilize the help of the faith-based initiative. Ever since presidents Clinton and Bush got the partnership ball rolling, the federal government, some state governments, and some local governments have designated certain officials and offices, often with a label like "faith-based initiative," to be ready to help you locate suitable funding, understand restrictions and freedoms, and establish the necessary accountability practices. Google "faith-based" and the name of the government program or agency that is of interest and you should be able to locate which official or office can help guide your next steps.

Go after government funding for the sake of those who need your good service. The point isn't simply to find another source of funds but to extend the good you do in your community. If your services honor God by being excellent and effective, then it's good for everyone that more people can access them because of government financial assistance. And by being part of the network of services the government supports—if participation is right for your church—you help to keep churches from being marginalized.

The Institutional Religious Freedom Alliance advocates to Congress and the presidential administration for the religious freedom that faith-based organizations need so they can serve and flourish. Through the Sacred Sector Initiative, IRFA equips ministries to understand religious freedom, to adopt appropriate policies and practices, and to speak up to the public and government about their services and the freedoms they need. For more information, visit www.irfalliance.org.

45

Legal Protections for Churches Engaged in Compassion

H. Robert Showers, Esq.

As legal and cultural landscapes continue to shift, risk management for churches and nonprofits is no longer an optional planning tool used only by those with extra time and resources. It's a necessity. Without it, churches and nonprofits run the risk that their beloved ministry may one day come to a grinding and unexpected halt when the IRS questions their charitable receipts, or when a member announces he is gay, or when a trusted childcare volunteer is exposed as an abuser.

Here is some guidance on legal issues that every church and nonprofit should be aware of.

Legal Risks for Food Pantries and Distribution Centers

Both nonprofit food banks and their donors are protected from lawsuits claiming negligence under the Bill Emerson Good Samaritan Food Donation Act. Under the Good Samaritan Act, the nonprofit is only liable for actions of gross negligence, intentional misconduct, or violations of food or product regulations for food/product-related injury by a recipient. Still, the food pantry should establish clear written guidelines outlining what types of food donations it will receive and what inspection procedures its employees and volunteers will follow. This will demonstrate that the pantry has taken reasonable steps to ensure the items are still within applicable regulations and not dented, moldy, spoiled, or otherwise damaged.

Regarding nonfood items, the standard is a bit vague, as potential liability would depend on any number of factors. However, a good first step is to develop a clear written policy about what items are and are not acceptable and to review the policy with staff, volunteers, and the public. Such a policy should consider the location of the center and its target demographics to determine what items would be of the greatest mutual benefit. Additionally, the center should monitor product recall lists to ensure donated items aren't on the list, removing all recalled items from the center's shelves. Finally, the center should have waivers and releases to the effect that consumers assume the liability and understand that the center hasn't inspected items for safety.

Receiving Donated Property

The primary concerns for a church when a gift of real property is being offered are (1) whether the donor has clear title to the property and (2) consideration of potential environmental concerns. "Clear title" means that the donor is the owner of the property, they have full authority to convey it to the church, and there are no liens on the property (i.e., mortgage or judgment liens). Further, the donor should be able to provide, or allow the church to obtain, both a recent survey plat of the property showing the current metes and bounds, and an environmental survey of the property to ensure that the property is appropriate for the church's purposes. If the church intends to use the property for ministry purposes, it will also need to work with a knowledgeable attorney to determine whether the desired use is permitted within the current zoning ordinances or whether it will need to seek a special use permit or special exception from the local government.

To determine whether the donor will be able to take a deduction, the parties will need to have the real property professionally appraised. Finally, you need to "look a gift horse in the mouth" and do a Phase 1 Environmental Site Assessment or you could assume massive liability unawares.

Unrelated Business Income Tax (UBIT)

Many excellent fund-raising ideas involve pursuing some sort of venture that brings the potential for a nonprofit or church to realize income that is not related to its tax-exempt purpose. While income is not a negative thing, this type of income generates a tax, otherwise known as the Unrelated Business Income Tax (UBIT). This can happen in a variety of situations, from a nonprofit youth camp that leases its facilities for weekend business conventions, to a church that sells Christmas trees at twice the market cost to raise money for a missions trip, or a church that leases its parking lot to a local university during the school year.

First, familiarize yourself with the following principles that apply to the UBIT:

1. the income is from a trade or business
2. the trade or business is regularly carried on
3. the income is not substantially related to the exempt purpose of the entity

Second, know the exceptions. For example, while UBIT generally applies to income from land, there are exceptions available when the use is substantially related, and when the property is not debt financed. If your church or nonprofit wants to undertake an unrelated (or even a related) business venture on a larger scale, you should also consider the possibility of conducting that business through a wholly owned subsidiary entity.

Third-Party Facility Use

If your church or nonprofit chooses to use its facilities to serve the community, you will need to take proper steps at the outset to avoid a number of potential problems. Allowing someone onto your property is, in many ways, an intimate act and should only be done with careful planning. One of the first mistakes many churches make is to allow use of their premises without any written agreement as to the terms or the types of uses permitted and prohibited. For example, if a church won't allow gay marriages to be performed on its premises, it can't enforce that restriction unless the restriction is included in a facility-use policy, or unless its restrictions are somehow otherwise tied to the terms controlling the use of the property.

Allowing use of your premises can also impact your tax exemption and may endanger your status if you dedicate too much use to nonexempt purposes. Your church may also come under the purview of your state's public accommodation nondiscrimination laws. Although these laws often have exceptions for religious organizations, more and more states are prohibiting discrimination based on sexual orientation by places of public accommodation. Be sure to consult an attorney to determine if holding your premises open for public use could cause problems by conflicting with your exempt purpose and religious beliefs.

Child and Youth Protection

Youth and childcare programs often form a significant part of a nonprofit or church's ministry. It's easy to get involved with serving children in the community, but much trickier to develop proper safeguards to shield your program from liabilities. There are at least four key steps that you should implement.

First, you must have a program to screen workers and volunteers. Getting people to work with youth can be a challenge, so it's tempting to welcome anyone who's willing to help with open arms and to check them out later. Check them out *before* you welcome them.

Second, after you've conducted proper background and reference checks, make sure to train your workers properly. If volunteers and employees don't know how to report suspected abuse or even spot it, your liability increases significantly.

Third, make sure you supervise your workers properly. Training isn't sufficient—supervision ensures that all staff and workers are following the policies and plans you have in place.

Finally, practice protocols that dictate exactly how to report and investigate alleged abuse. When the allegation is made, you need to have a system to address the allegation quickly and clearly, without hesitation.

International Ministry and Fund-Raising

More and more frequently churches and nonprofits are doing ministry through partnerships and relationships with overseas organizations and individuals. US churches and nonprofits are raising funds in the United States to support those laboring internationally. While these are often noble pursuits, they can run afoul of laws restricting the transfer of funds to such organizations by a US tax-exempt organization.

Because the IRS has no way of knowing whether the recipient of the money overseas is a truly exempt organization, they are much more skeptical about international transfers. Their suspicion isn't without merit. Cases abound of scam artists around the globe who hoodwink well-meaning US donors. Though the project seems genuine, the funds are diverted for personal benefit. Add to that the additional scrutiny of the Office of Foreign Asset Control looking for potential violations of trade embargoes and sanctions, and it can be highly risky for a church or nonprofit to send money—whether in large or small sums—to foreign recipients. For these types of relationships, it's important to consult with an attorney since they are best structured on a case-by-case basis.

As a rule of thumb, however, the IRS is looking for factors that demonstrate the US charitable organization's control over the use and direction of the funds. Any such transfers must be structured so it is apparent the US charity is not just a temporary resting place for funds as they exit the country.

Disclaimer: This information in this chapter is provided for general information purposes only and is not a substitute for legal advice particular to your situation. No recipients of this memo should act or refrain from acting solely on the basis of this memorandum without seeking professional legal counsel. Simms Showers, LLP expressly disclaims all liability relating to actions taken or not taken based solely on the content of this memorandum. Please contact H. Robert Showers, Esq. at hrshowers@simmsshowerslaw.com or at 703-771-4671 for legal advice for nonprofits, churches, and businesses that will meet your specific needs.

Additional Legal Resources

Coleman, Justin, and H. Robert Showers. "'Always Look a Gift Horse in the Mouth': How to Avoid an Excess Benefit Transaction." *Simms Showers, LLP* (blog), August 31, 2017. https://www.simmsshowerslaw.com/always-look-a-gift-horse-in-the-mouth-how-to-avoid-an-excess-benefit-transaction/.

Hebda, Daniel. "Unrelated Business Income Tax Primer for Nonprofits." *Simms Showers, LLP* (blog), August 3, 2016. https://www.simmsshowerslaw.com/unrelated-business-income-tax-primer-for-nonprofits/.

Showers, H. Robert. "Church Third-Party Use Agreements: What You Don't Know Can Hurt You!." *Simms Showers, LLP* (blog), August 3, 2016. https://www.simmsshowerslaw.com/church-third-party-use-agreements-what-you-dont-know-can-hurt-you/.

Showers, H. Robert. "Granting Money from a US Charity or Church to a Foreign Individual or NGO: Substantial Risks and Best Practices." *Simms Showers, LLP* (blog), August 3, 2016. https://www.simmsshowerslaw. com/granting-money-from-a-u-s-charity-or-church-to-a-foreign-individual-or-ngo-substantial-risks-and-best-practices/.

Showers, H. Robert. "Minimize Child Abuse—How to Do Excellent Background Checks for Child and Financial Protection—Part 1." *Simms Showers, LLP* (blog), July 12, 2017. https://www.simmsshowerslaw.com/minimize-child-abuse-how-to-do-excellent-background-checks-for-child-and-financial-protection-part-1/.

Showers, H. Robert, and Bethany Horvat. "Protecting Your Church in Troubled Times: A Guide to Establishing Church Security Protocols." *Simms Showers, LLP* (blog), February 14, 2018. https://www.simmsshowerslaw.com/protecting-your-church-in-troubled-times-a-guide-to-establishing-church-security-protocols/.

Showers, H. Robert. "Successful Church Assimilation of Sex Offenders." *Simms Showers, LLP* (blog), August 3, 2016. https://www.simmsshowerslaw.com/successful-church-assimilation-of-sex-offenders/.

Showers, H. Robert. "What You Don't Know Will Hurt You: Myths and Misconceptions About Church/Nonprofit Employment Liability." *Simms Showers, LLP* (blog), August 3, 2016. https://www.simmsshowerslaw.com/what-you-dont-know-will-hurt-you-myths-and-misconceptions-about-churchnonprofit-employment-liability/.

Smith, Elyse. "'Go Out to All the Nations,' But Sign This Waiver First." *Simms Showers, LLP* (blog), August 3, 2016. https://www.simmsshowerslaw.com/go-out-to-all-the-nations-but-sign-this-waiver-first/.

46

Responsible Compassion

Dave Donaldson

This is an interview with Dave Donaldson, co-founder of Convoy of Hope and CityServe International.

Q: What experiences shaped your understanding of the term "responsible compassion"?

Donaldson: After the death of my father, our family moved into a fixer-upper he had purchased a year earlier. One day our pastor, Ray Horwege, huddled us kids on the front yard, gathering us like a quarterback ready to call a play. The yard had become a weed-infested patch of dirt. Pastor Horwege told us the church board had voted to bless us with a front lawn. We jumped with glee over the thought of having real grass to play on. Our euphoria was soon dampened. "There's just one catch," he continued. "You won't receive the entire lawn at once. We'll start with one strip of grass. If you care for that piece and keep it green, we'll keep adding strips until you have a full lawn." Days later the first strip of sod grass was laid in our front yard, close to the house. The neighbors gawked with curiosity, and one even asked, "Who's buried under there?"

At first, the grass received much attention and appeared to respond favorably to our tender loving care. Yet over time, other activities such as golfing, camping, and, oh yes, school took precedence over caring for that strip of grass. Eventually the bright green grass faded into a brownish-yellow layer of dirt. Pastor kept his word and never brought us another strip of grass. He taught us a priceless lesson: if someone is gracious enough to give you something, you have a responsibility to be a good steward of that gift. Genuine compassion requires responsible giving *and* receiving.

Q: What's the responsibility of the person receiving compassion?

Donaldson: The Israelites marched toward a goal—the Promised Land. Once they got there, God stopped sending the heavenly manna, and the people raised their own crops. The manna and quail had been a temporary provision until the people were able to fend for themselves. We see this echoed in the story of Ruth. Hebrew farmers were to make some of their produce available to the poor: " 'When you reap the harvest of your land, do not reap to the very edges of your field or gather the gleanings of your harvest. Leave them for the poor and for the foreigner residing among you. I am the LORD your God' " (Leviticus 23:22). As illustrated by Ruth, she worked in Boaz's field and gleaned after the reapers to provide for her family until she was later adopted into his household. It's interesting that one of the things that attracted Boaz to Ruth was her work ethic.

> Endless handouts can erode a person's self-worth, allow their dreams to die, and create a lifestyle where survival becomes the only goal.

Relief must be part of a continuum of care that leads a person and family towards sustainability. Endless handouts can erode a person's self-worth, allow their dreams to die, and create a lifestyle where survival becomes the only goal.

The Bible encourages us to, "carry each other's burdens" but also admonishes, "each one should carry their own load."[17] The apostle Paul wanted the church of Galatia to discover the proper balance of personal responsibility, whether as a person who gives or one who receives compassion.

Some contend, "Why shouldn't able-bodied homeless persons clean up streets, remove graffiti, and pull weeds?" Of course, this so-called culture of dependency doesn't apply to every person living on public assistance. There are millions who need and deserve society's safety net. Perhaps they can't work due to physical or mental illness.

The Bible addresses the need to discern who truly deserves help: "Give proper recognition to those widows who are really in need" (1 Timothy 5:3). History teaches us that redistributing wealth without training people how to create it themselves is careless compassion. As Marvin Olasky says, "Aid given with 'no strings attached' and 'no questions asked' may feed the ego of the giver . . . but it can often hurt more than it helps."

Q: What's the role of one's own family in responsible compassion?

Donaldson: Jesus condemned the Pharisees because they donated funds toward public causes while neglecting the needs of their own families.[18] Of course, Jesus was speaking to their self-promotional motive for giving, but He also underscored a family-first policy. Historically, when people needed financial support, charities tried to raise it from relatives and others with personal ties. This approach enforced family accountability and set a pattern for the next generation. Sadly, the nuclear family is disappearing along with the family safety net.

Over the years, when I've met a person in crisis I've asked, "Where is your family? Can they help you?" Overwhelmingly the response has been, "I no longer have a relationship with them," or "They're in no better shape than I am." The absent father and disjointed family have led to a titanic paternal shift in our society: the head of the household is now Uncle Sam.

Q: What's the role of government in responsible compassion?

Donaldson: I attended a conference in Washington, DC. A congresswoman walked to the platform amidst a wave of applause. To the attendees she was a model advocate for the poor, working tirelessly to garner more funds and programs for the less fortunate. "I'm pleased to announce that we've grown to over thirty million people on food stamps." The news brought a thunderous ovation, and many leaped to their feet. Remaining seated I queried, *They're celebrating more people on food stamps?*

Today, the Supplemental Nutrition Assistance Program (SNAP) boasts over forty million people who are dependent on government for food security. Jubilation over more people hooked on the government's Kool-Aid only exposes our warped understanding of genuine compassion. Having personally grown up on welfare after my father's death and mother's debilitation, I know how it can be both a blessing and a curse. It was a blessing to live in a country that caught us when everything beneath us collapsed. It was a curse to watch my mom pay for groceries with stamps, to sit in the emergency ward while rich kids went first, and to beg for money to pay for Little League equipment. Granted, there are those who work the system and are lazy, unwilling to change their situation, but if you peel the layers down far enough, you won't find many people living off the public dole who are celebrating.

Some contend that if the government would step aside, the faith community would be waiting in the wings to "take its rightful and responsible place" in helping the disenfranchised. Frankly, this is a pipe dream since most churches don't have enough compassion programs in place to care for their own flock, let alone the masses dependent on government social service programs. Realistically, this transformation won't happen overnight and will require the federal government to maintain its safety net while the faith community strengthens and expands its programs to care for the "least of these." This revolution of compassion must start with a renewed vision to phase out government social programs and develop fresh approaches that will enable churches and other community-based organizations to take the lead in fighting poverty.

For example, government can lend a hand by helping to make this transition economically feasible for social service providers. One the best ideas is for the federal government to offer a five hundred dollars tax credit for mentoring a person currently in the welfare system. Or if a family houses the mentee individual and/or family, then the tax credit would increase based on the number of persons cared for by the family. This can all be coordinated and monitored by a government-approved and qualified community-based organization. Based on personal experience, I can tell you that families mentoring families is the best way to lift people out of welfare and into sustainable, fulfilling, and productive lives. "A father to the fatherless, a defender of widows, is God in his holy dwelling. God sets *the lonely in families*" (Psalm 68:5–6, emphasis added).

This approach is the best stewardship of public funds since in the long-term it will save billions of tax dollars and produce citizens who are building social capital instead of draining it.

Q: How does the church's role differ from that of the government in social welfare?
Donaldson: Hebrews 11:1 says, "Faith is the substance of things hoped for, the evidence of things not seen" (NKJV). Simply put, faith makes hope possible; faith is the root system of hope. Since

1965, our government has spent trillions of dollars combating poverty, yet we still lead all industrialized nations in nearly every category of social brokenness. Our government is staffed with many qualified, compassionate, and godly people, but as an institution, it's been trying to provide hope without faith. Truth be told, it can't provide hope because that isn't the function of government; it's the role of the church.

As former-President George W. Bush liked to say, "We must support programs that change habits and the heart." Even Alcoholics Anonymous, founded by a Christian evangelical group known as the Oxford Group, included reliance on a higher power in their twelve-step program.

The government's big-machine approach to alleviating suffering is a failed experiment. The church can offer the personal approach to compassion, recognizing that "one size does not fit all."

A possible model program of collaboration between government and the church is Access to Recovery (ATR). While serving on the federal government's Commission Center for Substance Abuse Treatment, it became painfully clear to me that alcoholism and addictions were roots that sprouted spousal abuse, unemployment, homelessness, crime, and poor health. To address the addiction problem, the government issues vouchers that clients can redeem at church-based counseling centers called Access to Recovery (ATR). This is a viable government and church-based partnership to help people escape the straitjacket of addictions.

There are many more examples such as the church teaching abstinence for prevention and adoption as a solution to children raising children that can reduce the bloated welfare system.

Q: Has the discovery of organizations misusing funds produced any good results?

Donaldson: It has. It has taught us the need for stewardship in giving. Wise stewards of God's blessings can investigate charities using organizational watchdogs like Generous Giving, Signatory, and National Christian Foundation. At the same time, it's sad that a handful of abusers are creating a scenario that hurts all compassion organizations. Most organizations are responsible with the way they use their funds and are transparent about how they spend the money. Responsible giving isn't ceasing to give but taking a little more care to give wisely.

Q: How does this apply to people who are serving in compassion roles?

Donaldson: It goes without saying that compassion work can be discouraging. As Mark Twain once wrote, "The cat, having sat upon a hot stove lid, will not sit upon a hot stove lid

> Responsible giving isn't ceasing to give but taking a little more care to give wisely.

again. But he won't sit upon a cold stove lid either." When we've poured ourselves into a cause and it fails to bear much fruit, we feel discouraged. This can predispose us not to try again. It's discouraging when you pour enormous amounts of compassionate energy into lifting a person out of addictive habits, only to have them return to that destructive lifestyle.

The father of a college student was helping his son move into the dorm room. While he was unpacking boxes of books, the son decided to hook up his computer. But when they tried to turn it on, nothing happened—a blank, dark screen. Trying to figure out what was wrong, the father crawled under the desk and discovered the problem: the power strip was plugged into itself! If we're plugged into our own power supply, we're sure to experience compassion fatigue. In any form of compassion ministry, we must be plugged into God, the eternal source of wisdom, strength, and joy. Ultimately, if we aren't serving the least of these for Jesus, then people will disappoint us, and compassion fatigue will seep into the most vigorous saints and worthy causes.

Q: What's the result of practicing responsible compassion?

Donaldson: I once asked the late, great Bill Bright, founder of Campus Crusade, "What is the key to God's favor?" Bright replied, "God blesses those whom He can trust. Therefore, become more and more trustable." Life's graduation ceremony is when we stand before God and hear Him say, "Well done, good and faithful servant! You have been faithful with a few things; I will put you in charge of many things. Come and share your master's happiness!" (Matthew 25:21)

The world is filled with peddlers of doubt and fear, but the triumphant church of Jesus Christ is a purveyor of hope that together can solve our most pressing social problems and restore genuine and responsible compassion in our communities.

Part 7

THE GREAT COMMISSION: WORD AND DEED

Performing the Great Commission with compassion
becomes automatic with a lifetime commitment
to move everyone, every day, closer to Jesus.

—Barry Meguiar

47

The Great Commission: Word and Deed

Barry Meguiar

The Great Commission doesn't tell us to go into the world and feed the poor. Neither does it tell us to go into the world and pray or read the Bible. While all of these are critical aspects of our walk with the Lord, they aren't our preeminent task. Jesus came with one purpose . . to seek and save the lost, that none should be lost.

Throughout the ages, the focus of the church has evolved through various stages to where it is today. During the last half of the nineteenth century, the focus of the church transitioned to a social gospel, with the intention of blending faith and works. Unfortunately, this led us into being good Christians, while leaving the world in darkness . . . and now chaos!

As it happens, it's far easier to have compassion than it is to lead people to Jesus. The theme of "Some Send, Some Go" has reinforced the notion that donating money in support of compassionate causes is equal to saving the lost. Giving to eradicate the haunting scenes of starving children around the world is a wonderful thing, but it can also be a prideful thing. It's not unusual to hear Christians boasting of feeding and clothing the poor, without giving God the glory, and with no thought of where those they feed and clothe will spend eternity.

As destructive as this is in the life of a Christian . . . it gets worse. In fact, it's affecting the entire church today. Most Christians now see themselves as recipients and supporters of ministry but are not involved in ministry themselves. Pastors have moved from equipping the saints for ministry to asking the saints to support ministry. All too often, giving to compassionate causes is taking precedent over the Great Commission, even when these causes aren't proclaiming the gospel.

Christian give hundreds of millions of dollars to support secular compassion programs, believing they're pleasing God in the process—but they're not! Secular compassion programs don't use one dollar of those gifts to lead people to Jesus, and all too often, only a small portion of those gifts benefit the poor.

God calls us to be good stewards in all aspects of our lives. While stewardship affects how we spend our time and live our lives, we most often think of stewardship as it relates to how we handle our finances. The

> How many people are being led to Jesus by everything you do and say and support financially? That's the question you need to answer!

first 10 percent of our gross income is given as a tithe to support the work of the church we attend, and that's not optional. We pay our tithes and give our offerings over and above that 10 percent, as good stewards of what God has placed in our hands.

The downside comes when we allow ourselves to believe that good stewardship means giving to good causes, because being good doesn't get you or anyone else to heaven. All of life is about redemption! Whatever you do or say or support that doesn't lead people to Jesus is poor stewardship, and God will hold you accountable. God isn't only pleased when you give money; He's pleased when your investment gives a good return. How many people are being led to Jesus by everything you do and say and support financially? That's the question you need to answer!

Giving a cup of cold water to those who are thirsty is a nice thing to do; all of us should do that. We're called to be generous, but unless you connect God with your generosity, it's just a cup of cold water. Nothing redemptive has taken place. "Truly I tell you, anyone who gives you a cup of water in my name . . . will certainly not lose their reward" (Mark 9:41). At the end of your life, the words you want to hear are, "Well done, good and faithful servant" (Matthew 25:21).

On a personal basis, the world is full of rewards and recognition for good people doing good things. The slippery slope is when Christians view themselves as being good Christians when simply doing good things. The scriptural term for that is self-righteousness, and it's definitely not good. "The steps of a good man are ordered by the LORD" (Psalm 37:23, NKJV) for one purpose—to seek and save the lost, that none should be lost.

> **Feeding and clothing the poor has nothing to do with seeking and saving the lost unless it's done in the name of the Lord.**

Feeding and clothing the poor has nothing to do with seeking and saving the lost unless it's done in the name of the Lord. With wrong motivation, some organizations work in opposition to the spread of the gospel. The first question you should ask of anyone seeking your support for their compassion work is: "How many people did your organization lead to the Lord in the last year?" If they can't answer that question, they've answered the question.

There's nothing we can do to earn our way into heaven. Ephesians 2:8–9 tells us, "For it is by grace you have been saved, through faith—and this is not from yourselves, it is the gift of God—not by works, so that no one can boast." If Christians across America boast of all they do "for the Lord," that's not redemptive.

At the same time, James 2:26 tells us that, "Faith without deeds is dead." Mark 16:20 clarifies this message, explaining that the Lord works with us to confirm His Word with signs following: "Then the disciples went out and preached everywhere, and the Lord worked with them and confirmed his word by the signs that accompanied it." Matthew 5:16 really says it all: "Let your light shine before others, that they may see your good deeds and glorify your Father in heaven."

Performing the Great Commission with compassion becomes automatic with a lifetime commitment to move everyone, every day, closer to Jesus, by loving everyone in Jesus' name! If you're a Christian, the only thing that will matter a hundred years from now is how many people are in heaven because of how you used the influence and resources God gave you. Everything else is hay and stubble!

Afterword

Jump

Dave Donaldson

What more can Wendell and I possibly add to the wealth of inspiration, wisdom, and insights contributed to the *CityServe* book by over forty influential leaders?

How about an action word?

During the 2006 Winter Games, the thirty-two-year-old ski jumper stared down a long snow-packed ramp that would catapult him over eight hundred feet into the air, hopefully to land safely on his narrow-bladed skis—no parachute, no safety net, nothing to soften the landing if the wind currents suddenly shifted.

While the skier waited motionless for the light to turn green and the horn to sound, the commentator made an off-script remark I'll never forget. "It's highly unusual for a thirty-two-year-old to still be jumping." My first thought as a former battered pupil of Evel Knievel was, *A nasty fall from elevated heights at an elevated age could take a while to recover.* Instead the commentator explained, "In ski jumping, the older you get the higher it looks."

Hopefully this book has inspired you to climb to the precipice of your highest leap of faith to take your For-Prophet seat and lead your church into a compassion revolution from your neighborhood to the nations. Leader, the forces of evil that have preyed upon your community—splintering families, shattering lives, and stealing hope—want you to believe it's too high because you're too old or too young, too weak, too hurt, too broke, too unmanned, or too defeated.

Do you not know? Have you not heard? The LORD is the everlasting God, the Creator of the ends of the earth. He will not grow tired or weary, and his understanding no one can fathom. He gives strength to the weary and increases the power of the weak. Even youths grow tired and weary, and young men stumble and fall; but those who hope in the LORD will renew their strength. They will soar on wings like eagles; they will run and not grow weary, they will walk and not be faint. (Isaiah 40:28–31)

Jump!

Notes

1. All these statistics and are more are available at: https://www.chlpi.org/wp-content/uploads/2013/12/Food-Waste-Toolkit_Oct-2016_smaller.pdf.

2. www.census.gov.

3. https://www.cnbc.com/2018/06/26/refugee-crisis-a-record-number-of-those-forcibly-displaced-in-2017.html.

4. https://www.cnbc.com/2018/06/26/refugee-crisis-a-record-number-of-those-forcibly-displaced-in-2017.html.

5. UNHCR Refugee Agency.

6. UNHCR Refugee Agency.

7. https://www.pwc.com/gx/en/managing-tomorrows-people/future-of-work/assets/reshaping-the-workplace.pdf.

8. https://www.bloomberg.com/news/articles/2017-04-20/a-quarter-of-millennials-who-live-at-home-don-t-work-or-study.

9. https://www.inc.com/gordon-tredgold/29-surprising-facts-about-millennials-and-what-motivates-them.html.

10. Luke 12:48, NKJV.

11. Luke 12:16–21, NKJV.

12. https://www.hudson.org/search?q=jobs

13. Marvin Olasky, *Renewing American Compassion: A Citizen's Guide* (New York: Free Press, 1996), 16.

14. Doris Kearns Goodwin, *Lyndon Johnson and the American Dream* (New York: St. Martin's Griffin, 1991).

15. Ezekiel 37:1–14.

16. www.businessinsider.com/biggest-transfer-of-wealth-in-history-2014-6.

17. Galatians 6:2, 5.

18. Mark 7:9–13.

Acknowledgements

The *CityServe* book includes material from over forty contributors and required a bold vision and constellation of people to make it successful. The general editors, Wendell Vinson and Dave Donaldson, first want to acknowledge Julie Horner, senior director of Publishing for My Healthy Church. From the outset, Julie inspired and guided the *CityServe* book to fruition.

We're grateful for the expansive quality and diversity of contributors who shared their insights, innovations, and church-based compassion models. We believe their contributions will make the *CityServe* book a staple resource for every leader's physical and digital bookcase.

Joel Kilpatrick did a lot of the heavy lifting by interviewing many of the contributors and constructing chapters out of a wealth of material. Joel is one of the top editors in the nation and was a godsend to this ambitious project.

Ryan Odle, church engagement director for CityServe International, performed brilliantly as project manager by herding a pack of cats to arrange interviews, gather materials, and act as a liaison to Assemblies of God's Publishing, My Healthy Church.

When Julie asked Dave, "Who do you and Wendell want as editor?" Dave replied, "Is it possible to get the best, Terri Gibbs?" Dave had worked with Terri on his previous book, *Relentless*, and knew she would go the extra mile to make all of us look good. Some other notable individuals who assisted with the production include Barbie Long, Randall Howard, Jeff Roman, Trevor Birch, Champion Slye, and Brooke Donaldson.

The general editors also wish to thank these current and previous Assemblies of God executives: Dr. George O. Wood, Doug

Clay, Alton Garrison, Jim Bradford, Rick DuBose, and Donna Barrett, along with Chris Railey, senior director of Leadership and Church Development Ministries. These leaders are all champions of church-based compassion.

The CityServe ministry and this book are made possible because of the inspirational leadership of the SoCal Network's executives: Rich Guerra, John Johnson, Gordon Houston; the CityServe International board members: Dave Pavlin, Chuck Bengochea, and Burl Evans; and the CityServe SoCal team: Don Crabtree and executive director, Karl "The Viking" Hargestam. We give special thanks to other advisors and supporters: Anne "Auntie Anne" Beiler, Dan de León, Rick Bezet, Darren DeLaune, Doug Heisel, Wendel Cover, Fred and Joyce Evans, and Sal and Cynthia Giamarra.

We're grateful to our families who supported us through their prayers, enthusiasm, and patience during this challenging, but rewarding, venture.

Finally, *CityServe: Your Guide to Church-Based Compassion* captures only a sampling of the faithful leaders working in the trenches to bring hope and healing to broken lives and communities. To these warriors, who are persevering in this compassion resolution, we hope the Lord Jesus Christ will use this book and its accompanying web-based platform to affirm and inspire you to press on with joy and victory from the neighborhood to the nations.

Contributors

Tommy Barnett

Tommy is a world-renowned speaker, author, and compassion leader. He pastored Dream City Church in Phoenix, Arizona, for thirty-eight years before transitioning to co-pastoring with his son Luke Barnett. Dream City Church has seen extensive transformation and impact in the surrounding community through its 260-plus outreach ministries. Barnett is also the founder of the Los Angeles Dream Center, which he co-pastors with his son Matthew Barnett. The LA Dream Center was the beginning of a worldwide movement of Dream Centers focused on localized compassion initiatives that provide help and hope to drug addicts, orphans, single mothers, gang members, and the homeless to name a few.

Jonas and Anne Beiler

Jonas and Anne are co-founders of Auntie Anne's Inc., an acclaimed international pretzel franchise. Jonas is a licensed family counselor, founder of the Family Resource and Counseling Center, and the best-selling author of *Think No Evil*. Anne is widely known as an inspirational speaker and has been a guest on numerous radio and television shows including *Secret Millionaire*. She is the author of *Twist of Faith*, which chronicles her inspiring life story.

Chuck Bengochea

Chuck is a successful businessman who has held many influential positions including CEO of Honeybaked Ham, CEO of Family Christian Stores, and controller of the Fountain Business Division at the Coca-Cola Company. He now serves on several corporate boards and coaches business executives. He is a founding member of CityServe International.

Rick Bezet

Rick is the founder and lead pastor of New Life Church in central Arkansas. In 2001, Rick set aside his future as a professional golfer to follow God's call to start a church. Now, many years later, New Life Church has multiple locations and services to an audience exceeding twenty thousand people. Rick is one of the founding pastors of the Association of Related Churches (ARC). He shares his passion and vision for church planting and leadership around the globe. Rick and New Life Church have been actively involved in CityServe International from its inception.

Greg Burris

Greg is the creator of Give 5, a civic matchmaking program that connects retired baby boomers with volunteer opportunities to "move the needle" on key community issues. Burris was previously the city manager for Springfield, Missouri. In that position he was responsible for approximately 2,300 full- and part-time employees, a $315 million annual budget, and $1.4 billion in assets.

Danita Bye

Danita is a sought-after speaker for conferences, TED Talks, and corporate functions. She is a best-selling author, and business and sales leadership consultant. Bye's latest book, *Millennials Matter: Proven Strategies for Building Your Next-Gen Leader,* resources and equips business professionals to develop the next generation into high-capacity leaders.

Stanley Carlson-Thies

Dr. Stanley Carlson-Thies is an author and the founder and senior director of the Institutional Religious Freedom Alliance (IRFA), a division of the Center for Public Justice. He's an authority on the relationship between religious organizations and government, and has written many publications and books on the subject. He held influential roles in the White House Office of Faith-Based and Community Initiatives for both President George W. Bush and President Barack Obama.

Darren DeLaune

Darren is the senior executive pastor of New Life Church in Conway, Arkansas. DeLaune implements and executes the vision and values of NLC while overseeing the ministries and leadership teams on a weekly basis. He's also involved in coaching pastors and planting churches throughout Arkansas and is actively involved in shaping and building CityServe in Arkansas and around the globe.

Dan de León

Dan is senior pastor of Templo Calvario, a prominent bilingual church in Santa Ana, California. Under his leadership, Templo Calvario has established seventy-five campuses in the United States and Latin America. He is a general presbyter of the General Council of the Assemblies of God. He has spoken before the US Senate and served on influential committees at the request of the president. He was privileged to be one of the keynote speakers at Promise Keepers conferences including Stand in the Gap in Washington, DC. He was the former host of the *Club 700, The 700 Club* in Spanish.

Lee de León

Lee is the president and CEO of Templo Calvario Community Development Corporation (CDC). The CDC focuses on education, parenting, financial empowerment, and mobilization of the faith community. He is a trusted leader, advisor, and convener for government entities, corporations, and the faith community in Santa Anna, California.

Bridget Dierks

Bridget is the vice president of programs for the Community Foundation of the Ozarks (CFO) in Springfield, Missouri. She has been with the organization for twelve years and is an expert in grant research and programming. At the CFO, she works to improve the quality of life for citizens in the southern Missouri region by supporting resource development, community grantmaking, collaboration, and public leadership. She also assists one thousand students annually with four hundred separate scholarship programs.

Steve Donaldson

Steve is the co-founder of Convoy of Hope and senior director of Convoy's Rural Compassion division, which trains and resources rural pastors to address severe poverty in their communities. Steve is the innovator of many relief and development initiatives now modeled by organizations around the globe.

Joyce Dexter

Joyce is the director of Lake City Church's food bank in Coeur d'Alene, Idaho, an innovative and high-impact ministry. The food bank provides both immediate assistance and life skill classes to guide and empower recipients toward healthy living and sustainability.

Jim Franklin

Jim is pastor of Cornerstone Church in Fresno, California, a pillar of the community housed within the city's Historic Wilson Theater. He is also the host of *Jim Franklin Live*, an in-depth radio program dealing with social, moral, and political issues. Jim and Cornerstone direct the CityServe HUB for the Fresno region.

Sharen Ford

Dr. Sharen Ford is the adoption consultant at Focus on the Family and oversees their Wait No More! program content. A nationally recognized child welfare consultant, she is the retired manager for permanency services of the Colorado Department of Human Services. Dr. Ford is also the former president of the National Association of State Adoption Programs (NASAP) and the Association of Administrators for the Interstate Compact on Adoption Medical Assistance (AAICAMA).

Alton Garrison

Alton is the assistant general superintendent of The General Council of the Assemblies of God. He is also a speaker, best-selling author, and director of the Acts 2 Journey, which helps churches renew their spiritual vitality and reach their full ministry potential. Previously he served as executive director of U.S. Missions for the Assemblies of God, as superintendent of the Arkansas District Council of the Assemblies of God, and as pastor of First Assembly of God, North Little Rock, Arkansas.

Wayde Goodall

Dr. Wayde Goodall is the former dean of the College of Ministry, codirector of the graduate program, associate professor of church leadership, and department chair of pastoral ministries at Northwest University in Kirkland, Washington. Dr. Goodall and his wife, Rosalyn, are coauthors of *Marriage and Family*, which has received international recognition. As the president and founder of World-Wide Family, Inc., he is an influential voice on marriage and family counseling.

Doug Green

Doug is the founding pastor of North Hills Church in Brea, California. He is also a presbyter for his region within the Assemblies of God and serves on the board of trustees for Vanguard University in Costa Mesa, California. For nearly two decades, Doug volunteered as a chaplain for the Brea Police Department.

Rich Guerra

Rich is the superintendent of the Assemblies of God SoCal Network, which includes over four hundred churches and two hundred thousand adherents. Previously he served as the senior pastor of a megachurch in Visalia, California, where his innovative approaches to community engagement earned him the city's Citizen of the Year award. Rich's vision for the Galaxy of Compassion helped to inspire and resource the founding of CityServe SoCal.

Steve Haas

Steve is the vice president and chief catalyst at World Vision. He works with church leaders, contributing to strategic planning on major humanitarian initiatives and communicating about global issues that affect those living in poverty. Steve labored along the Thailand border as a relief worker aiding Vietnamese and Cambodian refugees. Previously he served on the pastoral staff of Willow Creek Community Church, where he developed small group ministry along with local and international ministries.

Rod Haro

Rod is the founding and lead pastor of The Worship Centre in Fowler, California, which is located in a former gambling casino. The Worship Centre has seven campuses across the Central Valley of California. Rod launched the second CityServe HUB and has effectively modeled building and empowering church PODs (Points of Distribution).

Doug Heisel

Doug is pastor of New Life Church in the Bay Area, California, a wealthy and mainly unchurched suburb of the San Francisco Bay area. The multicampus church is strong in ministering to marketplace leaders.

Bill High

Bill is the CEO of The Signatry a global Christian foundation that helps individuals set up donor-advised funds and helps churches establish ministry foundations to receive cash and noncash gifts. He is a founder of iDonate.com, a software designed to help the nonprofit community market and receive asset-related gifts.

Fitz Hill

For nearly twenty years, Dr. Fitz Hill served as an assistant and head collegiate football coach for the Arkansas Razorbacks and San Jose State Spartans. Dr. Hill transitioned from coaching to become the president of Arkansas Baptist College in downtown Little Rock, Arkansas. After a decade of leading the college, he accepted a tenured faculty position in the College of Business while also leading the Scott Ford Center for Entrepreneurship and Community Development. Dr. Hill is currently serving a seven-year term on the Arkansas State Board of Education while assisting in leading New Life Church's downtown campus.

Julie Horner

Dr. Julie Horner is the senior director of Publishing for My Healthy Church, the Publishing division of the Assemblies of God. Horner is also an adjunct professor in the Business Department of Evangel University, Springfield, Missouri.

John Hughes

John is the director of CityServe's national grant center. He comes to CityServe with twenty years of experience as the CEO of Metro Community Ministries located in San Diego. John has won over fifty million dollars in grants from both government and private foundations. He is the co-founder of the Faith-Based Leadership Training Institute at San Diego State University, a former adjunct professor at the University of San Diego, and a lecturer at San Diego State University. He is currently an adjunct professor at Bethel Seminary in San Diego.

John Johnson

John is the assistant superintendent of the SoCal Network for the Assemblies of God. He oversees the network's global mission and compassion initiatives and helps to equip the local church to be a pillar in its community. Prior to working in the network office, Johnson was the senior pastor of a multisite church in Covina, California. From its inception, John has played a key role in the birth and growth of CityServe International.

Tom Knox

Tom is the founder and CEO of CareFamily, an organization that helps seniors receive effective and comfortable in-home care from highly qualified caregivers. Tom has served as senior vice president for the Christian Broadcasting Network (CBN), chairman of Regent University, and board member for the Commonwealth of Virginia's Council on Human Rights.

Mark Lehmann

Mark is the lead pastor of Cornerstone Church in Bowie, Maryland. He is also the assistant superintendent of the Assemblies of God Potomac Ministry Network, made up of churches and ministries in Maryland, Washington, DC, Virginia, and West Virginia. Mark launched Kingdom Investors to engage the business sector in supporting missions projects around the globe.

Barry Meguiar

Barry is the president of Meguiars, Inc. and the host of *Car Crazy*. He is the recipient of the Petersen Automotive Museum's Automotive Icon Award because of his lifelong influence on and passion for the car hobby, which spans the entire automotive world from car manufacturers to prominent car events, and for his sponsorship of thousands of car shows worldwide. He is also the founder of Revival Outside the Walls, which resources and equips individuals to live out their faith in daily life.

Ryan Odle

Ryan leads church engagement for CityServe and manages the 1Equals2 campaign. He previously served as an executive assistant at Convoy of Hope in Springfield, Missouri.

Marvin Olasky

Marvin is the editor-in-chief of *World* magazine, website, and podcast. He has authored more than twenty books including the influential work, *The Tragedy of American Compassion*. He is also dean of World Journalism

Institute, holder of the distinguished Chair in Journalism and Public Policy at Patrick Henry College, and an Acton Institute senior fellow.

Jay Pathak

Jay is the lead pastor of Mile High Vineyard Church, which has campuses in Arvada, Denver, Lakewood, and Westminster, Colorado. He and Dave Runyon coauthored *The Art of Neighboring* to empower a church movement based on loving your neighbor.

Mike Quinn

Mike is the founder and lead pastor of NewBreak Church in San Diego, California, which has positively influenced nearly every sector of the city by "Connecting people with God through authentic relationships to serve communities." He is a lead team member for the Church Multiplication Network (CMN), which is dedicated to strategically equip, fund, and network church leaders to establish new faith communities and multiply the church. NewBreak is affiliated to CityServe in the San Diego region.

Jonathan Reckford

Jonathan, the CEO for Habitat for Humanity International, came to Habitat with extensive experience after holding executive and managerial positions at Goldman Sachs, Marriott, the Walt Disney Company, and Best Buy. Habitat for Humanity International partners with communities around the world to help families achieve strength, stability, and independence through the provision of a home.

Gene Roncone

Gene is the lead pastor of Highpoint Church in Aurora, Colorado, a network of Christian ministries and outreaches with multiple locations across the city. He is actively involved in the local community, serving on several city boards and committees focused on problem solving. He has received Aurora's Humanitarian of the Year award and commendation from Colorado's House of Representatives for his efforts. He also hosts several national podcasts and has authored three books: *Explore the Call*, *Prevailing Over Impossibility*, and *A Season for Legacy*.

Dave Runyon

Dave is the co-founder and director of CityUnite, an organization that helps government, business, and faith leaders unite around common causes. He also serves as a consultant for businesses that have a desire to make a difference in their communities.

Robert Showers, Esq.

Robert is a principal in the firm of Simms-Showers, LLP, where he is responsible for the operation of the DC Metro office located in Leesburg, Virginia. Previously he was a principal in the firm of Gammon & Grange, P.C., where he managed the litigation department. He is a leading expert in diverse practice areas from church to constitutional law.

Brian Steele

Brian is the pastor and executive director over the Phoenix Dream Center. He has worked closely with the Barnett family over the years to start Dream Centers around the world. The Phoenix Dream Center is a center of hope in the community that addresses needs from foster care prevention to rescuing women from sex trafficking.

Cary Summers

Cary is the founder of the Museum of the Bible in Washington, DC. Previously he served as president and CEO of Herschend Family Entertainment/Silver Dollar City Corporation, one of the world's largest theme attraction operators. He also served as vice president for Bass Pro Shops and as general manager of Abercrombie and Fitch. He also serves as CEO of Nazareth Village in Israel, a recreation of the first-century village where Jesus grew up.

Paul Thompson

Paul is the executive director of The BetterWorld Trust and senior adjunct faculty at the Center for Creative Leadership. He has extensive experience providing organizational and leadership development to businesses both in the nonprofit and for-profit sectors.

Randy Valimont

Randy is the pastor of Griffin First Assembly in Griffin, Georgia. He has achieved global influence as a speaker and author and through his television and radio ministries, *Fresh Touch* and *Wontok Radio.* He is chairman of Calcutta Mercy, which provides holistic care to struggling families in Calcutta, India.

Doug Wead

Doug is a *New York Times* best-selling author of over thirty books and an accomplished speaker and historian. For over twenty years he has been researching and writing about the families of American presidents. He has interviewed six presidents, seven first ladies, and coauthored a book with President George H. W. Bush. He has served as an adviser to two American presidents and was a special assistant to the president in the George H. W. Bush White House. He has also served as co-chairman of the Charity Awards with first ladies Lady Bird Johnson, Rosalynn Carter, Nancy Reagan, Barbara Bush, and Laura Bush. Today he is a regular commentator on FOX, CNN, and MSNBC.

Rich and Robyn Wilkerson

Rich and Robyn are the founders of Peacemakers and Peacemakers Family Center in Miami, Florida. They are best-selling authors of several books including *Inside Out: How Everyday People Become Extraordinary Leaders.* Over 1.5 million students have attended Rich's presentations in over 1,600 public school campuses in the United States and Canada. While the Wilkersons' evangelistic ministry has taken them around the globe, they remain committed to serving in the heart of Miami through cutting-edge approaches to community transformation.

Scott Wilson

Scott is the senior pastor of The Oaks Church in the south Dallas, Texas, area. An acclaimed speaker, author, and church leadership mentor, he created the Oaks School of Leadership, a specialized ministry training program to provide young leaders with hands-on experience while earning college credits. The Oaks Church has a significant presence in the community that can be seen through their outreach ministries and Wilson's multiple invitations to deliver the invocation before the Texas House of Representatives.

About the General Editors

Dave Donaldson, CityServe International, co-founder, chairman of the board

Dave has invested his life in inspiring, equipping, and resourcing leaders in more than one hundred countries to bring aid and opportunity to millions of underresourced people. As the former national director for Operation Blessing and co-founder of Convoy of Hope, Dave forged global partnerships with churches, organizations, and businesses to mobilize tens of thousands of volunteers worldwide.

A veteran of Washington, DC, Dave coordinated government briefings between the government and faith-based leaders and served on the C-SAT Council for Substance Abuse and Mental Health Services Association (SAMHSA). He also hosted the first National Summit on Foster Care and Adoption with the US Children's Bureau and has served on numerous boards including the National Football League (NFL) sanctioned National Courage Awards. He is a former trustee at Vanguard University and an advisor to Missouri State University's graduate college.

In 2016, Dave retired from Convoy of Hope to co-found CityServe International (CSI). As initiatives of CSI, Dave hosts trips to Israel and spearheads efforts to provide aid and education for refugees in the Middle East. In 2019 Dave and CityServe launched "Neighborhoods to the Nations" to unify churches and organizations around church-based compassion initiatives, and to provide an advocacy office in Washington, DC.

Dave is the author of the bestselling *Rock Solid* discipleship program and coauthor of *Revolution of Compassion* and *Relentless.*

Dave earned his MA from Fuller Theological Seminary. He and his wife, Kristy, reside in California and Washington, DC, and have four adult children.

Wendell Vinson, pastor, Canyon Hills, CA; co-founder, CityServe International

Wendell and Lynda Vinson became pastors of Canyon Hills Church, Bakersfield, California, over thirty years ago when it was a small congregation in need of revitalization. Today Canyon Hills is one of the leading multisite churches in Southern California, pioneering fresh approaches to church planting, church renewal, and taking the gospel to unreached tribes.

The Vinson's unwavering compassion to love people to Jesus inspired innovative ways to better serve their community, such as Fort Faith, an award-winning children's ministry center; Champion's Club, a state-of-the-art center designed specifically for children with special needs; Florence Gardens Senior Living Center, an affordable housing development for seniors; and Frazier Woods Conference Center. Canyon Hills is a forerunner in the CityServe network with the ongoing renovation of a two-hundred-thousand-square-foot commercial shopping mall that serves as an inner-city outreach center and CityServe warehouse HUB.

Wendell has trained pastors around the globe, advised world leaders, and helped to coordinate government briefings in Washington, DC, as part of the White House Office of Faith-Based and Community Initiatives.

He currently serves or has served as a member of the board of trustees for Vanguard University, Costa Mesa, CA; Covenant Foundation of California; Convoy of Hope, Springfield, MO; Covenant Community Services Kern County; Kern Leadership Alliance; and Mission One Eleven.

Wendell and Lynda have two adult children and are the proud grandparents of two grandchildren.

For more information about this book and other helpful resources, visit www.MyHealthyChurch.com